9/99

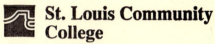

REVOLUTIONARY WOMEN IN THE WAR FOR AMERICAN INDEPENDENCE

ൠ

E F Ellet.

REVOLUTIONARY WOMEN IN THE WAR FOR AMERICAN INDEPENDENCE

ଔଃ

A One-Volume Revised Edition of Elizabeth Ellet's 1848 Landmark Series

Edited and Annotated by
LINCOLN DIAMANT

Westport, Connecticut
London

Library of Congress Cataloging-in-Publication Data

Ellet, E. F. (Elizabeth Fries), 1818–1877.
    Revolutonary women in the War for American Independence: A One-Volume
Revised Edition of Elizabeth Ellet's 1848 Landmark Series / edited and annotated
by Lincoln Diamant.
        p.   cm.
    Includes bibliographical references and index.
    ISBN 0–275–96263–6 (alk. paper)
    1. United States—History—Revolution, 1775–1783—Women.
2. Women—United States—History—18th century.   3. United States—
History—Revolution, 1775–1783—Biography.   I. Diamant, Lincoln.
II. Ellet, E. F. (Elizabeth Fries), 1818–1877.   Women of the
American Revolution.   III. Title.
E276.E45   1998
973.3′082—dc21   98–5391

British Library Cataloguing in Publication Data is available.

Library of Congress Catalog Card Number: 98–5391
ISBN: 0–275–96263–6

First published in 1998

Praeger Publishers, 88 Post Road West, Westport, CT 06881
An imprint of Greenwood Publishing Group, Inc.

Printed in the United States of America

The paper used in this book complies with the
Permanent Paper Standard issued by the National
Information Standards Organization (Z39.48–1984).

10 9 8 7 6 5 4 3 2 1

If attention is not paid to the ladies, we are determined to foment our own rebellion.

—Abigail Adams
(to John Adams at the First Continental Congress)

CONTENTS

III. THE WAR IN THE SOUTH

INTRODUCTION

Revolutionary women . . . shared with cheerfulness and gaiety the privations and sufferings to which the situation of their country exposed them. In every stage of this severe trial, they displayed virtues that have not always been attributed to their sex. With a ready acquiescence, with a firmness always cheerful, and a constancy that never lamented all the sacrifices . . . they yielded up the conveniences furnished by wealth and commerce, consenting to share the produce of their labour. They even gave up without regret a considerable portion of the covering designed for their own families, to supply the wants of a distressed soldiery; and heroically suppressed the involuntary sigh which the departure of their brothers, sons and husbands for camp, rendered from their bosoms.

—Chief Justice John Marshall (1804)

WOMEN HAVE ALWAYS played a part in war. But in the important American Revolution, only a handful of the approximately 800,000 adult females living in what soon became thirteen united states, ever pulled a musket trigger or helped to serve a cannon. Custom frowned on such Amazonian heroics, which is not to say that the female role in this struggle was unimportant to its outcome. It merely underlines how most women went about either unnoticed or unsung. "Yet without some conception of them," asserts Elizabeth Ellet in the opening paragraphs of her major three-volume work, *The Women of the American Revolution*, "the Revolution cannot be appreciated."

At the time, Mrs. Ellet's voice was a singular one; while she may not have been the first American woman historian, she certainly was the first American historian of women. Even a century and a half ago, when Revolutionary War reminiscences were still green, it was no easy matter for Elizabeth Fries

Lummis Ellet to track down and assemble authentic records for this large group of biographical sketches. Some were brief, others exhaustive. Her success turns what today might be otherwise considered a quaint reprint into a vibrant example of American historical narrative.

The mid-nineteenth century proved an excellent starting point for the beginnings of American oral history. In 1848, almost pacing Mrs. Ellet, the stroke-ridden, Westchester County, New York lawyer John McClain McDonald became a familiar figure in his touring carriage, conducting more than six hundred verbatim interviews with 241 county residents who could still provide personal recollections of the Revolution.

For her three volumes, Mrs. Ellet specifically sought out and related the wartime experiences of woman after woman in each of the thirteen states, tracing the war's devastating effect on families on both sides of the conflict. Allowing for a certain amount of understandable mid-nineteenth century red-white-and-blue hyperbole, Mrs. Ellet's presentation remains thoughtful and colorful.

As the Revolutionary struggle waxed and waned, and waxed afresh, traditional "female chores" kept American women busier than ever. Their varied daily activities in town and on the farm and frontier were always family related. Within the family, formal or rudimentary levels of education and book learning regularly admonished a woman to become and remain a supportive, and cheerfully hardworking wife and mother. New Revolutionary responsibilities on the home front merely added to a burden never easily shouldered. But on different levels, each of Mrs. Ellet's biographical subjects played her own particular part. Their regular wartime activities could range from tasks like spinning, weaving, and sewing clothing and uniforms to preparing cartridges and bandages and collecting urine for gunpowder processing.

Such routines merely supplemented conventional tasks of farm and town life, activities that became infinitely more difficult in the wartime absence of able-bodied husbands and sons. In order to exercise their new roles, many of Mrs. Ellet's subjects found themselves uncomfortably turning their backs on established tradition, religious precept, and social development as they faced eight long years of a difficult and often tumultuous wartime existence.

Raised and educated to generally consider themselves inferior to men, suitable only for conducting affairs of the home, often missing any intellectual stimulation beyond a Sunday sermon, patriotic American women suddenly had to suppress any feelings of inadequacy and throw themselves wholeheartedly into the political and military arena. Female "energy, industry, and perseverance," Mrs. Ellet reminds us, "were necessary to the fulfillment of daily duties and were to form the character and shape the destinies of the republic. It was the part of women to reclaim what the ravages of war laid waste . . . and to lay a moral foundation on which the structure of a nation's true greatness might be built."

Thus in a time of domestic crisis, the revolutionary women of British North America met the challenge, abundantly displaying—in Mrs. Ellet's words—"magnanimity, fortitude, self-sacrifice, and heroism . . . with one heart determined to die or be free." Often defiantly asserting American independence in the face of a repressive enemy, wives and mothers seized the critical opportunity to set their feet on the long road to greater individualism. In so doing, they gave a dramatic eight-year demonstration that men held no monopoly on the qualities of courage, self-reliance, and fortitude.

Not every woman remained at home throughout the war. Many went to live alongside their husbands under primitive conditions in the army's encampments. They were not only the wives of important officers but spouses (and children) of ordinary soldiers. These participants in Continental camp life included women like Lucy Knox, wife to Artillery General Henry Knox, who—Mrs. Ellet wryly tells us—was saluted (or disliked) by many male acquaintances as a truly "independent woman." And despite a slightly cocked eyebrow, Ellet tells the romantic story of the cross-dresser Private Deborah Sampson (alias Robert Shurtleff).

In passing, homage should also be paid to the thousands of equally valiant but anonymous women, not included in Mrs. Ellet's presentation. All these unheralded women chose to share the dangers of the field with their men. George Washington, amid all his other concerns on the march, fought a losing battle to keep soldiers' families from piling aboard the army's supply and baggage wagons. Many of them were fleeing from areas nominally occupied by the British or ravaged by guerilla combat.

Without complaint, this horde of camp followers undertook the mundane but essential tasks: cooking, washing, sewing and darning, helping to forage or care for the sick and wounded, bearing and rearing children, and other "distaff duties." Such hardworking, but ration-consuming females (with their children) were usually viewed by the American general officers as an inevitable military encumbrance. Their numbers varied with each campaign and change in the fortunes of war.

On both sides during the American Revolution, women numbered from 5 percent to 10 percent of the total camp population. Apart from the inevitable presence of a handful of loose "white-stockinged women"—drummed out of camp when officially apprehended and against whom General Washington regularly warned his young troops—most camp followers were tolerated and mainly ignored by the brass. Exceptions were made during major army movements when officers attempted to keep camp and town populations apart.

This concern was graphically demonstrated on 4 August 1778, following the British withdrawal from Philadelphia, when the Continentals were poised for their triumphal reentry into the largest city in North America. Always acutely aware of appearances, the otherwise imperturbable Washington forbade any additional women to come into the camp and sought to expel many already there. "In the present state of the army," said the commander in chief, "every encumbrance proves prejudicial. The multitude of women in particular, especially those who are pregnant, or have children, are a clog upon every movement." Whereupon Washington led his nine thousand Continental troops down Broad Street into the newly liberated capital of the year-old republic, past the wildly cheering Philadelphians.

But at the same time a vastly separate parade of carefully segregated camp women and their children was snaking its way through the City of Brotherly Love by a completely different route, past empty stableyards into back alleys and quaint little streets. Washington had simply ordered: "Not a woman belonging to the army is to be seen." (For an even more graphic description of a raggedy column of captive Hessian women and children, slogging their way through Cambridge, Massachusetts, see HANNAH WINTHROP below.)

Until the advent of Mrs. Ellet's 1848 book and the early stirrings of the women's suffrage movement, this typical "out of sight, out of mind" approach could have also been a watchword of American historiography.

Following a British army tradition dating back before the French and Indian Wars, the enemy's camp, too, contained a large number of women and children, usually exceeding commander in chief Lord William Howe's stipulated regimental quotas of six women for each company of thirty-eight men and nine officers.

In 1777, a British army ration return, covering eleven regiments, contains a total of 22,068 men; it also lists 1,648 camp women (on half rations) and 539 children (on one-fourth rations). The last two categories approach 9 percent of the total camp population. In New York City in 1779, the four thousand–man British garrison was accompanied by a staggering 1,550 women and 968 children! During the enemy occupation of Newport, Rhode Island, Hessian mercenary General Friedrich von Wurmb criticized his command with understandable exaggeration: "This corps has more women and children than men, which causes considerable vexation."

A British historian recently remarked, presumably with a smile, that the American Revolution was the successful handiwork of a highly organized group of radical white male Protestants, who won political independence for the United States even though supported by less than one-third of the colonial population. But Mrs. Ellet keeps reminding us that this minority group, at camp and at home, also contained a great number of fervent females.

Men held center stage and controlled almost every event. Only on the rarest occasion did a woman have the opportunity to perform the common colonial act of firing a musket in anger. That is why, in a war where females were not expected to participate in impromptu heroics, an appreciative Congress eventually honored and rewarded three indomitable women—Mary Hays ("Molly Pitcher"), Margaret Corbin ("Captain Molly"), and Deborah Sampson. They shattered the accepted eighteenth-century image of genteel females, either by happenstance or covert design. All three got to fire a musket—or a cannon—at the enemy.[1]

The new United States demonstrated its gratitude by awarding each of these three women a modest military pension—and in the case of one husband, the first authorized veteran's spousal benefit. The man was Benjamin Gannett of Sharon, Massachusetts, who after the war married the fearless woman who, disguised as a man, had served almost two undetected years in the Continental army's regular Massachusetts Line. An enforced hospitalization finally brought an end to Miss Sampson's patriotic masquerade. As far as we know, Deborah Sampson Gannett was the only male impersonator swept into the front ranks of America's fighting men by undeniable revolutionary enthusiasm.

A half century after the last cannon shot of the Revolution, Elizabeth Fries Lummis Ellet, one of the most prolific American female (or male) writers of the nineteenth century, began her assembly of a diverse collection of biographical sketches presenting the lives and exploits of a host of revolutionary women. Their sentiments and active support played a major role in helping win the eight-year war (1775–1783)—a critical period in which the pace of American history quickened.

Mrs. Ellet "respectfully and affectionately inscribed" to her mother the initial two volumes of *The Women of the American Revolution*—issued in 1848 by the New York publishers Baker & Scribner. Two years later a third volume supplemented the set. Its new preface gave Mrs. Ellet an opportunity to restate her creative purpose and respond to early critics of her geographic balance. "One of the neglected portions of our country," she wrote, "is the upper part of South Carolina, where the Revolutionary struggle was more painful and destructive, owing to the division among the inhabitants. . . . It seemed therefore a duty to rescue from oblivion well-authenticated facts which were likely to be of value to the future historian."

Mrs. Ellet's additional volume also allowed her to tactfully soften her initial evaluation of such women as Lucy Knox. The three-volume set was followed almost immediately by the similarly titled, *Domestic History of the American Revolution*—issued in 1850 by the same publishers. This supplementary, even more anecdotal volume re-mines, somewhat repetitively, Mrs. Ellet's original source material, while bluntly asserting her "just aversion to the romancing trash of the present day, under which the simple realities of our struggle for national existence seem in danger of being buried."

With a slight shift of attention to the frontier, the indefatigable and unabashedly expansionist author next brought out in 1852 *Pioneer Women of the West*—published by the now independent Charles Scribner & Co. Mrs. Ellet had uncovered a major American historical lode and assiduously proceeded to dig and tunnel.

All her biographical research and compilation took place in what was for her a remarkably fertile period. Hardly out of her twenties, Mrs. Ellet kept herself continuously busy with dozens of manuscript sketches, magazine and newspaper articles, and other editorial projects. Clearly she was a "demon writer"—and a good one at that.

—Lincoln Diamant

NOTE

1. One can only speculate why Elizabeth Ellet makes no mention of two of these three military participants in the Revolution. We have elected to add biographical sketches of Mary Ludwig Hays and Margaret Corbin, overlooked in her original text.

THE AUTHOR

Complacent political and military historians, following the traditions of their craft, left women out of their chronicles of the American Revolution; Mrs. Ellet in a domestic history of that cataclysm partly restored the balance of justice.

—Charles and Mary Beard in *The Rise of American Civilization* (1927)

THE FIRST BIOGRAPHICAL sketch of this book is properly that of Elizabeth Fries Lummis Ellet herself. A closer look at Mrs. Ellet reveals an unusually prolific and spirited American author. Last of a file of almost a dozen women—beginning in 1805 with Mercy Warren—who wrote in one form or another about the Revolution, Mrs. Ellet conducted the most serious historical research. All her predecessors were content to reconstitute previously assembled writings as new articles or books, each with a general emphasis on men. Mrs. Ellet set out to change all that. Reviewing the available documents and letters, corresponding assiduously with descendants of many of her biographical subjects, she chose for her broad canvas both high- and low-profile female Americans during the War of Independence.

Her work offers a realistic picture of ordinary and extraordinary women. She replaces the traditional focus on the wealthy, powerful and illustrious with something more profound—a belief that the Revolution, a new kind of political institution, required a new kind of detailed historical writing in which American females were viewed as more than just passive or decorative participants in a life-or-death struggle. To this ideal, Mrs. Ellet's two prefaces give eloquent testimony. While hers was not exactly a household name like Stowe or Alcott, it was not far off the mark.

ELIZABETH FRIES LUMMIS

Elizabeth Fries Lummis was born to Sarah Maxwell Lummis, daughter of Captain John Maxwell, a proudly remembered veteran officer of the American Revolution. Sarah Maxwell became the second wife of Philadelphia physician William Nixon Lummis—a pupil of the noted Dr. Benjamin Rush. In 1810, following the death of his first wife and his remarriage, Dr. Lummis decided to play a part in frontier land development. He moved his family to the tiny and sparsely settled lakeside area of Sodus Point, New York, on the south shore of Lake Ontario. The new Lummis home (reportedly burned by the British during the War of 1812 and subsequently rebuilt) lay north of New York State's Finger Lakes region, about thirty miles east of Rochester.

Elizabeth, by her own report, was born at Sodus Point, 18 October 1818. (The question persists as to whether this professed date actually shaves six years off her true age.) In 1818, James Monroe was still enjoying his first term in the White House; the second British attempt to crush the infant United States—again by way of Canada—was still fresh in popular memory. On Elizabeth's father's side, she was distantly related to the charismatic Revolutionary War veteran John Fries, who had won a last-minute reprieve from President John Adams for a 1799 death sentence. Fries's treason trial arose from his leadership of an abortive federal tax rebellion by 140 Pennsylvania farmers.

Elizabeth's nearby neighbor was the venerable "revered and beloved" daughter-in-law of Anne Frisby Fitzhugh of Maryland, who became one of the future author's biographees. As this Fitzhugh relative recounted dramatic family legends of the Revolution, she soon became one of Elizabeth Lummis's "earliest and highly esteemed friends." It was all part of a politically romantic heritage that would find expression in what was destined to be a remarkably diverse and abundant literary career—unusual for an American woman of that period.

Her family eventually enrolled Elizabeth in the Female Seminary at Aurora, New York, forty miles from her home. There, like many other genteel young ladies of the time, she received language instruction in French, German, and Italian plus classes in world history, all under the watchful eye of a sympathetic Quaker teacher from England. Elizabeth was a precocious teenager with a vivid imagination. Her lifelong writing career began almost at once.

Elizabeth's first published work—in 1834, at the age of sixteen—was her (anonymous) translation of *Euphemio of Messina,* a tragedy by the contemporary Italian revolutionary poet Silvio Pellico. Her English version of the play was followed by a Venetian-based historical tragedy of her own, *Teresa Contarini.* She also composed a small volume of poems that appeared in 1835; by then the successful and confident young author was (presumably) only seventeen.

After graduating from the seminary in 1835, the eighteen–(or twenty-four?)-year-old Elizabeth, traveling to New York City to call on publishers, met and subsequently married William Henry Ellet, a thirty–year-old Columbia College chemistry professor. It was to be a happy union, without any children. In the fall of 1836, the couple moved to Columbia, South Carolina, where Dr. Ellet would teach chemistry for twelve years at South Carolina College. But despite a wide circle of acquaintances generated by William's teaching and Elizabeth's continued literary endeavors, the "Yankee" Ellets must have always appeared somewhat exotic in this area of the antebellum Palmetto State.

Elizabeth pursued her own work, corresponding with New York and Boston publishers and turning out three books: *The Characters of Schiller* (1839), *Scenes in the Life of Joanna of Sicily* (1840), and *Rambles About the Country* (1840). She also contributed a steady outpouring of literary material to such magazines as *American Monthly, Southern Literary Messenger,* and Edgar Allan Poe's New York *Broadway Journal.*

In 1848 the Ellets returned to New York City to continue their twin careers. For a decade, William served as a consultant to the Manhattan Gas Company, while Elizabeth's published output soared. She continued to submit critical reviews and articles to New York and Boston newspapers and leading periodicals like *Graham's, The Democratic Review,* and *The Saturday Evening Post.* She filled what remained of her spare time with translating European legends and fairy tales, for which she found a ready juvenile market.

She had always possessed a keen sense of American history. For several years in South Carolina, she was busily engaged in assembling the relevant information for an extended work on local history. With her return to New York, she refocused on a far broader canvas. Treading lightly in the footsteps of the handful of women writers (starting with Mercy Warren in 1805) who had delved into America's brief history, Elizabeth embarked on a major project.

Spurred by countless long and detailed family-history conversations she had enjoyed during her stay in the South, Elizabeth now expanded her particular theme—the turbulent Revolutionary role played by noteworthy women from every state.

Considering her subject matter, the period in which she assembled her materials, and her previous romantic productions, Elizabeth's new work remained relatively free of cant or sentimentality. Less than sixty-five years had elapsed since Cornwallis's momentous surrender at Yorktown; the Revolutionary founding fathers and battlefield heroes were still subjects of second-generation household stories. Such heroes of the northern states were well known to Elizabeth; her southern sojourn brought her into contact with many new names, fresh faces, and unrecorded wartime exploits.

It did not take long for Elizabeth to fully embark on her grand design—a major work dealing with American Revolutionary women from every region of the conflict. Mrs. Ellet unabashedly re-created an onstage female role in a historical pageant that had always been presented from a masculine perspective. She tested the waters with a long article on the subject in *Godey's Lady's Book*; overwhelming response told her she had found a major market with a work that would subsequently run into many printings. She could now throw herself wholeheartedly into reassembling her growing mass of material.

Establishing a web of correspondence and research, Elizabeth dug into the available Revolutionary archive seeking authentic stories about women. Her unambiguous purpose was clearly recapitulated in her prefaces:

Many among the actors in that momentous drama whose deeds should have been recorded, are scarcely mentioned. . . . No full history has ever been written. . . . No pen has done justice to the memory of many who, by the impression of mind and character, have nobly served their age, and whose influence is still felt and acknowledged. In almost every part of the country, mention is naturally made of women unknown to history, yet well remembered in popular tradition. . . . While much that might have illustrated the influence of women on the domestic character and feeling of those days has been lost or obscured by time, it appeared yet possible by persevering effort to recover something worthy of an enduring record.

Elizabeth's work moved ahead against an already busy literary schedule—combined with a small torrent of critical reviews, a study of women artists, novelettes, and stories. With its understandable overemphasis on heroic exploits in the lives of South Carolina women, Elizabeth's grand concept for *The Women of the American Revolution* and its sequels slowly took shape. It was also inevitable that Mrs. Ellet would unintentionally omit more than a few deserving candidates for her otherwise exhaustive women's history. As she discovered in the course of her 1840s research—and ruefully testified to in print—source material on the Revolution was already proving scanty. Although she struggled, in letter after letter, to painstakingly identify descendants, striving to achieve as complete a female record as possible, Mrs. Ellet's prefaces acknowledge the possibility of important omissions. "The apparent dearth of information," she confesses, "was at first almost disheartening. Except for the letters of Mrs. Adams, no fair exponent of the feelings and trials of the women of the Revolution had been given to the public."

But assuming that nineteenth-century readers of both sexes might not be ready for a vision of too many strong and capable women, the author disarmingly bows towards a more traditional view of the "inherent difficulty in delineating female character, which impresses itself on the memory of those who have known the individual, by delicate traits that may be felt, but not described." Mrs. Ellet's actual text, however, suggests a certain hollowness in that sentiment.

As she soon discovered (and attempted to redress in her final volume), every region of the Revolutionary struggle had its own roster of worthy local heroines. For every teenaged Emily Geiger—who carried General Greene's urgent dispatches over South Carolina back roads to General Sumter—there was some completely overlooked young woman like Sybil Ludington, whose midnight gallop across New York's Putnam County in 1777 helped to rouse her father's militia against the British raid on nearby Danbury.

Slowly and carefully, Mrs. Ellet compiled the material for her biographical sketches—Revolutionary women who stood both behind and alongside their men. While Mrs. Ellet was no modern feminist, it is not coincidental that *The Women of the American Revolution* was issued within a few months of the first national feminist congress at Seneca Falls, New York. Eighteen-forty-eight was also the year in which massive social upheaval toppled governments in Europe. Elizabeth Ellet's timely work was one more milestone on the frustratingly long road to final admission of female Americans to the franchise and the political mainstream of the United States.

As Mrs. Ellet prepared her manuscripts for 1848–1850 publication, mounting sectional recrimination and bitterness—exacerbated by the Mexican Peace Treaty, Clay's compromises, and the Fugitive Slave Act—were rapidly converting the more than two-centuries-old institution of slavery into a boiling cauldron of controversy. It would soon engulf the nation, shaking the federal system to its roots.

Probably mindful of her many Carolinian friends, Mrs. Ellet eschewed any reflections on the distant drum of Northern and Midwestern abolitionism. Caught between bifurcating ideologies in a nation relentlessly edging toward apocalyptic civil war, she elected to emphasize and celebrate its original patriotic—and undeniably romantic—unity of purpose.

Nevertheless, Mrs. Ellet's narrative does involve a number of patriotic negroes (she uses, like Harriet Beecher Stowe, the lower case "n"). But her focus rests on recounting the ways in which those subservient individuals supported their masters—and more often, mistresses—in achieving American independence. Of a time when one out of every five inhabitants of a colony like Virginia was a female of color, Mrs. Ellet makes no mention of the thousands of male and female slaves who took advantage of rare opportunities to run off to supposed freedom within the British lines—even from so benign a plantation owner as Thomas Jefferson. (For many, that brief moment of liberty collapsed when British officers in occupied Charleston and Savannah sold the ex-slaves to new masters in the West Indies.)

Mrs. Ellet's concentration on the unifying aspects of our Revolutionary history also discouraged her from acknowledging ethnic milestones like the long wartime service of the soldiers of the first Rhode Island Regiment and their camp women. All of them were black.

Regarding the New York, Pennsylvania, Kentucky, and Carolina frontier families Mrs. Ellet chose to chronicle, she had little but scorn for all the Native American Indians who aligned themselves with the British in a desperate but futile attempt to delay the inevitable "over the mountain" colonization that wrested away tribal land and hunting grounds. In her almost universal condemnation of the natives, Mrs. Ellet was in unimpeachable company; even Jefferson had described in the Declaration of Independence how the King of Great Britain had done all in his power to bring down on Americans "the merciless Indian savages, whose known rule of warfare is an undistinguished destruction of all ages, sexes, and conditions." Seven decades later, when Mrs. Ellet wrote her book (with no mention of a substantial number of Native American volunteers with Washington's army), the bitter war against the Indian nations continued.

Dr. Ellet died in 1859. His wife maintained her unflagging literary career with books and magazine articles for another eighteen years, along the way becoming editor of the new *Cyclopaedia of Domestic Economy, and Practical Housekeeper*. She continued to live in New York City, became deeply involved in charitable efforts with the city's poor and homeless women and children, and eventually converted from her Episcopal faith to Catholicism. Her death from Bright's disease at the age of fifty-nine (or sixty-four) on 3 June 1877 was marked by tributes in all the New York newspapers. She was buried in Brooklyn's Green-Wood Cemetery.

More than any writer before her and many thereafter, Elizabeth Ellet gave American women a vivid appreciation of their crucial role in the earliest history of their country.

—LINCOLN DIAMANT

AUTHOR'S 1848 PREFACE

IN OFFERING THIS work to the public, it is due to the reader no less than the writer to say something of the extreme difficulty which has been found in obtaining materials sufficiently reliable for a record designed to be strictly authentic.

Three-quarters of a century have necessarily affected all recollection of many imposing domestic scenes of the Revolution, and cast over many a veil of obscurity through which it is hard to distinguish their features. Whatever has not been preserved by contemporaneous written testimony, or derived at an early period by immediate actors in the scenes, is liable to the suspicion of being distorted or discolored by the imperfect knowledge, the prejudices, or the fancy of its narrators. It is necessary always to distrust, and very often to reject, traditional information.

Much of this character has been received from various sources, but I have refrained from using it in all cases where it was not supported by responsible personal testimony, or where it was found to conflict in any of its details with established historic facts.

Inasmuch as political history says but little—and that vaguely and incidentally—of the women who bore their part in the Revolution, the materials for a work treating of them and their actions and sufferings must be derived in great part from private sources. The apparent dearth of information was at first almost disheartening. Except for the letters of Mrs. Adams, no fair exposition of the feelings and trials of the women had been given to the public; of the Southern women, the few fragmentary anecdotes of female heroism to be found in some historical works complete the amount of published information on the subject.

Letters of friendship and affection—those most faithful transcripts of the heart and mind of individuals—have been earnestly sought, and examined wherever they could be obtained. But letter writing was far less usual among our ancestors than it is at the present day; and the uncertainty and sometimes the danger attendant upon the transmission of letters were not only an impediment to frequent correspondence but excluded from what did exist much discussion of the all-absorbing subjects of the time. Of the little that was written, how small a portion remains in this—as it has been truly called—manuscript-destroying generation!

While much that might have illustrated the influence of women and the domestic character and feeling of those days had been lost or obscured by time, it appeared yet possible, by a persevering effort, to recover something worthy of an enduring record. With the view of eliciting information for this purpose, application was made severally to the surviving relatives of women remarkable for position or influence, or whose zeal, sacrifice, or heroic acts had contributed to promoting the establishment of American independence.

My success in these applications has not been such as to enable me to fill out entirely my own idea of the work I wished to present to the reader. Some of the sketches are necessarily brief and meagre, and perhaps few of them do full justice to their subjects. There is, also, inherent difficulty in delineating female character, which impresses itself on the memory of those who have known the individual by delicate traits that may be felt but not described.

The actions of men stand out in prominent relief and are a safe guide in forming a judgment of them; a woman's sphere, on the other hand, is secluded, and in very few instances does her personal history, even though she may fill a conspicuous position, afford sufficient incident to throw a strong light upon her character.

This want of salient points for description must be felt by all who have attempted a faithful portraiture of some beloved female relative. How much is the difficulty increased, when a stranger essays a tribute to those who are no longer among the living and whose existence was passed for the most part in a quiet round of domestic duties!

It need scarcely be said that the deficiency of material has in no case been supplied by fanciful embellishment. These memoirs are a simple and homely narrative of real occurrences. Wherever details were wanting to fill out the picture, it has been left in outline for some more fortunate limner. No labor of research, no pains in investigation—and none but those who have been similarly engaged can estimate the labor—have been spared in establishing the truth of the statements. It can hardly be expected that inaccuracies have been altogether avoided in a work where the facts have to be drawn from numerous and sometimes conflicting authorities, but errors, if discovered, may be hereafter corrected.

Many authorities, including nearly all the books upon the Revolution, have been consulted. My grateful acknowledgment is due to Mr. Jacob B. Moore, librarian of the New York Historical Society, for valuable advice and for facilities afforded me in examining the books and manuscripts under his charge. Others have rendered valuable assistance in the same way, affording me the opportunity of examining family papers in their possession. To them and to those numerous friends who have encouraged me by their sympathy and kind wishes in this arduous but interesting task, I offer most heartfelt thanks. If the work whose progress they have cherished should be deemed a useful contribution to American history, they will be no less gratified than myself that its design has been accomplished.

—Elizabeth F. Ellet

AUTHOR'S 1850 PREFACE

IT CAN HARDLY be necessary to apologize for the appearance of a third volume of this work, in view of the favor with which the first two have been received and the general interest manifested in the subject.

The materials for these additional memoirs are derived altogether from private sources; many among the actors in that momentous drama, whose deeds should have been recorded, are scarcely mentioned by name in historical books, and no full history has ever been written of some parts of the confederation. It seemed, therefore, a duty to rescue from oblivion well-authenticated facts which were likely to be of value to the future historian.

One of the neglected portions of our country is the upper part of South Carolina, where the revolutionary struggle was more painful and destructive, owing to the division among the inhabitants. Those who have charged me with partiality to this state will perhaps be startled to see so many sketches of just one of its districts; for my own part, I wish only that I could have obtained as efficient assistance in the illustration of other states.

To Daniel Green Stinson, Esq., of Chester District, South Carolina, I am indebted for information respecting the women of the Catawba region. Tales of the war were the amusement of his childhood; his early associations were with survivors of that period, and in youth he frequented places where they were accustomed to meet and talk over their battles and adventures. In later years, the Revolutionary pensioners of the neighborhood came to him, as the magistrate, to get their papers drawn up. The task, therefore, of recording the forgotten brave was to him one of peculiar interest, and with unwearied assiduity he collected reliable accounts from various sources, with manuscript records of the day—comparing them with care, visiting aged persons in his vicinity, and writing to those at a distance—sending me from time to time the results of his patriotic labors, and enabling me to present a graphic picture of the war in that region, and such a picture of the condition and feeling of those times of bloody contest between neighbors and acquaintances as can be found in no historical work.

I have also found advantage in appealing to the recollections of individuals for suggesting the names of women whose influence was most prevalent and enduring in the communities where they lived. Isolated instances of heroism—interesting in themselves—may be recorded in journals, but no pen has done justice to the memory of many who, by the impression of mind and character have nobly served their age, and whose influence is still felt and acknowledged. In almost every part of the country, mention is naturally made of women unknown to history yet well remembered in popular tradition as having been prominent. These will usually be found to be representative of classes, and as such, it becomes doubly important to preserve the faithful record of them.

Mercy Warren and the intellectual group around her illustrate the higher order of women in Massachusetts; Mary Slocumb is typical of the spirited dames of North Carolina—embodying the spirit and experience of an even larger portion of our country.

Traditions, however entertaining, should have no place in an authentic record if they are unsupported by indisputable testimony or if they are at variance with history or probability. No small portion of my labor has been in sifting truth from error, and if the scrutiny may be thought too rigid, excluding what might fairly have been admitted, it is better to err on the safe side.

"Truth," says a distinguished correspondent, "is so noble and persuasive a quality in historical composition, that no pains should be spared to preserve it from the least shadow or tint, that can impair its dignity, or tarnish its beauty." In some cases contradictory statements were received from different sources, and the most cautious investigations were necessary to ascertain on which side lay the truth. Sometimes the total demolition of a pleasing story upon examination of authorities gave warning to be ever distrustful.

It may be proper to take this opportunity of answering objections urged by persons whose opinions should command respect. A British critic has charged me with having mentioned instances of cruelty among the Royalists without due notice of their forbearance and clemency frequently exercised. I am aware that it is difficult to avoid apparent partiality in narrating incidents received from descendants of the patriots, who, even if influenced by the remains of political animosity, would naturally remember the noble acts and sufferings of their ancestors, while forgetful of the provocations given, or injuries inflicted, by individuals of their own party.

It must be confessed too, that the very boldness of the women who took an active part, and the impunity with which they indulged in severe speeches to the royal officers, form a strong argument for the humanity and respect with which they were generally treated.

So far am I from being unwilling to do justice to the other side that I only regret my inability—from want of details promised but not yet received—to also portray the devotion, self-sacrifice, and courageous enterprise in the cause of the destitute and suffering by which Royalist women softened the grim features of war and lighted a period of darkness and distress.

—Elizabeth F. Ellet

THE WOMEN OF THE REVOLUTION

ALL AMERICANS ARE accustomed to view with interest and admiration the events of the Revolution. Its scenes are vivid in their memory, and its prominent actors are regarded with the deepest veneration. But while the leading spirits are thus honored, attention should be directed to the source whence their power was derived—to the sentiment pervading the mass of the people.

The force of this sentiment, working in the public heart, cannot be measured; because, amidst the abundance of materials for the history of action, there is little for that of the feeling of those times. And, as years pass on, the investigation becomes more and more difficult. Yet it is both interesting and important to trace its operation. It gave statesmen their influence and armed heroes their victory. What could they have done but for the home sentiment to which they appealed and which sustained them in the hour of trial and success? They were thus aided to the eminence they gained through toils and perils. Others may claim a share in the merit, if not the fame, of their illustrious deeds. The unfading laurels that wreathe their brows had their root in the hearts of the people and were nourished with their lifeblood.

The feeling wrought so powerfully in the community depended, in great part, upon the women. It is always thus in times of popular excitement. During the years of the progress of British encroachment and colonial discontent, when the sagacious politician could discern the portentous shadow of events yet far distant, there was time for the nurture, in the domestic sanctuary, of that love of civil liberty which afterwards kindled into a flame and shed light on the world.

The talk of women in American homes was of the people's wrongs and the tyranny that oppressed them, till the sons who had grown to manhood with strengthened aspirations towards a better state of things and views enlarged to comprehend their invaded rights, stood up prepared to defend them to the utmost.

Patriotic mothers nursed the infancy of freedom. Their counsels and their prayers mingled with the deliberations that resulted in a nation's assertion of its independence. They animated the courage and confirmed the self-devotion of those who ventured all in the common cause. They frowned upon instances of coldness or backwardness; and in the period of deepest gloom, cheered and urged onward the desponding. They willingly shared inevitable dangers and privations, relinquishing without regret prospects of advantage to themselves, and parted with those they loved better than life, not knowing when they were to meet again.

It is impossible now to appreciate the vast influence of woman's patriotism upon the destinies of the infant republic. We have no means of showing the important part she bore in maintaining the struggle and in laying the foundations on which so mighty and majestic a structure has arisen. History can do it no justice, for history deals with the workings of the head rather than the heart. And the knowledge received by tradition, of the domestic manners and social character of the times, is too imperfect to furnish a sure index.

We can only dwell upon individual instances of magnanimity, fortitude, self-sacrifice, and heroism, bearing the impress of the feeling of Revolutionary days, indicative of the spirit which animated all, and to which, in its various and multiform exhibitions, we are not less indebted for national freedom than to the swords of the patriots who poured out their blood.

" 'Tis true," says a writer in one of the papers of the day [*New Jersey Gazette*, 11 October 1780]. "No mean merit will accrue to him who shall justly celebrate the virtues of our ladies! Shall not these defenders of our country, supply a column to emulate the Roman women, stripped of their jewels when the public necessity demanded them?" Such tributes were often called forth by the voluntary exertions of American women. Their patriotic sacrifices were made with an enthusiasm that showed the earnest spirit ready on every occasion to appear in generous acts. Some gave their own property and went from house to house to solicit contributions for the army. Colors were embroidered by fair hands and presented with the charge never to desert them, and arms and ammunition were provided by some liberal zeal.

They formed themselves into associations renouncing the use of tea and other imported luxuries and engaged to card, spin, and weave their own clothing. In Mecklenburgh and Rowan counties, North Carolina, young ladies of the most respectable families pledged themselves not to receive the addresses of any suitors who had not obeyed the country's call for military service.

The needy shared the fruit of their industry and economy. They visited hospitals daily; sought the dungeons of the provost[1] and the crowded holds of prison ships; and provisions were carried from their stores to the captives whose only means of recompense was the blessing of those who were ready to perish. Many raised grain, gathered it, made bread, and carried it to their relatives in the army or in prisons, accompanying the supply with exhortations never to abandon the cause of their country.

The burial of friends slain in battle or chance encounters often devolved upon them, and even enemies would not have received sepulture[2] without the service of their hands.

When the resources of the country scarcely allowed the scantiest supply of clothing and provisions, and British cruisers on the coast destroyed every hope of aid from merchant vessels; when, to the distressed troops, their cup of misfortune seemed full to overflowing, and there appeared no prospect of relief, except from the benevolence of their fellow citizens; when even the ability of these was almost exhausted by repeated applications—then it was that the women of Pennsylvania and New Jersey, by their zealous exertions and willing sacrifices, accomplished what had been thought impossible. Not only was the pressure of want removed, but sympathy and favor of the fair daughters of America, says one of the journals, "operated like a charm on the soldier's heart—gave vigor to exertion, confidence to his hopes of success, and ultimate certainty of victory and peace."

General Washington, in his letter of acknowledgment to the committee of ladies, says, "The army ought not to regret its sacrifices or its sufferings when they meet with so flattering a reward, as in the sympathy of your sex; nor can it fear that its interests will be neglected, when espoused by advocates as powerful as they are amiable." An officer in camp writes, in June 1780: "The patriotism of the women of your city is a subject of conversation with the army. Had I poetical genius, I would sit down and write an ode in praise of it. Burgoyne, who, on his first coming to America, boasted that he would dance with the ladies, and coax the men to submission, must now have a better understanding of the good sense and public spirit of our females, as he has already heard of the fortitude and inflexible temper of our Men." Another observes: "We cannot appeal in vain for what is good, to that sanctuary where all that is good has its proper home—the female bosom."

How the influence of women was estimated by John Adams appears in one of his letters to his wife:

I think I have sometimes observed to you in conversation, that upon examining the biographies of illustrious men, you will generally find some female about them, in the relation of wife, mother, or sister—to whose instigation a great part of their merit is to be ascribed. An example is Aspasia, wife of Pericles. She taught him, it is said, his refined maxims of policy, his lofty imperial eloquence, nay, even composed the speeches on which so great a share of his reputation was founded. I wish some of our great men had such wives; what a pity it is that our Generals in the Northern District[3] had not Aspasias for their wives!

I believe the two Howes have not very great women for wives; if they had, we should suffer more from their exertions than we do. This is our good fortune; a smart wife would have put Howe in possession of Philadelphia a long time ago.

The sentiments of women towards the brave defenders of their native land were expressed in a female address widely circulated at the time and read in the churches of Virginia: "We know that, at a distance from the theatre of war, if we enjoy any tranquillity, it is the fruit of your watchings, your labors, your dangers. Shall we hesitate to evince to you our gratitude? Shall we hesitate to wear clothing more simple, and dress less elegant, while at the price of this small privation we shall deserve your benediction?"

The same spirit appears in a letter found among some papers belonging to a lady of Philadelphia. It was addressed to a British officer in Boston and written before the Declaration of Independence:

My only brother I have sent to the camp, with my prayers and blessings. I hope he will not disgrace me; I am confident he will behave with honor, and emulate the great examples he has before him. I have retrenched every superfluous expense in my table and family; tea I have not drunk since last Christmas, nor bought a new cap or gown since your defeat at Lexington; and what I never did before, have learned to knit, making stockings of American wool, and this way do I throw in my mite for the public good.

I know this—that as free I can die but once; but as a slave I shall not be worthy of life. I have the pleasure to assure you that these are the sentiments of all my sister Americans. They have sacrificed assemblies, parties of pleasure, tea drinking and finery, to that great spirit of patriotism that actuates all degrees of people throughout this extensive Continent. If these are the sentiments of females, what must glow in the hearts of our husbands and brothers, and sons? They are as with one heart determined to die or be free.

It is not a quibble in politics, a science which few understand, that we are contending for; it is this plain truth, which the most ignorant peasant knows, that no man has a right to take their money without their consent. You say you are no politician. Oh, sir, it requires no Machiavellian head to discover this tyranny and oppression. It is written with a sunbeam; everyone will see and know it. We shall be unworthy of the blessings of Heaven if we ever submit.

From all portions of the country thus rose such expression of woman's ardent zeal. Under accumulated evils, the manly spirit that alone could secure success might have sunk but for the firmness and intrepidity of the weaker sex. It supplied every persuasion that could animate to perseverance and secure fidelity.

The noble deeds in which this irrepressible spirit breathed were not unrewarded by persecution. In these days of tranquillity and luxury, imagination can scarcely compass the extent or severity of the trials endured; and it is proportionately difficult to estimate the magnanimity that bore all, not only with uncomplaining patience but with a cheerful forgetfulness of suffering in view of the desired object. The alarms of war—the roar of the strife itself—could not silence the voice of woman, lifted in encouragement or prayer. The horrors of battle or massacre could not drive her from the post of duty. The effect of this devotion cannot be questioned, though it may not now be traced in particular instances. These women were, for the most part, known only to those who were themselves actors in the scenes or who lived in the midst of them. The heroism of the Revolutionary women has passed from remembrance with the generation who witnessed it; or is seen only by faint and occasional glimpses through the gathering obscurity of tradition.

As we recede from the realities of that struggle, it is regarded with increasing interest by those who enjoy its results, while the elements that were its life-giving principle, too subtle to be retained by the grave historian, are fleeing fast from apprehension. Yet without some conception of them, the Revolution cannot be appreciated. To render a measure of justice—inadequate as it must be—to a few of the American females whose names deserve to live in remembrance, is the object of this work.

—ELIZABETH F. ELLET

NOTES

1. Jail official.
2. Interment.
3. The ambitious ten-month American invasion of Canada had ended in military disaster. —Editor's note. All footnotes herein are provided in the spirit of Elizabeth Ellet's generous Prefatory invitation: "Wherever details were wanting to fill out the picture, it has been left in outline for some more fortunate limner."

PART ONE

THE WAR IN THE NORTHEAST

THE SUCCESSFUL BRITISH imperial struggle to wrest control of Canada from the French ended with the capture of Montcalm's Quebec in 1759. Four years later the Treaty of Paris formally ended the French and Indian Wars on the North American continent, but the final removal of the French threat created new problems for the Crown. In the Commonwealth of Massachusetts particularly, men, women, and youngsters of every class, shouting useful slogans like "No taxation without representation," began to reconsider and aggressively test the basic economic and political assumptions that had always bound them to the Mother Country more than three-thousand miles and six sailing weeks away.

In Boston, riots and acts of civic protest like the Massacre and Tea Party polarized the population and sowed the seeds of political commotion all along the seaboard. When the colonial leaders of this well-organized awakening began to stockpile arms and ammunition and started retraining the militia (now called "Minute Men"), the British military decided things had gone far enough.

In the dead of night, part of their garrison sallied forth from Boston, killed a few of the local American militia at Lexington and Concord, and suffered a very bloody nose in return.

The war was on; it would last eight years.

Young men and older veterans of the wars with the French flocked by the thousands to the ad hoc American base at Cambridge.

The entrenchments they dug overnight on a hill outside Boston invited an enemy attack. The result was a serious setback for the British. The Battle of Bunker Hill was the last of the heavy fighting around Boston. The enemy resigned themselves to a siege that would last nine months. Meanwhile,

George Washington, a colonel in the Virginia militia, was appointed by Congress to organize and command the new Continental Army at Cambridge camp.

In March 1776, the arrival and installation of heavy artillery seized by the Americans from the British garrison at Fort Ticonderoga made the enemy's position in Boston untenable. Under a flag of truce, the British evacuated the city, regrouping in Nova Scotia.

New England, the initial cockpit of the Revolution, could breathe easier as the British shifted their military attentions elsewhere. The more than 825,000 men, women, and children living on the farms and in the towns of the Northeast could concentrate on the important home front task of helping to supply the rest of their struggling countrymen.

—LINCOLN DIAMANT

CHAPTER ONE

MASSACHUSETTS

ABIGAIL SMITH ADAMS

Abigail Smith was descended from the genuine stock of the Puritan settlers of Massachusetts. Her father, Reverend William Smith, was for more than forty years minister of the Congregational Church at Weymouth. The ancestors of her mother, Elizabeth Quincy, were first in honor among the leaders of the church.

Abigail was the second of three daughters (see MARY SMITH CRANCH below) and was born at Weymouth 11 November 1744. From her ancestry it may be inferred that her earliest associations were among those whose tastes and habits were marked by the love of literature. Since she had not been sent to any school because of the delicate state of her health, the knowledge she evinced in after life was the result of reading and observation, rather than what is commonly called education.

The lessons that most deeply impressed Abigail's mind were received from Mrs. Quincy, her grandmother, whose beneficial influence she frequently acknowledged. Her marriage to John Adams, nine years her senior, took place 25 October 1764. She quietly passed the ten years that succeeded, devoting herself to domestic life and the care of her young family. In 1775 she was called to pass through scenes of great distress, amid the horrors of war and the ravages of pestilence.[1] She sympathized deeply in the sufferings of those around her.

"My hand and heart," she says, "still tremble at that domestic fury and fierce civil strife. I feel for the unhappy wretches who know not where to fly for succor. I feel still more for my bleeding countrymen, who are hazarding their lives and their limbs!" To the agonized hearts of thousands of women, went the roar of the cannon booming over those hills! Many a bosom joined in breathing that prayer—"Almighty God! Cover the heads of our countrymen, and be a shield to our dear friends."

When the Boston neighborhood was no longer the field of military action,[2] Mrs. Adams again occupied herself with the management of her household and farm. In February 1778 her husband John was appointed joint commissioner at the Court of France and embarked with his eldest son, John Quincy. During the years that Mrs. Adams was deprived of his society, she devoted herself to the various duties devolving on her, submitting with patience to the difficulties of the times. In all her anxieties, her calm and lofty spirit never deserted her, nor did she regret the sacrifice of her own feeling.

The grace and elegance of Mrs. Adams, with her charms of conversation, were rendered more attractive by her frank sincerity. Her close observation, discrimination of character, and clear judgment gave her an influence which failed not to be acknowledged. Her husband ever appreciated her worth and, in the multiplicity of his cares and labors, was sustained in spirit by her buoyant cheerfulness and affectionate sympathy. It was hers to calm agitation, heal the rankling wounds of pride, and pluck away the root of bitterness. With intellectual gifts of the highest order, Mrs. Adams combined sensibility, tact, and much practical knowledge of life. Few can rise to such preeminence, but many can emulate the firmness that sustained her in all vicissitudes.

This is pictured in Mrs. Adams's letters, the publication of which[3] was the first attempt to give tradition a palpable form, by laying open the thoughts and feelings of one who had borne an important part in our nation's early history.

MARY SMITH CRANCH

Mary, Sarah Quincy Smith's eldest daughter, was married in 1762 to Richard Cranch. In 1775, the Cranch family moved from Boston to Braintree.[4]

The life of Mrs. Cranch, Abigail Adams's older sister (see ABIGAIL SMITH ADAMS above), was spent in deeds of charity and kindness. She was remarkable for her cheerfulness and fortitude. In those portions of the country that were the scene of military operations, the energy, heroism, and magnanimity of such women were called by necessity into continual exercise.

MARY DRAPER

Mary Draper was the wife of Captain Moses Draper, of Dedham,[5] and lived on a farm. Mrs. Draper felt the deepest sympathy for the hardships inevitably encountered by the newly raised troops, and considered the limited means she possessed not as her own property but belonging to her distressed country. At the first call to arms, she exhorted her husband to lose no time in hastening to the scene of action; and with her own hands bound knapsack and blanket on the shoulders of her only son, a stripling of sixteen, bidding him depart and do his duty. To the entreaties of her daughter that her young brother might remain at home to be their protector, she answered that every arm able to aid the cause belonged to the country: "He is wanted and must go. You and I, Kate, have also service to do."

"Food must be prepared for the hungry; for before tomorrow night, hundreds, I hope thousands, will be on their way to join the Continental forces. Some who have traveled far will need refreshment, and you and I, with our Molly, must feed as many as we can."

This undertaking, though of no small labor, was presently commenced. Captain Moses Draper was a thriving farmer; his granaries were well filled, and his wife's dairy was her special care and pride. All the resources at her command were requisitioned to contribute to her benevolent purpose.

Assisted by her daughter and the domestic, she spent the whole day and night, and the succeeding day, in baking brown bread. The ovens of that day were not the small ones now in use, but were suited for such an occasion, each holding bread sufficient to supply a neighborhood. By good fortune two of these monster ovens appertained to the establishment, as is frequently the case in New England. These were soon in full blast, and the kneading trough was plied by hands that shrank not from the task.

At that time of hurry and confusion, none could stop long enough to dine. The volunteers were under the influence of strong excitement and were all in such haste to join the army that they stayed only to relieve the cravings of hunger, though from want of food, and fatigue, many were almost exhausted. With the help of a disabled veteran of the French war, who had for years resided in her family, Mrs. Draper soon had her stores in readiness. A long table was erected by the roadside; large pans of bread and cheese were placed upon it and replenished as often as was necessary; while Old John brought cider in pails from the cellar, which, poured into tubs, was served out by two lads who volunteered their services.

Thus were the weary patriots refreshed on their way. When Mrs. Draper's own stock of provisions began to fail, she applied to her neighbors for aid. By their contributions her hospitable board was supplied, till in a few days the necessity for extraordinary exertion had passed, and order and discipline took the place of popular tumult. When each soldier carried his rations, the calls on private benevolence were less frequent and imperative.

But ere long came the startling intelligence, after the Battle of Bunker Hill, that a scarcity of ammunition had been experienced. The inhabitants of Massachusetts were called upon to send to headquarters every ounce of lead or pewter at their disposal, saying that any quantity, however small, would be gratefully received.

It is difficult at this day to estimate the value of pewter as an ornamental, as well as indispensable convenience; the more precious metals had not yet found their way to the tables of New Englanders, and throughout the country, services of pewter covered the tables, even in the mansions of the wealthy. Mrs. Draper was rich in a large stock of pewter, which she valued as the ornament of her house.

But the call reached her heart, and she delayed not, thankful that she was able to contribute so largely to the requirements of her suffering country. Her husband, before joining the army, had purchased a mold for casting bullets. Mary Draper's platters, pans, and dishes were soon in the process of transformation into musket balls.

˙ DEBORAH SAMPSON GANNETT

It cannot be denied that this romantic girl exhibited something of the same spirit as Joan of Arc, the lowly herdsmaid who, amid the round of her humble duties, felt herself inspired with resolution to go forth and do battle in her country's cause—exchanging her peasant garb for mail, helmet, and sword.

There is something very moving in the aspect of Deborah's secret soul, at length impelling her to the actual accomplishment she had pondered in daydreams. The ignorance and error mingled with this enthusiasm should increase our sympathy, without diminishing the share of admiration we would bestow—had everything been evinced in a more becoming manner. In the case before us, the isolation from ordinary domestic and social ties favored the impulse that prompted her to a course so extraordinary.

Deborah Sampson was the youngest child of poor parents, who lived in Plymouth County. Their poverty, rendered hopeless by pernicious habits, was the least of the evils suffered by the unfortunate Sampson children. They were removed from their parents and placed in the homes of different families, where a prospect was afforded of their receiving proper care and instruction to fit them for eventually maintaining themselves.

Deborah found a place in the house of a respectable farmer, whose wife bestowed upon her as much attention as is common in such cases. She was provided with food and clothing but no advantages of education. There was no one to teach her, but she seized every opportunity for acquiring knowledge. She even borrowed books from the children who passed the house in which she lived, on their way to school, and persevered with untiring exertion in her private studies, till she had learned to read tolerably well.

On the completion of her eighteenth year, the law released Deborah from her indenture. Her first arrangement upon becoming the mistress of her own movement was to secure herself the advantages of instruction. Her improvement was rapid beyond example; in a few months she had acquired more knowledge than many of her schoolmates had done in years.

Meantime, the Revolutionary struggle had commenced. The gloom that had accompanied the outburst of the storm hung over the whole land. News of the carnage at Lexington and the sound of cannon at Bunker Hill reached every dwelling and vibrated on the heart of every patriot in New England. The zeal which urged the men to quit their homes for the battlefield also found its way to a female bosom. Deborah felt as if she would shrink from no effort or sacrifice in the cause which awakened all her enthusiasm.

She entered with the most lively interest into every plan for the relief of the army and bitterly regretted that, as a woman, she had not the privilege of a man in shedding her blood for her country. By keeping the district school for a summer term, Deborah had amassed the sum of twelve dollars; she purchased a quantity of coarse fustian[6] and, working at intervals when she could be secure from observation, made up a suit of man's clothing. Each article, as it was finished, was hid in a stack of hay. Having completed her preparation, she announced her intention to go where she could obtain better wages for her labor.

The lonely girl departed, but only to the shelter of the nearest woods, before putting on the disguise she was so eager to assume. Deborah now pursued her way to the American army, where she presented herself on 1 October 1778[7] as a young man anxious to join his efforts to those of his countrymen in their endeavors to oppose the common enemy.

Resolute to continue in the service, Deborah enlisted for the whole term of the war. She was enrolled in the army under the name of Robert Shurtleff and was one of the first volunteers in the company of Captain Nathan Thayer of Medway, Massachusetts.

Accustomed from childhood to labor upon the farm and in outdoor employment, Deborah had acquired an unusual vigor of constitution. Her frame was robust and of masculine strength, and having thus gained a degree of hardihood, she was also able to acquire great expertness and precision in the Manual of Arms exercise and to undergo what a more delicately nurtured female would have found impossible to endure. Soon after joining the company, the recruits were supplied with uniforms in a kind of lottery; that drawn by Robert did not fit. Taking needle and scissors, he soon altered it to suit him. To Mrs. Thayer's expression of surprise at finding a young man so expert in using the implements of feminine industry, his answer was that his mother having no girls, he had been often obliged to practice the seamstress's art.

For three years our heroine appeared in the character of a soldier. During this time, her exemplary conduct and the fidelity with which her duties were performed gained the confidence and approbation of her officers. She was a volunteer in several hazardous enterprises and was twice wounded. The first time was by a sword cut on the left side of her head. Many were the adventures Deborah passed through; sometimes placed unavoidably in circumstances in which she feared detection, she nevertheless escaped without the least suspicion being awakened among her comrades. The soldiers were in the habit of calling Deborah "Molly," in playful allusion to her want of a beard, but not one of them ever dreamed that the gallant youth fighting by their side was in reality a female.

About four months after her first wound, she received another severe one, being shot through the shoulder.[8] Strange as it may seem, she also this time escaped unsuspected; soon recovering her strength, Deborah was again able to take her place at the post of duty.

Her immunity, however, was not destined to long continue. While in Philadelphia, she was seized with the brain fever, then prevalent among the soldiers. For the few days that reason struggled against the disease, her sufferings were indescribable; most terrible of all was her dread lest consciousness should desert her and the secret she had guarded so carefully be revealed. She was carried to the hospital, and there could only ascribe the preservation of her secret to the number of patients and the negligent manner in which they were attended. Her case was considered a hopeless one, and she perhaps also received less attention on this account.

One day the physician of the hospital, a Dr. Binney, inquiring, "How is Robert?" received from the nurse in attendance the answer, "Bob is gone." The doctor went to the bed and, taking the hand of the youth supposed dead, found that the pulse was still feebly beating. Attempting to place his hand on the heart, Dr. Binney perceived that a bandage was fastened tightly around the breast. This was removed, and to the doctor's utter astonishment, he discovered a female patient, where he had least expected one. With a prudence, delicacy, and generosity ever afterwards warmly appreciated by the unfortunate sufferer, Dr. Binney said not a word of his discovery, but paid Deborah every attention and provided every comfort her perilous condition required.

As soon as she could be removed with safety, the doctor had Deborah taken to his own house, where she could receive better care. His family wondered not a little at the unusual interest manifested for the poor invalid soldier. The doctor had a young and lovely niece whose compassionate feeling led her to join her uncle in bestowing kindness on the friendless youth. Many censured the uncle's imprudence in permitting the two to be so much in each other's society and to take drives so frequently together. The doctor laughed to himself at the warnings and hints he received, and thought how foolish the censorious would be when the truth could come out. His knowledge, meanwhile, was buried in his own bosom; the niece was allowed to be as much with the invalid as suited her pleasure.

In the confiding abandonment of woman's love, the fair girl made known her attachment. To Deborah, no other way of amends seemed open, except confession of her real character, and to that, though impelled by remorse and self-reproach, she could not bring herself.

His patient's health now being nearly restored, the physician had a long conference with the commanding officer of the company in which Robert had served, and this was followed by an order to the youth to carry a letter to General Washington.[9] Deborah's worst fears were now confirmed. From the time of her removal into the doctor's family, she had cherished the misgiving, which sometimes amounted almost to certainty, that he had discovered her deception. In conversation with him, she anxiously watched his countenance, but not a word or look indicated suspicion, and she had again flattered herself that she was safe from detection. But when the order came for her to deliver a letter into the hands of the commander in chief, she could no longer deceive herself. There remained no course but simple obedience.

When she presented herself for admission at Washington's headquarters, she trembled as she had never done before the enemy's fire. She strove in vain to collect and compose herself and, overpowered with dread and uncertainty, was ushered into the presence of the chief. He noticed her extreme agitation and, supposing it to proceed from diffidence, kindly endeavored to reassure her. He then bade her retire with an attendant, who was directed to offer her some refreshment, while the communication of which she had been the bearer was read.

Within a short time she was again summoned into the presence of Washington. He said not a word but handed her in silence a discharge from service, putting into her hand at the same time a note containing a few brief words of advice and a sum of money sufficient to bear her expenses to some place where she might find a home. The delicacy and forbearance thus observed affected her sensibly.

Deborah, once again in female garb, returned to Massachusetts, and after the termination of the war, she married Benjamin Gannett, a farmer from Sharon. She bore him three children. Through the rest of her life, Deborah Gannett—voted a war veteran's pension by Congress in 1805—remained the object of much admiration from her friends and the general public.

DOROTHY QUINCY HANCOCK

Dorothy, born in 1750, was the daughter of Edmund Quincy. At the age of twenty-four, she married John Hancock, one of the great men of the age. The honor that encircled the name of her husband received added luster from the fair partner of his fortunes. Mrs. Hancock was not only admirable in the duties of mistress of her household, but in hours of disease and pain, she soothed her husband and calmed his sensitive and irritable temper.

She had her share, too, of the terrors and dangers of the war. When the British made their attack at Lexington and Concord, she was at the latter place with Mr. Hancock and fled with him to Woburn.[10] In after years, she was accustomed to depict many a scene of Revolutionary days in which she was herself an actor or a spectator. She would often describe the manners and appearance of the British officers who had been quartered in Boston, dwelling particularly on the military virtue of Earl Percy—who slept in a tent among his soldiers encamped on Boston Common in the winter of 1774–1775 and whose voice could be heard at the dawn of day, drilling his troops.[11]

Later, at Cambridge, she was one of those who extended courtesies to the ladies of Burgoyne's army, then under the convention of surrender.[12]

SARAH FULLER HULL

Born about 1755, Sarah Fuller was the daughter of a Newton judge. She married the officer, William Hull, a young lawyer from Connecticut. At the outbreak of war, she was one of those women who followed their husbands to camp, resolving to partake of their dangers and privations.[13]

She was with the army at Saratoga and joined the other American ladies in kind and soothing attention to the fair captives after the surrender.

She did the honors of her husband's marquee,[14] receiving his guests of distinction with the grace, dignity, and affability that attracted general admiration. In her later eminent station,[15] Mrs. Hull displayed so much good sense, with more brilliant accomplishments, that she improved the state of society in her neighborhood without provoking envy by her superiority. The influence of her strong intellect, with cultivated taste and refinement, presided in her circle. Those who visited her found a generous welcome and departed with admiring recollections of Mrs. Hull and her family.

LUCIA FLUCKER KNOX

When Major Henry Knox, a resident of Boston, was parading the company to the command of which he had just been elected, he was seen—among many who admired the young officer—by Miss Lucia Flucker, daughter of the secretary of the Province of Massachusetts. Knox's noble and martial appearance[16] naturally attracted the attention of the young lady, and on a personal acquaintance, a mutual sentiment grew up and ripened into love. There existed such a difference in point of station between the young people, as rendered the idea of their marriage a wild vision. Lucy was an Episcopalian, Henry a Presbyterian.

The social position of her father, who had long been in high office, was an elevated one. His family was prominent among the aristocracy of the land, at a time when distinctions in society were strongly marked and clung to as a test of loyalty to the government. The idea that a daughter of this family should favor the pretensions of one inferior to her—even though he kept one of the few large bookstores of which Boston could boast—was not to be tolerated; still less that she should look upon a lover soon to be branded with the name of "rebel."[17] Further interruption was threatened by the growing troubles of the times. Amid the popular discontent, Lucy's father, Thomas Flucker, adhered to the Royal side.

It is fair to suppose that the opinions of the young officer influenced those of the maiden, at least so far as to induce in her a candid examination into the merits of the question; the result of which was that, with all the ardor of her enthusiastic suitor, Lucy espoused the cause of her oppressed country. In the gathering storm, the time came when her decision was to be made. It was made with the true woman's faith and self-devotion, and Lucy pledged herself to the fortunes of a soldier's wife.

Her parents and friends grieved sincerely after what they termed her "apostasy" and used arguments and entreaties to dissuade her from a course which they believed must be destructive to all her worldly prospects. Lucy's father believed she had consigned herself to an unworthy fate and predicted she would suffer in the troubles to come, while her sisters would enjoy the luxury and station she had unwisely renounced. How dimly did they discern the future!

The proud Royalists, who had borne honors conferred by the British government, were compelled to fly from their country, forfeiting the wealth they deemed secure or, after long delay, inadequately compensated for their sacrifices. The poor and self-denying patriots, who gave up affluence and ease for their country's sake, stand eminent in the light of her triumph, crowned with undying fame.

The separation from her nearest and dearest relatives involved in Lucy's choice caused her intense grief and severe struggle, but the path of duty was plain before her, and she bore the trial with firmness, indulging the hope that when the unhappy contest was over, all would again be united.

Mr. Flucker and the remainder of his family removed to England soon after the Battle of Lexington, and Lucy Knox, with her new husband, joined the American army at Cambridge. From this time on, she adhered to a determination to encounter the perils and hardships of a military life. Neither her courage nor her powers of endurance failed.

When Boston was occupied by the British, she escaped with her husband, and in their precipitate retreat, it is said that she concealed the sword he wore through the rest of the war by quilting it within the lining of her cloak. In various journals we find notice of Mrs. Knox's presence in camp. She was constantly with the army and always located near the scene of the action, that she might receive the earliest intelligence and should be at hand lest any accident render her presence necessary.

This was undoubtedly the most anxious and eventful period of her life; truly an ever varying scene of trouble and triumph, disaster and rejoicing. Many were its privations and trials, yet a certain wild pleasure was not wanting in the changeable camp life, when mental faculties were in full play, and expectation was continually excited as to what the morrow—or the succeeding hour—would bring. Mrs. Knox often remarked that she lived more in one year at this period of intense excitement, than in a dozen of ordinary life. And trying as were many scenes through which patriotic wives were called to pass, there were times when a brief repose was granted from the toils and terrors of grim war, and care was cast aside for the moment. General and Mrs. Knox felt strong confidence that all would eventually be well. It is represented that her cheerful manner did much to diffuse discontent.

During the siege of Yorktown, Mrs. Knox remained with Mrs. Washington at Mount Vernon (see MARTHA DANDRIDGE (CUSTIS) WASHINGTON below) with her eldest son, then an infant. Often in after years she described the agitating suspense of that momentous period and the trembling that seized them both on the arrival of the daily express. Sad it is that no formal record remains of the ministrations of women in softening war's grim features. The good they did, however, was at the time acknowledged with respectful gratitude. There is reason to believe that General Knox often deferred to his wife's judgment, regarding her as a superior being, and it is said that her influence and superiority were owned to by Washington himself. Her mind was undoubtedly of a high order and her character a remarkable one. She appears to have possessed an ascendency over all with whom she associated. Her style of dress, which was somewhat peculiar, and her dignified manner gave her an appearance of being taller than she really was.

The influence of Madam Knox (as she was called) on all within the circle of her acquaintance was decided.

She shared the lot of all remarkable persons in having enemies as well as friends. With rare powers of conversation, a memory stored with interesting incidents, and much knowledge of the world, Lucy Knox was—when she pleased—one of the most entertaining of women. Yet she sometimes awed without charming, or gave offense by an air of independence or by the boldness of her manners. Her thoughts were expressed without reserve to those with whom she conversed and sometimes without due regard to the sensibilities of others.[18]

Mrs. Knox is said to have possessed a great talent for management and to have been fond of matchmaking. The military life of which she partook, and her association with those in command, perhaps imparted a tone to her character and deportment. In person she is described as being tall and large; and in manner, lofty and dignified. She preferred the society of men to that of her own sex and, according to accounts given by those who remember her, mingled little with females and had few intimates among them.

When they were in Boston, a frequent companion was Mrs Sarah Hull (see SARAH FULLER HULL above) reported to be of a spirit congenial to Mrs. Knox's own. Both appear to have been what are called "independent women." No portrait of Mrs. Knox remains that does her any justice. It is said that the celebrated Gilbert Stuart had made considerable progress on a portrait but one day suddenly became dissatisfied with what he had done and rubbed it out. Something about Mrs. Knox upset him. He was, as is known, much governed by impulse and could not be prevailed on to renew the attempt.

Mrs. Knox had ten children—only three of whom lived beyond infancy. For eleven years after the Revolution, General Knox served the new country as soldier and secretary of war before retiring with Lucy to her extensive inherited family holdings in Maine. After his death, she lived eighteen more years, until her own passing in 1824.

MRS. OLIVER POND

On the morning after the Battle of Lexington, a company of nearly one hundred militiamen halted before the house of Colonel Oliver Pond of West Dedham.[19] They had marched all night, were covered with dust, and were faint from fatigue and want of food. Their haste was urgent, and the mistress of the house, whose hospitality they claimed, was unprepared for the entertainment of so large a party. Her husband was absent with his own militia, and Mrs. Pond had only one female assistant and the hired man.

But the willing heart can do wonders. In a few minutes Mrs. Pond had a huge brass kettle over the fire, filled with water and Indian meal for hasty pudding. In the barnyard were ten cows ready to contribute their share to the morning's meal. A store near the farm was well supplied with brown earthen dishes for sale and pewter spoons tied in dozens. The military guests volunteered their aid. Some milked the cows, others stirred the pudding, while the two domestics collected all the other milk in the neighborhood. Thus in the short space of an hour, by the energetic efforts of one kind-hearted woman, a hundred weary, hungry soldiers were provided with refreshment.

They ate, and marched on to the place of their destination, receiving encouragement—it cannot be doubted—from this simple manifestation of good will.

SARAH QUINCY SMITH

The mother of Abigail Adams, it is said, took her last illness in 1775 from a soldier who had returned sick from the army and whom she visited at Braintree.[20]

Mrs. Smith was the daughter of the Honorable John Quincy of Braintree. Without the least tincture of what is called pride of family, she possessed a true dignity of character with great kindness of heart, and her efforts to relieve those in need extended to all objects of distress within her reach.

Prudent and industrious in her own domestic management, she was attentive to provide employment for her poor neighbors and was mild, frank, and friendly in her intercourse with her fellow parishioners, who regarded her with unbounded esteem and affection.

MERCY OTIS WARREN

Mercy Warren, at seventy-seven, was the author of an acclaimed three-volume history of the American Revolution. She was perhaps the most remarkable woman who lived in the Revolutionary period. Mercy was the eldest child of Colonel James Otis of Barnstable, Massachusetts, in the old colony of Plymouth, and was born 25 September 1728. The Otis family came to the country about 1630 and settled first in Hingham.

The youth of Miss Otis was passed in the retirement of her home in a routine of domestic employments. Her love of reading was early manifested, and such was her economy of time that, never neglecting her domestic cares or the duties of hospitality, she found leisure to improve her mind by careful study.

At that period, the opportunities for female education were extremely limited, and the more prized on that account. Miss Otis gained nothing from schools. Her only assistant in the intellectual culture of her earlier years was the minister of the parish, from whose library she was supplied with books and from whose counsels her tastes were in large measure formed. It was from reading—in accordance with his advice—Raleigh's *History of the World* that her attention was particularly directed to history, the branch of literature to which she later would devote herself.

In later years, her younger brother James, who was himself an excellent scholar, became her advisor and companion in literary pursuits. There existed between them a strong attachment, which nothing ever impaired—even in the wildest moods of that insanity with which, in later life, that great patriot was afflicted. Her voice had power to calm him, when all else was without effect.[21] The favorite employments of reading, drawing, and needlework formed the recreation of the quiet life in the home which Miss Otis rarely quitted.

When about twenty-six, Mercy Otis became the wife of James Warren, then a merchant of Plymouth. Her new avocations and cares were not allowed to impair the love of literature which had been the delight of her youth. With this fondness for historical studies and the companionship of such a brother and husband, it is not strange that the active and powerful intellect of Mrs. Warren should become engaged in political affairs.

These were now assuming an aspect that engrossed universal attention. Decision and action were called for on the part of those inclined to one or the other side. How warmly Mrs. Warren espoused the cause of her country, and how deeply her feelings were enlisted, appears in her letters. Besides those from members of her own family, the collection includes correspondence with Samuel and John Adams, Jefferson, Dickinson, Gerry, Knox, and others. These men asked her opinion in political matters and acknowledged the excellence of her judgment.

Colonial difficulties, and the signs of the times, continually formed subjects of communication between Mrs. Warren and her female friends. Mrs. Adams says to her in 1773: "You, Madam, are so sincere a lover of your country, and so hearty a mourner in all her misfortunes, that it will greatly aggravate your anxiety to hear how much she is now oppressed and insulted. To you, who has so thoroughly looked through the deeds of men, no action, however base or sordid, no measure, however cruel and villainous, will be matter for any surprise. The Tea, that baneful weed, is arrived: great and, I hope, effectual opposition has been made to the landing."[22]

The friendship that existed between these two gifted women was truly beautiful and touching. Commenced in early youth, it continued unchanged through the vicissitudes of their long and eventful lives, unshaken by troubles, unchilled by cares, unalienated by misunderstanding. Their thoughts were communicated to each other with perfect freedom and openness, and they found in joy and sorrow a solace, or an added pleasure in each other's sympathy and affection.

Another of Mercy Warren's correspondents, Mrs. Macauley, lived in England. In a letter written 20 December 1774, Mrs. Warren describes the progress of the Revolutionary spirit, and speaks forcibly of the aspect of things:

America stands armed with resolution and virtue; but she still recoils at the idea of drawing the sword against the nation from whence she derived her origin. Yet Britain, like an unnatural parent, is ready to plunge her dagger into the bosom of her affectionate offspring. But may we not yet hope for more lenient measures? The ball rolls westward fast and though we are daily threatened with the depredations of Britain, with foreign auxiliaries, and the incursions of the savages, yet each city from Nova Scotia to Georgia stands ready to preserve inviolate—and to convey to our children—the inherent rights of men, conferred on all by the God of nature, and the privileges of Englishmen claimed by Americans from the sacred sanction of compacts.

The following year Mrs. Warren writes: "I hinted that the sword was half-drawn from the scabbard; since then, it has been unsheathed. Almost every tongue is calling on the justice of Heaven to punish or disperse the disturbers of our country's peace, liberty, and happiness."

To John Adams she says: "May nothing ever check that glorious spirit of freedom, which inspires both the patriot in government and the hero in the field with courage to maintain our righteous cause. I will breathe one wish more, the restoration of peace—peace on equal terms; for pusillanimous and feeble as I am, I cannot wish to see the sword put up quietly in the scabbard, until justice is done to America."

During the years that preceded the Revolution, and after its outbreak, Mrs. Warren's house appears to have been the resort of much company. As she herself says, "By the Plymouth fireside were many political plans originated, discussed, and digested." Although the home was in Plymouth, her place of residence occasionally changed during the war. Wherever she was, the friends of America were always welcome to the shelter of her roof and the hospitalities of her table.

In her letters to Mr. Adams, the forty-seven–year-old Mrs. Warren describes the officers with whom she became acquainted. In October 1775 she wrote:

The Generals Washington, [Charles] Lee, and [Horatio] Gates, with several other distinguished officers from headquarters, dined with me at Watertown[23] three days since. The first of these I think one of the most amiable and accomplished gentlemen—both in person, mind, and manners—that I have met with.[24] The second, whom I never saw before, I think plain in his person to a degree of ugliness, careless even to unpoliteness—his garb ordinary, his voice rough, his manners morose; yet sensible, learned, judicious, and penetrating: a considerable traveler, agreeable in his narrations, and a zealous, indefatigable friend to the American cause; but much more from a love of liberty, and an impartial sense of the inherent rights of mankind at large, than from any attachment to any particular persons or countries.[25] The last is a brave soldier, a high republican, a sensible companion, an honest man of unaffected manners and easy deportment.[26]

Every page from the pen of Mrs. Warren is remarkable for clearness and vigor of thought. Thus her style was not vitiated by the artificial tastes of the day, yet her expression is often studiously elaborated, in accordance with the prevalent fashion. This is the case in her letters written with most care, while in others her ardent spirit pours out its feelings with irrepressible energy, portraying itself in the genuine and simple language of emotion. . . .

The late convulsions are only the natural struggle which ensues when the genius of liberty arises to assert her rights in opposition to the ghost of tyranny. I doubt not this fell form will ere long be driven from our land. Then may the western skies behold virtue, which is generally the attendant of freedom. Seated on the throne of peace, where may she ever preside over the rising commonwealth of America.

About this time was published Mrs. Warren's *The Group*, a satirical dramatic piece in two acts, in which many of the leading Royalist characters of the day were humorously introduced. A strong political influence has been ascribed to this and other satirical poems from her pen. It may be imagined that such bold and keen satire would produce a marked sensation and be severely felt by the persons against whom it was aimed. The author herself seems to have had some misgivings, lest her patriotic feelings might have carried her too far.

But the powers of Mrs. Warren were devoted to nobler objects than chastising the follies of the day. She gave her tenderest sympathies to the sufferings of her friends and poured the balm of consolation into many a wounded heart. Nor was her kindness limited to the circle of her acquaintances. Every sufferer from the cruel war had a claim her heart acknowledged, and her benevolence went forth on its gentle mission among strangers. She addressed a letter of condolence to the widow (see JANET LIVINGSTON MONTGOMERY below) of the brave General Richard Montgomery, 20 January 1776, in which the consolatory suggestions are those of a patriot and a Christian.

While you are deriving comfort from the Highest Source, it may still brighten the clouded moment to reflect that the number of your friends is not confined to the narrow limits of the province[27] but by the happy union of the American Colonies, suffering equally by the rigor of oppression, the affections of the inhabitants are cemented; and the urn of the companion of your heart will be sprinkled with the tears of thousands who revere the commander at the gates of Quebec,[28] though not personally acquainted with the General.

The friendships formed by Mrs. Warren were not short-lived; the letters addressed to her evinced the warmth of attachment she inspired, and her own true heart never swerved from its faith. The interchange of sentiment continued for years and, when interrupted, resumed with the same affectionate ardor as soon as the obstacles were removed. She was constantly visited by her friends, and continued to watch the progress of the struggle and to treasure her observations for the historical work she had in contemplation.

Early in 1777 she writes to her friend Mrs. Macauley: "The approaching spring appears big with the fate of empires, and the wheels of revolution move in swift progression. They may smite the diadem from the brow, and remove some tyrant from his throne before he is aware." A soul like Mrs. Warren's must have been continually saddened by grief and pity, in the view not only of the miseries of but the depravity prevalent as one of its consequences. Yet while she mourned the follies and crimes of many to whom her country looked for succor, she followed with ardent admiration the careers of those incorruptible idealistic patriots who kept their faith unshaken by misfortune or temptation.

Her *History of the American Revolution* was written, but not published, till some years afterwards. This work exhibits her as a writer in advance of the age; its sound judgment and careful research, with its clear and vigorous style, give it a high and lasting value, still unimpaired.

HANNAH WINTHROP

In an emotional correspondence with Mercy Warren, written before and after the outbreak of war, Hannah Winthrop, wife of a Cambridge doctor, caught the angry feelings of the civilian population. Her letters uncover a mind of no common order. Soon the subjects on which she wrote became momentous:

JANUARY 1773

"I think one of the most extraordinary political maneuvers this century has produced is the Ministerial mandate transporting the Newportians a thousand leagues for trial.[29]

Oh, America! You have reason to tremble and arouse, if we are not able to say to this Royal Vengeance, 'Hither shalt thou come, and no further.' Many are waiting impatiently the meeting of our Assembly; every eye will be on our political Fathers."

Again, in January 1774, Mrs. Winthrop's patriotic spirit breaks forth:

"The destruction of the detestable weed[30]—made so by cruel exaction—engages our attention. The virtuous and noble resolution of America's sons in defiance of threats of desolation and misery by arbitrary despots, demands our highest regard; may they yet be endowed with the firmness necessary to carry them through all their difficulties, till they come off conquerors. The union of the colonies, and the firm and sedate resolution of the people, is an omen for good unto us. And be it known unto Britain: Even American daughters are politicians and patriots, and will aid the good work with their female efforts."

And again, after the outbreak of hostilities, Mrs. Winthrop writes:

"Can America ever forget, nor will old time ever erase, the horrors of that midnight cry, preceding the bloody massacre at Lexington, when we were roused from the benign slumbers of the season, by beat of drum and ringing of bells at Cambridge, with the dire alarm that a thousand troops of George III had gone forth to murder the peaceful inhabitants of the surrounding villages. A few hours, with the dawning day, convinced us the bloody purpose was executed; the platoon firing assuring us the rising sun must witness the carnage. Not knowing what the event would be with the return of these bloody ruffians to Cambridge, and seeing another brigade[31] dispatched to the assistance of the former, looking with the ferocity of barbarians, it seemed necessary to retire to some place of safety, till the calamity was passed.

"After dinner we set out, not knowing whither we went. We were directed to a place called Fresh-Pond, about a mile from town, but what a distressed house did we find there, filled with seventy or eighty weeping and agonizing women, whose husbands had gone forth to meet the assailants. In addition to this scene of disorder, we were for some time in sight of the battle, whose glittering instruments of death proclaimed by their incessant fire that much blood must be shed; that many widowed and orphaned ones must be left as monuments of British barbarity.

"It was unsafe to return to Cambridge, as the enemy was advancing up the river and fixing on the town to stay in. Thus with precipitancy we were driven to the town of Anderson, following some of our acquaintances. We began our pilgrimage, alternately walking and riding, the roads filled with frightened women and children; some in carts with their tattered furniture, others on foot fleeing into the woods. But what added greatly to the horrors of the scene, was our passing through the bloody field at Menotomy, which was strewn with mangled bodies. We met one affectionate father with a cart, looking for his murdered son for burial, and picking up his neighbor's, who had fallen in battle. Let the inhabitants of America tremble to fall into the hands of such a merciless foe."

Two years later on 11 November 1777, when the fortunes of war had reversed, Mrs. Winthrop describes the entry into Cambridge of the now captive army of General John Burgoyne (see BARONESS FRIEDERIKE VON RIEDESEL below):

"We are at this time delayed with British and Hessian ——— what shall I call them?—who are now prancing at every corner of the town. Last Thursday, a very stormy day, a large number of British troops came softly through Cambridge to Prospect Hill. On Friday we heard the Hessians were to make a procession on the same route. We thought there was nought to do but view them as they passed. The sight was truly astonishing; I never had the least idea that the Creation produced such a sordid set of creatures in human figure—poor, dirty, emaciated men; also great numbers of women—who seemed to be the beasts of burden, having bushel baskets on their backs, by which they were bent double. The contents seemed to be pots and kettles, and various sorts of furniture, with children peeping through gridirons and other utensils; some very young infants who were born on the road; the women barefoot, clothed in dirty rags.

"Such effluvia filled the air while they were passing, that had they not been smoking all the time, I should have been apprehensive of being contaminated. After a noble-looking American advance guard, General Burgoyne headed this terrible group, on horseback. The other generals, all clad in blue cloaks, came after; followed by Hessians, Waldeckers, Anspachers, Brunswickers, etc.[32]

"The Hessian generals gave us a polite bow as they passed; but not so the British. The baggage wagons were drawn by poor, half-starved horses. To bring up the rear, another fine, noble-looking guard of brawny victorious American yeomanry, who assisted in bringing these sons of slavery to terms. Our own wagons, drawn by fat oxen driven by joyous-looking Yankees, closed the cavalcade.

"The generals and other officers went to Bradish's, where they quarter at present. The privates trudged through thick and thin to the hills, where we thought they were to be confined; but what was our surprise when, in the morning, we beheld an inundation of those disagreeable objects filling the streets of Cambridge. How mortifying is it—they, in a manner, demanding our houses for their genteel accommodation.

"It is said we shall have not less than seven thousand persons to feed in Cambridge and its environs, more than its inhabitants; two-hundred-fifty cords of wood will not serve them a week. Think then, how we must be distressed. Wood has risen to five pounds, ten shillings per cord, with but little to be purchased.

"Did the brave Gates[33] ever mean this? Did our legislature ever intend that the military should prevail above the civil? Is there not a degree of unkindness in so loading poor Cambridge, almost ruined[34] before this great army was let loose upon it! What will be the consequence, time will discover.

"Some polite ones say we ought not to look on them as prisoners—that they are persons of distinguished rank. Perhaps, too, we must not view them in the light of enemies; I fear this distinction will be soon lost. Surprising that any of our commanders should insist that the first university in America should be disbanded for the enemy's more genteel accommodation,[35] while we poor oppressed people seek an asylum in the woods against a piercing winter! Who is there to plead our cause? Insults, famine, and a train of evils present themselves to view. I never thought I could lie down to sleep surrounded by these enemies; but we strangely become inured to those things which appear difficult when distant."

Mrs. Winthrop's indignation does not seem to have quickly subsided; in February 1778, she writes to her correspondent:

"Methinks I hear Mrs. Warren wondering how they do at Cambridge? Perhaps her wonder may increase when I tell her the British officers live in the most luxurious manner possible, rioting on the fat of the land, and talking at large with the self-importance of lords of the soul.

"When General [William] Phillips[36] was traveling by Albany where it is very rocky and barren, he expressed astonishment that they should ever cross the Atlantic and go through such difficulty, to conquer so unfavorable a country which would not be worth keeping when conquered. But when they came onto the fertile banks of the Connecticut River, General [William] Whipple[37] said to him, 'This is the country which we are fighting for.' 'Ah,' replied General Phillips, 'this is a country worth a ten years' war.'

"General Burgoyne dined on Saturday in Boston. He rode through the town, properly attended down Court Street and through the Main Street. On his return he walked on foot to Charlestown Ferry, followed by as great a number of spectators as ever attended a Pope. He generously observed to an officer with him the decent and modest behavior of the inhabitants as he passed; saying that if he had been conducting prisoners through the City of London, not all the guards of majesty could have prevented insult. He acknowledges [Benjamin] Lincoln and [Benedict] Arnold to be great generals."

MRS. DAVID WRIGHT

After the departure[38] of Colonel Oliver Prescott's regiment of minute men,[39] Mrs. David Wright of Pepperell and the neighboring women collected at what is now Jewett's Bridge, over the Nashua River, between Pepperell and Groton, clothed in their absent husbands' apparel, and armed with muskets, pitchforks, and such other weapons as they could find. Having elected Mrs. Wright their commander, they resolutely determined that no foe to freedom, foreign or domestic, should pass that bridge.

Rumors were rife that the Regulars were approaching, and frightful stories of slaughter flew rapidly from place to place and from house to house. Soon there appeared on horseback Captain Leonard Whiting, of Hollis, New Hampshire, a noted royalist, who was treasonably engaged in conveying intelligence from Canada to the British in Boston.

By the command of Sergeant Wright, he was immediately arrested, unhorsed, searched, and the treasonable correspondence found concealed in his boots. He was detained prisoner and sent to Colonel Prescott, while his dispatches were forwarded to the local Committee of Safety.

The officer thus taken prisoner, being a polite gentleman, and probably somewhat experienced in the tactics of gallantry, endeavored unsuccessfully—when thus arrested and disarmed—to win his way past by kissing his fair captors. But they were proof against his arts, as well as his arms.

NOTES

1. Hostilities commenced 19 April 1775 at Lexington, Massachusetts, and terminated exactly eight years later.

2. The British withdrew from Boston by sea on 17 March 1776.

3. In 1840.

4. Now Quincy, Massachusetts.

5. Ten miles southwest of Boston.

6. A mixture of cotton and linen.

7. Deborah's pension application gives the year of her enlistment as 1781.

8. Deborah's memoirs say she was struck in the thigh; she walked with a limp the rest of her life.

9. At New Windsor, New York.

10. About a dozen miles northwest of Boston.

11. Percy personally paid the passage home for the widows of his soldiers who fell at Bunker Hill, with additional allowances once they were back in England.

12. Congress shuttled Burgoyne's raggedy seven thousand–man force as far east as Boston (see HANNAH WINTHROP's and BARONESS FRIEDERIKE VON RIEDE-SEL's description of the surrendered army's entry into Cambridge) and as far south as Virginia.

13. Hull served throughout the Revolution, participating in every northern campaign. By 1779, he had risen to the rank of lieutenant colonel.

14. A military tent.

15. Hull became a brigadier general in the War of 1812. Losing Fort Detroit to the British, he was court-martialed, cashiered, and narrowly escaped the firing squad.

16. By contemporary account, Knox—certainly in comparison to his future commander in chief—was actually short and decidedly corpulent.

17. Henry Knox was a leader of the "Tea Party," 16 December 1773.

18. She demonstrated particular disdain for General Greene's immensely popular wife, Catherine.

19. A dozen miles southwest of Boston.

20. Eight miles south of Boston.

21. A charismatic Boston lawyer and agitator, James Otis propounded the important pre-Revolutionary theory that any law in conflict with natural law is invalid. By 1771 Otis had begun to exhibit symptoms of serious mental illness. Yet at fifty he was able to seize a musket and participate at Bunker Hill. Otis was killed by a lightning bolt in 1783.

22. The aggressive Boston "Tea Party" was held in the closing days of 1773.

23. Four miles west of Cambridge.

24. On 15 June 1775, Congress had appointed Washington commander in chief of the Continental Army.

25. On 10 January 1780, responding to his repeated provocation, Congress dismissed Lee from the Continental service.

26. Gates, always intriguing against Washington for command of the Continental Army, had been made brigadier general by Congress 17 June 1775.

27. General and Mrs. Montgomery resided in New York state.

28. General Montgomery was slain at the gates of Quebec while leading a New Year's Day attack in 1776.

29. The previous summer—on 9 June 1772—more than sixty Rhode Island patriots boarded and burnt the grounded Royal revenue schooner *Gaspée*. The ship's customs interceptions had grown particularly galling to smugglers along Narragansett Bay. The British Cabinet demanded the extradition of all responsible, but no Rhode Islander ever came forward to claim the £500 bounty.

30. The Boston "Tea Party" had taken place a month earlier.

31. Earl Percy's relief column, sent to assist the British troops retreating from Concord and Lexington.

32. More than 40 percent of Burgoyne's invading army had been German mercenaries—hired out by their princes to the Hanoverian George III.

33. General Horatio Gates drew up the Saratoga surrender convention terms—never formally endorsed by Congress.

34. Cambridge had served as headquarters for the Continental Army for almost a year in 1775–1776.

35. Many from Burgoyne's "Convention Army" were quartered in the buildings of Harvard College.

36. Burgoyne's second in command. He was later exchanged for General Benjamin Lincoln (captured in the fall of Charleston, South Carolina), and died of typhoid fever at Petersburg, Virginia, in 1781.

37. A New Hampshire signer of the Declaration of Independence, Whipple had taken leave of Congress to join the fight against Burgoyne.

38. For Cambridge.

39. Prescott was a popular local doctor and brigadier general of the Middlesex militia, the brother of Colonel William Prescott, who led the action at Bunker Hill.

CHAPTER TWO

NEW HAMPSHIRE (AND VERMONT)

FRANCES BRUSH ALLEN

Frances Brush was the only child of a colonel in the British army stationed in Boston during the reign of Queen Anne. Her grandfather had seen military service under the Duke of Marlborough. Her mother Elizabeth was the daughter of another British officer. Colonel Brush died before the Revolutionary War, and his widow married Edward Wall of Westminster township, Vermont. Mr. Wall's residence lay in one of the most picturesque and well-cultivated regions of the Connecticut River valley, in an area originally part of the New Hampshire Grants. Such was his wealth and position that he spared no expense in the education of his stepdaughter, who was sent to Boston to complete her many accomplishments.

Fanny was a young woman of more than ordinary intellectual endowments, bold, striking, and original in her conceptions, and of singular facility and clearness in her expressions.

From early life she was brought up to disbelieve in the capacity or general intelligence of the masses for efficient self-government. All her prejudices were nurtured in favor of the British Constitution, as developed by Magna Charta and administered by a king and ministers responsible to the nation. This form of government she believed to be, above all comparisons, the best in the world.

Fanny Brush was in her eighteenth year when Ethan Allen, newly liberated from the Tower of London,[1] was returned to the United States, with the fame of his daring deeds not a little exalted by reports of his sayings and doings beyond the water. It was even said that he had angrily bitten off the head of a tenpenny nail while a prisoner in England. Of all the men of strong energy of thought or action who arrested public attention in the momentous period of the Revolution, there is scarcely one who compared to the zealous and erratic yet firm and indomitable Allen.

Born in Connecticut, he had early been active in the fierce contention between New Hampshire and New York for legal jurisdiction over the present area of Vermont. Allen's bold character had fitted the situation when the people of Vermont refused to submit to either side. He became the functionary of popular will in administering justice without law and obtaining independence without a government. He possessed traits in common with William Tell and Wat Tyler but was in himself unique and original, acting and thinking on the spur of occasion as few other men have ever done.

Allen's views on theology were as curious as his on politics, yet he had fixed points on both, and when the contest of 1775 drew on, he boldly grasped his sword, and by a sudden movement, summoned Ticonderoga to surrender "in the name of God and the Continental Congress." These were the two points of his faith, which led him forward in a series of bold and masterly movements and adventures, marked by an unquenchable love of civil liberty.

"I should like above all," Miss Fanny Brush remarked one evening in mixed company, "to see this Mr. Allen, of whom we hear such incredible things." Her remark reached the ears of the paroled Mr. Allen, who soon after paid a visit to her house and was introduced to Miss Brush.

There was mutually agreeable surprise. Both were manifestly pleased with the tone of thought and conversation which ran on with a natural flow and developed traits of kindred sympathies of intellect and feeling. It was late in the evening before Allen rose. He had not failed to observe the interest his conversation had excited in Miss Brush—only half his age—and said, as he stood erect before her, about to depart, "And now, Miss Brush, allow me to ask, how do you like this Mr. Allen?"

The wild and adventurous character of his early life had prevented him from forming any youthful attachment, and he had enacted his most daring scenes before he appears to have thought of any such connection. Now, seeking a reverse affinity within the mysterious chain of the marriage tie, these two individuals from the antipodes of American society accepted each other—one a bold, free-spoken democrat and stickler for the utmost degree of power to the people; the other, a well-educated and refined young woman of high aristocratic feelings.

In spite of all her deeply rooted prejudices, Fanny Brush had a grasp of thought that could examine questions of inherent right. To this she also brought abiding principles of Christian faith, serving as a guide to judge human duty to government. She also saw and acknowledged the wrongs being inflicted on America, and the justice of the cause in which the colonies had banded together for a higher measure of liberty.

Fanny thus became an intellectual convert to the doctrines of the Revolution. She and Ethan Allen were soon connected. Mrs. Allen proved a most useful and capable counselor to her husband in subsequent critical Revolutionary years. In boldness and originality, her mind was indeed a counterpart to that of her husband. Through her, Allen also felt the happy influence of manners, opinions, and sentiments at once dignified and frank, yet ever mild and persuasive. He did not confine his notions of human freedom and right to questions of government, to which he devoted himself so effectually during the struggle for independence. Mistaking the great theory of "A Substitute for the Lost Type of Righteousness in Man,"[2] he as boldly attacked the doctrine of Revelation as he had the divine right of kings. We only allude to this for the purpose of denoting the later ameliorating effects of Mrs. Allen's opinions, superior reading, and influence on his mind. He is believed to have relinquished these anti-Christian views prior to his death in 1789.

ELIZABETH SMITH PEABODY

Sarah Quincy Smith's daughter Elizabeth, born in 1750, was married to the Reverend Stephen Peabody of Atkinson.[3] Like her older sister Abigail Smith Adams, she possessed superior powers of conversation, with polished and courtly manners. Her reading was extensive, and when speaking to youthful listeners on some improving topic, she would frequently recite passages from Shakespeare, Dryden, and other English poets. She loved to instruct the ignorant, feed the poor, and comfort the afflicted; the young were particularly the object of her solicitude, thus dispensing light and joy wherever she moved.

She passed a useful and therefore a happy life. She formed an early and enduring friendship with Mercy Warren, for whose character and intellect she expressed the highest respect. Her correspondence contains frequent remarks upon the prospect of the country and the movements of the army.

"Lost to virtue," she says to John Adams, "lost to humanity must that person be, who can view without emotion the complicated distress of this injured land. Evil tidings molest our habitations, and wound our peace. Oh, my brother! Oppression is enough to make a wise people mad."

NOTES

1. In September 1775, the impetuous thirty-seven–year-old Ethan Allen, an early leader of Vermont's Green Mountain Boys, was seized by the British in Canada during a premature attack on Montreal—four months after his own legendary capture of Fort Ticonderoga. Clamped in irons, the execrated Allen was carried to England and imprisoned in Falmouth's Pendennis Castle for months. For political reasons undoubtedly connected with his leadership of Vermont's relentless separatist movement fighting domination by both New Hampshire and New York, Allen was returned to America by the British in 1776 and granted parole (which he occasionally broke) inside their lines, until finally exchanged in May 1778 and made a colonel in the Continental Army.

2. The subject of one of Allen's religious pamphlets; many were considered atheistic.

3. Thirty-five miles north of Boston.

CHAPTER THREE

RHODE ISLAND

MARY BOWEN

Mary Bowen, the sister of Jabez Bowen, Lieutenant Governor of Rhode Island, was celebrated for her charitable efforts in behalf of those who suffered in the war. Through her influence and exertions a petition was addressed to the American commandant at Providence for the lives of two soldiers—brothers—who had been condemned as deserters. The petition was successful, and the reprieve was read when the prisoners were already on the scaffold.

Miss Bowen was active in collecting contributions for clothing for the army and assisted in making up the material, exerting herself to interest others in the same good work. General Lafayette was one of her visitors and maintained a correspondence with her. Her information was extensive, her manner gentle and pleasing, and she had the respect and affection of all who knew her.

CATHERINE LITTLEFIELD GREENE

Catherine Littlefield, the eldest daughter of John Littlefield and Phebe Ray, was born on Block Island.[1] In 1753, after the death of her mother, she came with her sister to reside at the home of her aunt, the wife of the colony's governor, William Greene, at Warwick, twelve miles south of Providence. It was here that Miss Littlefield's happy girlhood was passed, and it was here also that she first knew Nathanael Greene.

She often went on visits to her remaining family on Block Island; Nathanael would come there to see her, and their time was spent in amusements, particularly riding and dancing—of which the future general was remarkably fond, not withstanding his father's efforts to whip out of him such idle propensities. He was not discouraged by the example of his fair companion, from any of these outbreaks of youthful gaiety,[2] for the recollections of all who knew her testify that there never lived a more joyous, frolicsome creature than Kate Littlefield. In person she was singularly lovely, of medium height, and light and graceful—although in after years she was inclined to embonpoint. Her eyes were gray and her complexion fair; her features regular and animated.

The facilities for female education being very limited, Miss Littlefield enjoyed few advantages of early cultivation.[3] Catherine was not particularly fond of study, though she read the books that came her way and profited by what she read. She possessed, moreover, a marvelous quickness of perception and the faculty of comprehending a subject with surprising readiness. Thus in conversation she seemed to appreciate everything said on almost any topic and frequently would astonish others by the ease with which her mind took hold of the ideas presented. She was at all times an intelligent listener; on one occasion, when in conversation with a Swedish botanist, she looked over his books and collection, making remarks from time to time which showed her an observer of no common intelligence.

This activity of mind, and her tact in seizing on points so as to apprehend almost intuitively, distinguished her throughout her life. This power of rendering available her intellectual stores, combined with her retentive memory, lively imagination, and great fluency in speech, rendered Catherine one of the most brilliant and entertaining of women. When to these gifts was added the charm of rare beauty, it cannot excite wonder that the possessor of such attractions should fascinate all who approached her.[4]

How, when, or by what course of wooing Nathanael won the bright, volatile, coquettish maiden cannot be ascertained. But it is probable that their attachment grew in the approving eyes of their relatives and met with no obstacle until sealed by the matrimonial vow. The marriage took place 20 July 1774, and the couple removed to Coventry.[5]

Little, it is likely, did the fair Catherine dream of her future destiny as a soldier's wife, or that the broadbrimmed hat of her husband covered brows that should one day be wreathed with the living laurels won by genius and patriotism. We have no means of knowing with how much interest she watched the overclouding of the political horizon or the dire advance of the necessity that drove the colonies to armed resistance. But when her husband's decision was made, and he stood forth a determined patriot—by embracing the military profession, separating himself from the Quaker community in which he had been born and reared—his spirited wife did her own part to aid and encourage him.

The papers of the day frequently notice Mrs. Greene's presence, among other ladies, at winter headquarters. Like Mrs. Washington, she passed the active season of the campaign at home. Hers was the Greene establishment at Coventry, where her husband had erected a forge and built himself what passed for a princely house on the banks of one of those small streams which form so beautiful a feature of Rhode Island scenery. Early in the war, when the army around Boston was inoculated for the smallpox, she gave her house for a hospital. Mrs. Greene was at home during the attack on Rhode Island, and every cannon on the hard-fought day which closed that memorable enterprise[6] must have awakened the echoes of those quiet hills.

When the army went into winter quarters, Mrs. Greene set out to rejoin her husband, sharing cheerfully the narrow quarters and hard fare of the camp. She partook of the privations of the dreary winter at Valley Forge, in that darkest hour of the Revolution; and it appears that, as at home, her gay spirits shed light around her, even in such scenes softening and enlivening the gloom which might have weighed many a bold heart into despondency. Some interesting little notes of Kosciuszko, in very imperfect English, show her kindness to her husband's friends and the pleasure she took in alleviating their sufferings. How much her society was prized by General Greene and how impatiently he bore separation from her, may be seen in his letters. They breathe the most entire confidence and affection. His respect for her judgment and good sense is shown in the freedom with which he expresses his thoughts and unfolds his hopes and plans. He evidently looked to her for support and sympathy in all his cares and troubles.

Notwithstanding Mrs. Greene's ardent wish to accompany the general in 1780, it seems that she was prevented from doing so. Mrs. Washington writes to her from Mount Vernon to say that General Greene was well and spent the evening with her on his way to Richmond. A letter from the commander in chief, written from New Windsor 15 December 1780, encloses for Mrs. Greene a letter from her husband and offers to forward hers. "Mrs. Washington," he says, "who is just arrived at these, my quarters, joins me in most cordial wishes for your every felicity, and regrets the want of your company. Remember me to my namesake; I suppose he can handle a musket."[7]

Mrs. Greene joined her husband in the South after the close of the active campaign of 1781 and remained with him till the end of the war. With the advent of peace, General and Mrs. Greene moved to Georgia, where a grateful Congress had awarded the general a large tract of land, but where he suddenly sickened and died.[8]

NOTES

1. Twelve miles off the coast of Rhode Island.

2. French Lieutenant Clairmont-Crèvecoeur, stationed in Rhode Island in 1780 with Rochambeau, observed that "if Quaker men are more solemn than those of other religions, Quaker girls make up for it with their gaiety and playfulness."

3. In 1777 her husband admonished Catherine to "spell well" when she penned a wartime request to Lucy Knox. "You are defective in this matter, my love," Greene wrote. "People are often laught [sic] at for not spelling well, but never for not writeing [sic] well."

4. Later, in close winter quarters at Morristown—and Valley Forge—"Cathrine's natural charm," observes a contemporary biographer, "won the admiration of countless of Nathanael Greene's fellow officers. A number of men fell in love with her, and she was not beyond encouraging them."

5. Fifteen miles southwest of Providence.

6. The British troops occupying Newport sallied forth 29 August 1778 to attack the withdrawing Americans under General John Sullivan; the all-black first Rhode Island Regiment distinguished itself in the violent battle that ensued.

7. The Greenes had named their eldest son for the commander in chief; the boy later drowned in the Savannah River.

8. Catherine was married again, to the wealthy planter who later backed Eli Whitney's revolutionary invention, the cotton gin.

CHAPTER FOUR

CONNECTICUT

ANNA WARNER BAILEY

At the burning of New London[1] by the traitor Arnold, a detatchment of the enemy army was directed to attack Fort Griswold on the opposite side of the river from the town. The garrison defending the fort, under the command of brave Lieutenant Colonel William Ledyard (see FRANCES LEDYARD below), was far inferior to the force of the assailants, but the gallant spirit of the commander and his men could not brook the thought of retreat before a marauding enemy without an effort at resistance.

They refused to yield and stood their ground until, overwhelmed by numbers after a fierce and bloody hand-to-hand encounter with the foe, they found it impossible to maintain the post. No mercy was shown by the conquerors; the noble Ledyard was slain—in the act of surrender—with the sword he had already placed in the hands of the commander of the assailants. After an indiscriminate butchery, such of the prisoners who showed signs of life were thrown into a cart. Heaped with mangled bodies, it was started down a steep and rugged hill towards the Thames River. The course of the cart was fortunately interrupted by stones and logs, and after the enemy had finally departed, friends came to the aid of the wounded, and several lives were preserved. But their sufferings before relief could be obtained were indescribable.

The morning after the massacre, a young girl named Anna Warner, who later married Elijah Bailey of Groton, left her home three miles distant from the fort and came in search of her uncle, who had joined the volunteers on the first alarm of invasion. He was known to have been engaged in the disastrous conflict and to be among those wounded unto death.

His niece found him in a house near the scene of slaughter. His wounds had been dressed, but it was evident that he could bear no further removal and that his life was fast departing. Still—perfect consciousness remained, and with dying energy, he entreated Anna that he might once more behold his invalid wife and their small child. Such a request was sacred to the affectionate amd sympathetic Anna, and she lost no time hastening home, where she caught and saddled the family horse and placed upon the animal her delicate aunt, whose strength could not have accomplished so long a walk. Taking her little cousin in her arms, Anna bore it the whole distance and presented the child to receive a final blessing from its expiring father.

REBECCA SANFORD BARLOW

Mrs. Barlow was the daughter of Elnathan Sanford and the sister-in-law of the poet, philosopher, and politician Joel Barlow—famous author of *The Columbiad* and other patriotic works. He is said to have owed much of the formation of his mind and character to his older brother Aaron's wife Rebecca; much of the poet's early life was spent in the society of his sister-in-law.

Rebecca and her husband lived in Redding in the southwestern corner of Connecticut, in an area the Indians called "Wampanoag." When the stirring scenes of the Revolution commenced, both Aaron and Rebecca were called to act their parts. The husband entered the army, and in a short time was promoted to the rank of colonel. His military duties required long absences from home, and his young wife was required to take full charge.

Rebecca was of strong mind and united the qualities of resolution and firmness. The courage she displayed in the midst of many trials won the admiration of those who knew her, presenting examples which ought to be recorded for the benefit of her countrymen. No feminine fears were strong enough to prevent the calm discharge of her duty to her family.

During the April 1777 raid by the British on the American arms depot at Danbury, news came to Redding that the British would reach Wampanoag that very night. The terrified inhabitants resolved on instant flight. Each family gathered together such of their effects as they could take with them and quickly quit the village, traveling the whole night to reach a place of refuge. Mrs. Barlow had two sick children and could not carry them away. To leave them was out of the question, so she and her family remained alone to face the enemy, deserted by all her neighbors. No enemy, however, came near the ground, the false alarm having been caused by the firing of some guns below the town.

At another time during the war, a brigade of American troops under the command of General Israel Putnam was quartered during the winter months at Redding. Only a short distance separated Colonel Barlow's home from Putnam's headquarters. The story of Mrs. Barlow's heroism in remaining alone in the village when an attack by the British was apprehended was of course told to the old general and gained his admiration for the intrepid young mother. He also heard much of her cheerful endurance of evils common to all, which she hoped might result in the accomplishment of great good to her country.

Feeling curiosity to make the acquaintance of one whose character met with his strong approbation, on a frosty morning in February, wearing the simple dress of a countryman, he took a stroll over the fields toward her house. He entered the kitchen without ceremony; his ostensible errand was a neighborly request that Mrs. Barlow be kind enough to lend him a little yeast for a baking. But she had none to give and told him so, without suspending her employment to even study her visitor. It was not until the general had departed that a servant told her who it was who had asked the favor. "Had I known him," she said, "I should have treated him with rather more civility. But I suppose it is of no matter, now."

The house where General Putnam made his headquarters was long celebrated on that account. It was eventually taken down so that an elegant mansion might be erected on the spot where it stood. The inhabitants of Wampanoag viewed with regret what they could only deem a sacrilegious destruction of a dwelling so hallowed by the rich reminiscences of a glorious struggle—for the freedom to build a more costly edifice on the same ground.

URSULA WOLCOTT GRISWOLD

For his narrow escape from a British naval patrol sailing up Long Island Sound to Saybrook in 1779, Connecticut's sixty-seven–year-old Deputy Governor Matthew Griswold was indebted to a happy thought by his wife Ursula. The family lived at Black Hall near Lyme, on the east bank of the Connecticut River opposite Saybrook Point, forty miles south of the state capital at Hartford.

Deputy Governor Griswold, a noted colonial lawyer, had made himself extremely obnoxious to the enemy, and the British shore party had been secretly dispatched to apprehend him. He was at home with his family and immediately expected to set forth for Hartford to meet with the legislature, which had commenced its session a day or two previous.

The Griswold family was suddenly alarmed to see a file of enemy marines marching from the beach towards the isolated farmhouse. There was no opportunity for flight; Mrs. Griswold bethought herself of a large meat barrel, or tierce,[2] which had recently been brought indoors, but not yet filled.

Quick as thought, Ursula decided that Matthew's proportions—which were by no means slight—must be compressed into the barrel, the only available hiding place. He was obliged to submit to being so stowed away and covered. The process occupied but a few moments, and the soldiers presently entered the house.

Mrs. Griswold was of course quite innocent of any knowledge of her husband's whereabouts, but mentioned that the legislature was in session at the capital, and that business required his presence. After searching the Griswold house and cellar without success, the soldiers departed. By the time they had regained their ship, the Deputy governor was already galloping up the road to Hartford.

FRANCES LEDYARD

After the capture of Fort Griswold during the British raid on New London, thirty-five men, covered with wounds and blood, trembling with cold and parched with thirst, lay all night on a bare wooden floor in the fort. They felt almost hopeless of succor, looking to death as a deliverance from intolerable anguish.

With the first ray of morning, a ministering angel came to their aid, one who also bore the name Ledyard, imperishably connected with the event. Fanny Ledyard was a near relative of the commander who had been so barbarously murdered (see ANNA WARNER BAILEY above). She brought warm chocolate, with wine and other refreshments, and while a doctor was dressing their wounds, Fanny went from one to another, administering her liquids and breathing in their ears simple words of sympathy and encouragement. To the day of their death, the soldiers who recovered from the wounds they had received at Fort Griswold were accustomed to speak of Fanny Ledyard in terms of fervent gratitude and praise.

NOTES

1. On 6 September 1781, Benedict Arnold—by then a major general in the British Army—led a destructive amphibious raid on the thriving Connecticut port town of New London. It was an unsuccessful attempt to divert American military attentions from Cornwallis's growing plight on the York Peninsula. Arnold's attack on his own hometown burnt more than 140 houses and twelve ships. It began with twin assaults on Forts Trumbull (logs) and Griswold (stone walls) on opposite sides of the Thames River. The forts were named for Connecticut's Revolutionary governor and deputy governor, respectively. American losses in heavy fighting were 215 killed, wounded, and captured; more than 70 soldiers were sabered or bayoneted to death at Fort Griswold after surrendering. British losses were 48 killed and 143 wounded.

2. A forty-two–gallon wooden cask.

CHAPTER FIVE

NEW YORK

CORNELIA Van CORTLANDT BEEKMAN

Mrs. Beekman's was no ordinary character. She was a true patriot and an important one in directing the judgment and movement of others. Her family was one of distinction, from which numerous branches have descended. Her ancestor, Oloff Stevenszen Van Cortlandt, died about 1683, leaving seven children. In 1685, his eldest son Stephanus obtained from Governor Thomas Dongan a patent for large tracts of land purchased from the Indians in Westchester and Dutchess counties.

For many years preceding the Revolution, the family resided in the Cortlandt Manor House, an old-fashioned stone mansion on the banks of the Croton River.[1] It was here that Cornelia, second daughter of Pierre Van Cortlandt and Joanna Livingston, was born in 1752. Her father, who was New York State's first lieutenant governor under George Clinton, served from 1777 to 1795. He was distinguished for his zealous maintenance of American rights. From him, Cornelia imbibed the principles to which she was so ardently devoted.

Her childhood and youth passed in peace and happiness in her pleasant home. At the age of seventeen, she was married to Gerard Beekman and moved to New York City, where her residence was on the street that today bears her husband's name. Cornelia was remarkable for force of will, resolution, and a lofty sense of honor. Steadfast in her principles, she had a mind of uncommon vigor, and a heart aligned to all kindly and noble feelings. Her husband was worthy of her choice in mind, character, and education.

Not many years of her married life had passed when the storm of war burst upon the land. Taught to share in their aspirations for freedom, she entered into the feelings of the people, with all the warmth of her generous nature. She always spoke with enthusiasm of an imposing ceremonial procession of the mechanics of the city, who deposited their tools in a large coffin made for the purpose. They marched to the solemn music of a funeral dirge and buried the coffin in Potter's Field, returning to present themselves, each with musket in hand, in readiness for Revolutionary service.

Finding her continued residence in the city disagreeable in view of the current state of popular excitement, the twenty-four–year-old Cornelia returned with her husband and children to the home of her childhood at Croton, until a new manor house could be completed at Peekskill.[2] This was to be a large brick building, situated on a flat north of the town, at the foot of Regular Hill, the place of encampment for the American army, within sight of Anthony's Nose.[3]

Here Cornelia Beekman resided all through the rest of the war. She was marked by the Royalists as an object of aggression and insult, on account of the part taken by her relatives and friends and her own ardent attachment to the American cause. Although often surrounded by peril and disaster, she would not consent to leave her home. Her zeal for the honor of her family and country inspired her with the courage that never faltered, disregarding evils she had so continually to bear.

When units of the British army ranged through upper Westchester County, she was particularly exposed to their injuries. But her high spirit and strong will supported her through many scenes of trial. Only once was she prevailed upon to leave her residence, being persuaded by her brother, Colonel Philip Van Cortlandt,[4] to retire with her family some miles back in the country for safety from an enemy scouting party on its way from Verplanck's Point. Contrary to her own judgment, she yielded to his counsel, and after being absent a day and night, she returned to her Peekskill manor house. She found it a scene of desolation! Not an article of furniture was left, save a solitary bedstead. A single glass bottle was the only drinking utensil. This disaster was borne with fortitude.

The leading officers of the American army had often been received and entertained at her mansion. But Mrs. Beekman's hospitality was not limited to persons of distinction; she was at all times ready to aid the distressed and administer to the necessities of those who needed attention.

In a particular instance, the firmness and prudence displayed by Mrs. Beekman proved to be of essential service. In the fall of 1780, Lieutenant John Webb, an aide to the commander in chief, spent some time at her house during the operations of the army on the banks of the Hudson. Riding down to Peekskill one day, he passed by Mrs. Beekman's home and requested her to oblige him by taking charge of his valise, which contained a new uniform and a quantity of gold. "I will send for it when I want it," he told her, "but do not deliver it without a written order from me."

He tossed the valise from his horse through the door and rode on to Peekskill, where he stopped to dine. A fortnight or so later, Mrs. Beekman saw an acquaintance, Joshua Hett Smith, whose fidelity to the Whig[5] cause was suspect, come riding quickly up to the house. She heard him ask her husband for Lieutenant Webb's valise, which a servant was directed to bring and give to Smith. Mrs. Beekman called out to ask whether the messenger had a written order from the officer. Smith replied, that he had no written order, Webb having had no time to write one. But, he added, "You know me well, Mrs. Beekman, and when I assure you that the Lieutenant sent me for the valise, you will not refuse to deliver it to me, as he is greatly in want of his uniform."

Mrs. Beekman had an instinctive antipathy to Smith and, with an intuition for which it is difficult to account, she felt convinced he had not been authorized to call for the article she held in trust. She answered, "I know you very well—too well to give you the valise without a written order." Smith was angry at her doubts and appealed to her husband, urging that the fact that he knew the valise was there, and that it contained the lieutenant's uniform, should be sufficient evidence that he came by authority. But his protestations had no effect on Cornelia Beekman's resolve, although even her husband was displeased at this treatment of the disappointed Smith, who thereupon rode away as rapidly as he had come.

It turned out that he had no authority to make the application, and it was subsequently ascertained that at the very time of this attempt, Major André was hiding in Smith's house.[6] How Smith knew that the uniform had been left with Mrs. Beekman is uncertain. But another account of the incident states that Lieutenant Webb, dining at the tavern in Peekskill, mentioned that Mrs. Beekman had taken charge of his valise and its contents. Webb later thanked Mrs. Beekman for the prudence that had saved his property, and had also prevented an occurrence which might have caused a train of disasters. He and Major André were of the same stature and form. Had Smith obtained possession of the uniform, André could have easily made his escape through the American lines.

Under the Providence that disposes all human events, the fate of a nation may here have been resting upon a woman's judgment.

MAGDALEN BEVIER

The sufferings of families during the depredations of the Indians and Royalists on the New York frontier, at Wawarsing[7] and its vicinity, were severe. The women bore their share in the efforts made for defense, loading guns for the defenders and carrying water to extinguish the flames of their dwellings.

In one such fiery attack upon the house of the widow Bevier, the woman and her daughter Magdalen sought refuge in the cellar. The daughter took with her the Dutch family Bible. When the flames approached, they decided to deliver themselves up to the savages and climbed out the cellar window. Magdalen threw her apron over her head, fearing to see her mother killed. As the daughter dreaded, her mother fell prey to a cruel tomahawk, and the Bible was wrested from Magdalen's hands and stamped in the mud, while she was made a prisoner. When afterwards released, she fortunately recovered the treasure she had saved from the flames, with only a few leaves soiled by the mud.

The house of Magdalen's relative, Jesse Bevier, at the Fantinekill, was afterwards also assailed but defended successfully by the spirit and resolution of its inmates. Their gunpowder was laid in basins on the table, and the women helped to load the pieces.

At length the old log house was fired by the Indians at a side where the little band of heroes could not bring their guns to bear. Their situation now became most alarming, and the women applied every drop of liquid in the house to check the progress of the flames. Taking milk, and even swill, in their mouths, they spurted it through the cracks of the logs, in hopes of protracting their existence till relief might come from Naponoch, a few miles away.

In this awful crisis, when death appeared inevitable, the pious wife and mother, knowing that with God all things are possible, proposed that they all should suspend their exertions and unite in petition to the Throne of Grace. Her son replied that she should pray but that they would continue to fight. Her brother-in-law, warned by the loud appeal of a dog, came to the assistance of the house. The Indians and Royalists, not knowing when they heard the firing of their sentry how large a force was coming, withdrew from the house just as the flames had extended to the curtains of the bed.

BLANDINA ELMENDORF BRUYN

Blandina Elmendorf, of Dutch descent, was the daughter of Petrus Elmendorf, a wealthy landowner in Hurley.[8]

Her father died when she was very young, and Blandina grew up in the care of her mother Mary, whose noble character, energy, and pious benevolence on behalf of the destitute and suffering rendered her widely known. It is said that Mrs. Elmendorf had studied medicine so that she might be qualified to practice that healing art when the men of the neighborhood were absent defending their country, with the physicians all requisitioned by the army. She appears to have possessed a mind of a superior order, with the advantages of cultivation.

From this intellectual and accomplished parent, Blandina received her early instruction, with the best education it was possible in that day to enjoy, with the advantage of attending a boarding school in New York City. There she learned to write and speak with ease and correctness in English, Dutch, and French. Her attainments caused her to be regarded as a learned lady in a time when even the privilege of the common country school was enjoyed by only a few, and so many of the daughters of the wealthy gained their instruction at home from books.

At the time of the rupture between Great Britain and the colonies, twenty-two–year-old Blandina had entered into a matrimonial engagement with Jacobus Bruyn. Before long, her fiancé was called into service as an officer in the American army, and the tranquil happiness to which the young lovers looked forward was not yet destined to be. Colonel Bruyn's duty took him to Quebec and elsewhere, and in less than two years brought upon him the hardships of a long captivity.

In the fall of 1777, Sir Henry Clinton made an attack on Forts Clinton and Montgomery,[9] supported by a British naval force under Captain James Wallace. The enemy action was successful. Colonel Bruyn, engaged in the defense of Fort Mongomery, was taken prisoner.[10]

This sad separation from her fiancé, the severest trial Blandina had hitherto been called to undergo, was but the beginning of her sorrows. The capture of Fort Montgomery was immediately succeeded by the British burning of Esopus, said to be the third place settled in New York colony. The town was beautifully situated on the fertile flats above Esopus Creek, with the Catskill Mountains seen in the distance. Esopus had been the scene of previous violence; a century earlier, the Indians of that region, who had been for some time discontented with their Dutch neighbors, made an attack on the town but were compelled to flee to the mountains by troops sent from New Amsterdam by Governor Stuyvesant.[11]

Sir William Howe described the British burning of Esopus[12] "a very spirited piece of service." The general commanding said, "The place was a nursery for almost every villain in the country. On our entering the town, they fired from the houses, which induced me to reduce the place to ashes, not leaving a house standing." "Thus, by the wantonness of power," wrote a Connecticut newspaper, "the third town in the state for size, elegance, and wealth, is now a heap of rubbish. Those who lately possessed convenient dwellings are now obliged to take up with such huts as they find can defend them from the cold blasts of approaching winter."

At this particular period, marked by the reverses that overspread with such gloom the prospects of the country, there was hardly a ray of hope to cheer the most sanguine or lighten the pressure of calamity. In this melancholy state of public affairs, individual misfortune was felt not the less keenly. The fate of Miss Elmendorf seemed linked with that of her suffering country. By the destruction of her native town, her mother's family was broken up and the members for some time dispersed. During this period, Blandina, modest and retiring in her manner and disposed to shrink from—rather than court—the public gaze, allowed the energy of her nature to remain constantly active in deeds of charity and kindness. It was her delight to minister to the sick, to relieve the wants of the poor, and to succor distress everywhere as far as her ability extended.

In New York City, her captured fiancé was soon sent into close confinement in a prison ship, where he could have no communication with his betrothed. He was eventually transferred from the horrors of these abodes of suffering, despair, and death.[13] Yet he was doomed for three more years to endure the weariness of paroled captivity, witnessing his country's struggles for liberty without being able to take part in the contest.

During this long and painful separation, the faithful affection of his fair and gentle mistress remained unchanged, until the season of disaster was succeeded by brighter times. In the spring of 1782 the lovers were finally restored to each other and united in marriage. In spirit and feeling, Mrs. Bruyn was a true and worthy daughter of the heroic age of the Republic.

JANE CANNON CAMPBELL

Jane Cannon was born on the first day of January 1743, the daughter of Matthew Cannon of County Antrim, Ireland. Her earliest years were spent upon Antrim's rocky coast. At the age of ten, with her family, she left Ireland for the North American colonies. Their first settling was at New Castle, Delaware, where they remained ten or eleven years, engaged in agricultural pursuits. Matthew and his family thereupon penetrated the wilderness to the central part of the Province of New York, fixing his home on the extreme frontier in present Otsego County, about seven miles from the village of Cherry Valley.[14]

A year after Matthew Cannon and his family moved to this new abode, his twenty-two–year-old daughter Jane married Samuel Campbell, a son of one of the first settlers of Cherry Valley. The young man was already distinguished for his energy of character and bold spirit of enterprise. At the commencement of the Revolution, both Mrs. Campbell's father and husband embraced the quarrel of the colonies with great ardor. They both served on the local Committee of Safety, and at an early period pledged themselves to the achievement of national independence. Both became actively engaged in the long and bloody warfare on the frontier.

Samuel Campbell was early chosen to command the local militia and at the general request, converted his own house into a garrison, where for two years, until a proper fort could be erected, the inhabitants of Cherry Valley gathered for protection. In all his patriotic efforts, Colonel Campbell not only had the sympathy of his wife but found her a zealous and efficient cooperator. Her feelings were ardently enlisted in behalf of her adopted country, and she was ready to give all her exertions to the cause, as well as to urge forward those who had risen against the oppressor.

In August 1777, Colonel Campbell, with his regiment, took part in the Battle of Oriskany,[15] the bloodiest in proportion to the number of men engaged of any in the Revolution. Colonel Campbell's brother was killed by his side, and he himself narrowly escaped death.

In November 1778, a force composed principally of Indians and Royalists invaded and utterly destroyed the settlement at Cherry Valley. Colonel Campbell was absent from home at the time. Mrs. Campbell's father Matthew, who was in her house, attempted almost singlehandedly to oppose the advance of the enemy. Notwithstanding that resistance was madness, the brave old man refused to yield until he was wounded and finally overpowered. Imagination alone can depict the terror and anguish of the mother trembling for her children in the midst of this scene of strife and carnage. With twenty or thirty others, the Campbell family was dragged away as prisoners by the triumphant Indians, and the house was presently in flames. The prominent position and services of Colonel Campbell had rendered him peculiarly obnoxious to the enemy, and it was well known that his wife had constantly aided his and her father's movements and that her determined character and excellent judgment had been of service to all the friends of liberty in that region.

Because of this, Mrs. Campbell and her children were considered important captives, and while most of the other women with their little ones were released after a day or two and permitted to return to what was left of their homes, no such mercy was extended to Mrs. Campbell. She was informed that she and her children must accompany their captors to the land of the Senecas. On the second day of her captivity, her mother was killed at her side; the aged and infirm lady was unable to keep pace with the rest. Mrs. Campbell carried in her arms an eighteen-month-old infant, and for the sake of all her little ones she dragged on her weary steps in spite of failing strength. This arduous, long, and melancholy journey began on the eleventh of November. Mrs. Campbell was taken down the valley of the Susquehanna, to its junction with the Tioga and thence into the western part of New York.[16] Mrs. Campbell's older children were separated from her en route, being given to Indians of different tribes, and upon her arrival at the Seneca "castle," her infant—the last link which visibly bound her to home—was also taken from her.

Long and dreary was the winter that followed. In one respect Mrs. Campbell was fortunate. She was placed with an Indian family composed of females, with the exception of one aged man, and with the tact that always distinguished her she began at once to make herself useful, thus early securing the confidence and even the admiration of these daughters of the forest. She taught them some of the arts of her civilized life and made garments, not only for the family to which she now belonged but also for those in the neighborhood, who sent corn and venison in return.

After a year and a half, a proposed exchange of Mrs. Campbell and her children for the captured wife and sons of Colonel John Butler[17] was agreed upon by Governor George Clinton and General Philip Schuyler. Early in the spring of 1779 Colonel Campbell despatched an Indian messenger to Colonel Butler at Fort Niagara. Butler soon came to the Indian council near Canadaseago to confer on the subject of giving up prisoners. In June Mrs. Campbell was sent to Fort Niagara where many persons took refuge, preparation being made for the expected attack by General John Sullivan which never took place. She was detained another year as a prisoner in the fort but had the solace of her children, all of whom save one were obtained from the Indians by Butler and restored to her. She associated freely with the wives of the British officers in the garrison, and in the summer of 1780 she received her first letter from her husband, carried by a friendly Oneida Indian. In June she was sent with her children to Montreal, where she recovered her missing child, a boy now seven years old, whom she had not seen since the day after the massacre at Cherry Valley. He had forgotten his native tongue.

At Montreal, the exchange of prisoners was effected, and in the fall Mrs. Campbell and her children finally reached Albany, escorted into that city by a detachment of troops under the command of Colonel Ethan Allen. Here Colonel Campbell awaited their arrival, and the trials of a two years' captivity were almost forgotten in the joy of restoration. At the close of the war, they returned to Cherry Valley and literally began the world anew.

MRS. JACKSON

Mrs. Jackson resided on a farm on New York City's Staten Island, a well-known "nest of Royalists." Although her husband did not join the American army, his zeal in the cause of his country led the enemy to think it proper to banish him. He was nine months confined in the provost,[18] and, for the remainder of a two-year sentence, was paroled on Long Island.

During his absence, the Jackson house was for a great part of the time the abode of British officers, who made themselves quite at home, but by firmness and spirit, Mrs. Jackson saved herself much inconvenience. From time to time, with the utmost secrecy, she was in the habit of sending provisions to the Americans on the opposite New Jersey shore, using the black man she employed to cross the water unsuspected by the watchful enemy. Once she kept a muzzled calf under her bed all day, before surreptitiously sending it to the American soldiers.

Mrs. Jackson sometimes came to New York City with friends, to visit prisoners in the provost. On such occasions they would be met at Whitehall[19] by a gentleman who, although of Whig principles, had been permitted to remain in the city. He would accompany the ladies to the prison, where he directed them, if they wished to convey any money to a captive, to drop it silently as they went past, while he walked just behind, so as to screen the action from observation by the stern provost marshal.[20]

JANET LIVINGSTON MONTGOMERY

Janet Livingston Montgomery was the sister of Congressman Robert R. Livingston[21] and the widow of Brigadier General Richard Montgomery. After her husband's death, Janet Montgomery lived in seclusion at Montgomery Place.[22]

Mrs. Montgomery is best remembered through her continued sympathetic correspondence with Mercy Otis Warren (see MERCY OTIS WARREN above). The letters dwell upon her irreparable loss, breathing a tender sorrow mingled with an ardent spirit of patriotism.

In a typical November 1777 exchange, Mrs. Warren writes:

It may further brighten the clouded moment to reflect that the number of your friends is not confined to the narrow limits of the State of New York. By the happy union of the American colonies suffering equally the rigor of oppression, the urn of the companion of your heart will be sprinkled with the tears of thousands who—though not personally acquainted with General Montgomery—revere the commander at the gates of Quebec.

To which Mrs. Montgomery replied:

My dear Madam—The sympathy that is expressed in every feature of your letter claims from me the warmest acknowledgments. The profession of friendship from one who so generously feels and melts at the woes of a stranger, not only soothes but flatters me. It is very kind of you, Madam, to seek for alleviating consolations in a calamity. Affectionate friends such as you have lightened the load of misery. With America, I weep the loss of the firm soldier, and the friend to freedom.

Let me repeat his last words when we parted: "You shall never blush for your Montgomery!" Nobly has he kept his word. I trust to the sustaining hands of friendship to assist me safely to rise superior to my misfortune, content to drag out the remainder of my life until the Supreme Being who has deprived me of my husband will kindly close this melancholy scene, and once more unite me with him in a world of peace where the tyrant shall no more wantonly shed the blood of his innocent subjects, and where vice and virtue will receive their proper reward.

MARY LINDLEY MURRAY

Mary Lindley was born to a Quaker family in Pennsylvania and resided in that colony for some years after her marriage to Robert Murray, a Quaker convert living near Lancaster. In 1753 the Murrays moved to New York, where Mr. Murray slowly became one of the city's wealthiest and most respected merchants. Mrs. Murray is remembered as a person of great dignity and amiable disposition.

Between 1764 and 1775, the Murrays lived in England. On their return to New York, Mr. Murray established a small country seat called The Grange, on what is now Murray Hill.[23] Mr. Murray was descended from a noble Scots family, and it was natural that he retained their prejudices. He continued to be disposed to royalism during his lifetime, while his wife joined with all her sympathies in the contest for the liberty of her native land.

On the American retreat from New York City, Major General Israel Putnam's troops were the last to leave. To avoid any enemy parties that might be advancing to cut them off, Putnam chose a road close to the Hudson River conducting him in a direction to join the rest of the army. A force of British and Hessians twice as large as Putnam's own was advancing toward the river road at the same time. But for a fortunate occurrence, the enemy would have encountered and cut off Putnam and his men.

In ignorance of their proximity, the British officers halted their troops at The Grange, where Mrs. Murray treated them to cakes and wine, and by means of her refreshment and agreeable conversation, beguiled them to stay a couple of hours. Governor William Tryon jested with her occasionally about her "American friends." Mrs. Murray might have turned the laugh upon him, for one half hour would have enabled the British to secure the road along the river, and cut off Putnam's retreat. The opportunity was lost, and it became a common saying among the American officers that Mrs. Murray had saved this part of their army.[24]

CATHERINE Van RENSSELAER SCHUYLER

Catherine Van Rensselaer was the only daughter of John Van Renssselaer, a Hudson River patroon and a patriot in the Revolutionary struggle. He was noted for his unusual kindness and forbearance towards the tenants of his vast estates. (It cannot be doubted that the present-day "anti-rent" struggles that have almost convulsed the state can be traced to the amiable but injudicious indulgence of this great landholder and his immediate heirs.)

Catherine became the wife and beloved companion of Philip Schuyler of Albany, cherishing his social virtues and adding luster to his fame. Those who shared Schuyler's hospitality or felt the charm of his polished manners could also testify to the excellence of her whose gentle influence was always apparent.

The qualities which shone in remarkable acts were consistently exercised by Catherine Schuyler. In the domestic sphere, at the head of a large family, her management was so perfect that the regularity with which all went on appeared to be spontaneous. Her friendships were warm and constant, and she always found time for dispensing charity to the poor; many families remembered with gratitude the quiet aid they received from her. Mrs. Schuyler possessed great self-control, and as the mistress of the household, her prudence was blended with unvarying kindness.

The mansion house in which the Schuylers resided was built under Catherine's supervision in 1760–1761, while her husband was in England on business. It was large and highly ornamented in the Dutch taste. During the French war it was a place of resort for British officers and travelers of note.

The Schuylers also maintained an elegant country seat near Saratoga—destroyed by General John Burgoyne. Catherine Schuyler's resolution and courage proved equal to any emergency. When the Continental Army was retreating before Burgoyne from Fort Edward,[25] Mrs. Schuyler went up herself in a carriage to see to the removal of her furniture. While there, she received directions from the general to set fire with her own hand to their extensive fields of wheat, and to request all the tenants to do the same thing—rather than suffer them to be reaped by the enemy. His injunction showed his confidence in her spirit and firm patriotism.

It was one of the ironies of the war that, after the British surrender, the captive general and his staff should be entertained in Albany by the same family whose country home and property he had laid waste (see BARONESS FREDERIKE VON RIEDESEL below). The courtesy and kindness shown by the Schuylers to Burgoyne and their generous forgetfulness of their losses were sensibly felt and acknowledged. This delicacy drew from the enemy general the observation, "You are too kind to me, who has done so much injury to you!" The reply was characteristic of the warmhearted victor: "Such is the fate of war; let us not dwell upon the subject."

LADY STIRLING (SARAH LIVINGSTON ALEXANDER)

Sarah Livingston was the daughter of Philip Livingston, second proprietor of Livingston Manor on the upper Hudson River. She was the sister of Governor William Livingston of New Jersey. Her husband was William Alexander, customarily addressed as "Lord Stirling,"[26] who served throughout the war as one of Washington's most dependable generals.

Fifty-three years old at the time of the Revolution, Lady Stirling usually accompanied her husband in the field, and while Lord Stirling was in the camp at White Plains in 1776, she was able to pay a visit to New York City, then in possession of the British, to see her eldest daughter Mary, the wife of Robert Watts. Lady Stirling was accompanied by her youngest daughter, Lady Catherine. Mr. Watts and his wife had remained quietly in the city, taking no active part on either side. Letters of mother and daughter describe the situation and show the temper of those Americans who continued in the city during its occupation by the enemy.

Lady Catherine, writing some time after the visit, is sanguine in her hopes of seeing her relatives become as zealous patriots as she herself: "Mr. Watts is among those who are heartily sick of the tyranny they have witnessed. As to Mary, her political principles are now perfectly rebellious. The sentiments of a great number of people have undergone a thorough change since they have been under the rule of the British Army. They have had many opportunities to see flagrant acts of injustice and cruelty which they had not believed their friends capable of. This convinces them that if the British conquer, we will live in abject slavery."

Lady Stirling refused to avail herself of permission from Sir Henry Clinton to take anything she pleased out of the city, fearing there would be a handle made of it if she accepted. "The last time I saw Mr. Andrew Elliot,"[27] she writes, "he told me I must at least take a box of tea. But I stuck to my text."

MARGARET TODD WHETTEN

Margaret Todd, born in New York City in 1736, married William Whetten of Devonshire, England. As a boy, before the French and Indian wars, Whetten had emigrated to this country without his parents. After commanding vessels trading with the West Indies, he settled in New York. At the commencement of the Revolution, he sold his ships, investing the greater part of the proceeds in the new paper currency of the state government and congress.

When the *Asia* fired on the city on 24 August 1776,[28] Whetten took the alarm like many of the city's inhabitants and moved with his family to New Rochelle.[29] He was a zealous patriot, though prevented by infirm health from taking an active part in the struggle. Here, far from finding a refuge from the perils of war, the Whetten family in New Rochelle soon discovered themselves to be in a situation of even greater danger. The American forces, contending the ground from one post to another, were for some time stationed near the troops of Lord Howe. The Whettens found themselves midway between the hostile lines, and during the movement of the two armies toward White Plains, devastation and famine marked the whole region through which they passed.

One night, after the family had retired, Mrs. Whetten was awakened by a noise without and called her husband, supposing some of the Americans had come to the village for provisions. He arose and, going to the door, was assailed by oaths and cries from some British soldiers demanding entrance. To the question "Are you King's men, or rebels?" Mr. Whetten replied, "I am a friend to humanity." The soldiers searched the house, stole some items, and went off.

The scarcity of provisions caused great suffering among the inhabitants of the village. Supplies that might reach the Continental troops were intercepted by the enemy, and the little bit the people had was often taken from them. The difficulty of procuring provisions at New Rochelle at length compelled the Whettens to return to New York. Mr. Whetten's health was declining rapidly, and he died a short time after. In the midst of danger and disaster, the family's care devolved upon his widow, who proved herself equal to the charge. Nearly all her money was in paper currency which Mr. Whetten had estimated as more valuable than gold. When the currency depreciated, Mrs. Whetten was often urged to exchange her paper for hard money but steadily refused. "I will never," she said, "undervalue the currency established by Congress." The consequence of this disinterested patriotism was the loss of all, but the high-spirited matron never regretted the sacrifice.

For some time, the family could not obtain possession of their own house, but through the friendly offices of Andrew Elliot, they were at length permitted to occupy it. A full account of their experience during their residence in the city for the succeeding six years of the war would present a graphic picture of the state of the times. Mrs. Whetten bore her part without shrinking, both in action and endurance. Her benevolent feelings prompted her to do good to all, especially oppressed anti-royalists, for whom her house was always an asylum. The British were sometimes quartered upon her, and she was required to board many American prisoners, who had reason to remember her kindness.

Once, when some of her countrymen, having dined with her, asked what compensation was due, she replied, "Nothing, if you all eat heartily." She made it her daily business to prepare food for the captured American soldiers and sent it regularly to the prisons, as well as to the hospitals. She went sometimes with her daughters to see the prisoners and encouraged them by cheerful conversation.

Occasionally they visited that modern Bastille, the Provost, where the marshal, the notorious William Cunningham, would now and then show his displeasure by kicking over the baskets of food they brought and beating the unfortunate prisoners with his keys. Mrs. Whetten and her daughters continually provided not only food but clothes for the captive soldiers not heeding the surliness of their gaolers or the risk of indignity to themselves. Cunningham told a gentleman that these ladies were the "the d—dest rebels in New York," but so true to the prisoners he could not often refuse to let them come.

Nor did Mrs. Whetten hesitate to risk her own safety by receiving persons suspected of serving the American cause. When a party of soldiers was sent to her house to arrest a suspected spy, she, having notice of their approach, had just time to slip a dressing gown and nightcap upon her guest, place him in a large easy chair, and put a bowl of gruel into his hand. When the guards came, Mrs. Whetten showed them the seeming invalid, and they left him, determined to return and take him as soon as he should be sufficiently recovered. The officer in charge of the soldiers was reprimanded and immediately ordered back, but by then the object of suspicion had disappeared.

The dread of being persecuted as obnoxious was no small part of the Whetten family's trials, for they knew how others had been treated under similar circumstances.

The time finally approached which was to end these dangers and sufferings. It was announced that New York was to be evacuated by the British.[30] The rejoicing of patriotic families who had lived so long in the midst of enemies was of course great at this cheering prospect. The house of Mrs. Whetten, called during the war "Rebel Headquarters," was the first in New York to which the news of peace was brought; a French gentleman, a prisoner who boarded with Mrs. Whetten, received from the French ambassador at Philadelphia a letter containing the earliest account. After the establishment of peace, the services of Mrs. Whetten to the American cause did not fail to receive thankful acknowledgment. A letter was written to her from General Washington expressing his warm gratitude on behalf of the country. He also desired leave to breakfast with her, and during the meal, while conversing about the scenes through which her family had passed, he thanked her for the kindness which she had shown the American prisoners at such risk to herself and the substantial aid she had rendered.

NOTES

1. An east Hudson tributary thirty-five miles north of New York City.

2. On the Hudson River, seven miles above her father's manor house at Croton.

3. A prominent mountain near the entrance to the Hudson River Highlands.

4. Commanding the second New York Regiment.

5. General term for the liberal reform faction in seventeenth- and eighteenth-century British and American parliamentary politics. The word derived from "Whiggamores," Scots Presbyterian protesters who marched on Edinburgh Castle in 1648 and later fought the accession of the converted Catholic Duke of York to the British throne (as James I).

6. Joshua Hett Smith's Haverstraw home provided André with a "safe house" after Benedict Arnold's secret meeting with the British spy.

7. Twenty-five miles west of Poughkeepsie.

8. A village three miles north of Kingston (originally Esopus), settled by the Dutch in 1652.

9. Twin forts on the Hudson, guarding a heavy iron chain across the river forty miles north of New York City. Fort Clinton was named for George Clinton, general in the Continental Army and also Governor of New York State; Fort Montgomery's name honored the fallen hero of the battle for Quebec.

10. Colonel Bruyn was one of more than one-hundred Americans captured in the battle. He was carried to New York City and initally locked up in the old Sugar House. The former sugar warehouses near Old Broadway were the most infamous of the city's military prisons.

11. The "Wiltwyck War" of 1663 was the most serious of many seventeenth-century conflicts between the Native Americans and Dutch settlers. It was New Amsterdam's practice to ship captured Indians as slaves to Curaçao.

12. Renamed "Kingston" in 1664 when the British seized New York from Holland, the town eventually became the first capital of the new state of New York.

13. Colonel Bruyn was lucky; an estimated eight thousand to eleven thousand American soldiers died during the war on the handful of rotting, overcrowded, unsanitary dismasted British prison hulks lying in East River's Wallabout Bay. Colonel Bruyn's rank certainly helped him.

14. Fifty miles west of Albany.

15. By turning back a British column from Fort Niagara this fierce engagement at Oriskany effectively contributed to the American success at Saratoga.

16. This was the land of the Six Nations of the Iroquois Confederacy, ravaged two years later by General John Sullivan's punitive expedition.

17. Butler, originally from Connecticut, became an active leader in the Mohawk Valley, commanding Indian/Royalist raids against the exposed frontier settlements at Wyoming, Wawarsing, and Cherry Valley.

18. One of New York City's military jails.

19. The southern tip of Manhattan Island.

20. "Stern" is a mild epithet for William Cunningham, called by some "a burly, ill-mannered scoundrel," who reportedly starved two-thousand American captives to death and hanged two-hundred-fifty others without trial.

21. A codrafter of the Declaration of Independence.

22. An estate on the east bank of the Hudson River, twenty miles above Poughkeepsie. The Royal Navy cannonaded the Montgomery home in October 1777.

23. An eminence at the middle of Manhattan Island, below present-day 42nd Street.

24. This tale, repeated by dozens of military historians, is one of the most enduring Revolutionary War myths. The enemy troops, flushed with victory, would have pressed ahead no matter how or where their officers were taking their ease.

25. A military post on the Hudson River 14 miles north of Saratoga and forty-two miles from Albany.

26. At a time when Old World military operations were generally led by titled noblemen, the energetic Sixth Earl of Stirling—American Major General William Alexander—was the only such officer in the republican army. Born in New York City in 1726, Alexander had unsuccessfully asserted before the House of Lords his claim to the hereditary Scots title.

27. Royal Collector of the Port of New York—highly esteemed by both parties for his integrity of character and urbanity of manner.

28. Lying off the Battery, Captain George Vandeput's HMS *Asia* lobbed several round shot into a group of townspeople wrestling heavy cannon off the ram-

parts of Fort George for use in new upriver fortifications. Three Americans were killed, for which Vandeput promptly apologized.

29. A Westchester County village twenty-five miles north of New York City.

30. Completed 25 November 1783.

PART TWO

THE WAR IN THE MIDDLE STATES

IN THE LATE spring of 1776, while British troopships regrouped at Halifax, awaiting the arrival in America of thousands of King George III's German mercenaries, Washington repositioned his available Continental troops and militia in and around New York City, digging earthworks throughout lower Manhattan and on the heights of Brooklyn.

But the huge amphibious force the enemy assembled and finally brought into New York Harbor in late summer proved irresistible. The subsequent Battles of Long Island and Brooklyn were disasters for the Americans. With adroit maneuvering and a lot of good luck, Washington managed to extricate his army from New York City, unwisely leaving a three-thousand–man garrison behind at Fort Washington on upper Manhattan.

After a standoff battle in October at White Plains, pursued by British Generals Howe and Cornwallis, Washington crossed the Hudson to New Jersey, leaving Fort Washington to be swallowed up by a Hessian attack. At a critical moment in the Revolution, the commander in chief lost almost one-third of his army. The captured Americans ended up in New York's stinking jails and rotting prison ships. Many were kept alive only through the brave intercession of a handful of Revolutionary women left behind in the American evacuation of the city. It was among the worst of the "times that tried men's souls."

As the enemy harried the fleeing Americans across northern New Jersey and into Pennsylvania, few would have dreamed that before the year's end, Washington would rally his starving troops to turn on their pursuers, re-crossing the Delaware to smash Cornwallis and his Hessians at Trenton and Princeton before heading for miserable winter quarters at Morristown.

In the spring of 1777, things looked a bit brighter, but the passage of both armies in New Jersey and elsewhere on the seaboard was marked by wanton destruction and death. The men, women and children—more than 750,000 in the Middle States—suffered greatly, particularly those living along main roads through the countryside.

The British occupation of Philadelphia (the new nation's capital) in 1777 and 1778 also took its toll on much of the civilian population. But while Washington battled the British along the Brandywine, the threat of an enemy invasion from Canada became a reality. General Burgoyne commanded seven-thousand British and German troops, but the eight-thousand Americans, led by Generals Gates, Schuyler, and Arnold, were too much for him; he surrendered his entire army. In a war with many turning points, this one was probably the greatest.

Despite this major victory in the north, the position of the bulk of Washington's army during the winter of 1777–1778 in the grim encampment at Valley Forge was precarious. But the freezing, starving, and ragged soldiers somehow endured. In the summer of 1778 when the British and their Philadelphia Royalist friends streamed out of the capital on foot, heading for New York City, the Americans also poured out of Valley Forge in hot pursuit.

Washington caught up with the enemy at Monmouth, where both sides drubbed each other in the longest battle of the war on the hottest day of the year. It was also the last major battle of the Revolution to be fought in the Northeast and Middle States.

—LINCOLN DIAMANT

CHAPTER SIX

NEW JERSEY

ELIZABETH ROGERS BORDEN

Early in 1778 at a period when American prospects were most clouded, with much of New Jersey overrun by the enemy, a British officer—said to be Lord Cornwallis—passed near Bordentown,[1] and visited Elizabeth Borden, endeavoring to intimidate her to use her influence to get her husband—militia Colonel Joseph Borden Jr., who was serving with their son in the American army—to quit that standard and rejoin the Royalists. Otherwise her property would be ravaged and her elegant Bordentown mansion destroyed.[2]

The fifty-three–year-old Mrs. Borden answered by bidding the foe to begin the threatened havoc. "The sight of my house in flames," she said, "would be a treat to me, for I have seen enough to know that you never injure what you have the power to keep and enjoy. I should happily regard the application of a torch to my dwelling as a signal of your departure!"

The house was burned in fulfillment of the threat, and the property laid waste. As the owner predicted, the retreat of the despoiler quickly followed.

HANNAH OGDEN CALDWELL

Few occurrences in the history of warfare have so strongly influenced the public feeling and excited so universal a sentiment of horror and deep resentment as the deliberate and barbarous murder of Hannah Caldwell. It was not only an act of vengeance upon an individual but was designed to strike terror into the country and compel the inhabitants to submission. Far from producing this effect, it aroused the indignation of the whole community, filling all with a desire to drive the invaders from their soil. It animated the brave with new energy, inspired the timid to feats of heroism, and determined the resolute to throng to the standard of liberty.

Hannah Ogden was the daughter of John Ogden of Newark, New Jersey, a descendant of Pilgrims. In 1763 Hannah married Reverend James Caldwell, pastor of the First Presbyterian Church in Elizabethtown.[3]

Hannah's personal appearance is described as conveying an abiding impression of benevolence, serenity, and a particular sweetness of disposition. She was of medium height, with dark gray eyes, auburn hair, and a complexion of singular fairness. She was of pleasing countenance and quiet, gentle, and winning manners. When the war broke out, Reverend Caldwell warmly espoused the cause of his country. In time he was appointed assistant commissary of the Continental Army, stood high in the confidence of Washington, and by his eloquent and patriotic appeals in times of despondency, contributed greatly to sustaining the drooping spirits of the soldiers. His zeal and activity did not fail to render him obnoxious to the enemy, and no effort was spared to do him injury. A price was set upon his head.

Due to the predatory incursions of the British, Reverend Caldwell with his family was compelled to leave home for a temporary lodging at Connecticut Farms,[4] four miles from Elizabethtown. It was during his residence at this place that British troops from New York, under the command of the Hessian general, Baron Wilhelm Knyphausen,[5] landed at Elizabethtown and began a march into the interior, marked by cruelty and devastation. Several houses were fired and the inhabitants left destitute of shelter and provisions. Informed of the enemy's approach, Reverend Caldwell put his elder children in a baggage wagon in his possession as commissary and sent them off to some friends for protection. His three youngest children, including an infant eight months old, remained with their mother. Caldwell had no fears for the safety of his wife and young family; he believed it impossible for resentment to be extended to a mother watching over her little ones.

Caldwell took an early breakfast, intending to join the force collecting to oppose the enemy. Having in vain endeavored to persuade his wife to go with him and seeing the gleam of British arms in the distance, he put spurs to his horse, and in a few moments was out of sight. Mrs. Caldwell herself felt no alarm. She had hidden several articles of value in the well bucket and had filled her pockets with silver jewelry. She then took her infant in her arms and retired to a downstairs room commanding a view of the road, and seated herself upon the bed.

An alarm was soon given that the enemy soldiers were at hand, but Mrs. Caldwell felt confident that no one would have the heart to do injury to the inhabitants of the house. Again and again she had said, "They will respect a mother." Suddenly a soldier left the road and crossed diagonally towards the house. Coming near the room in which Mrs. Caldwell sat, he put his gun close to the window, and fired. The ball entered Mrs. Caldwell's breast; she fell back upon the bed, and in a moment, expired, a sad victim to political hatred.

After the murder, other soldiers cut open Mrs. Caldwell's dress and rifled her pockets. Her remains were then carried to a house on the other side of the road, and her home was set afire, with all soon reduced to ashes. The ruthless soldiers went on with their work of destruction, pillaging and burning, piling beds and clothing in the road and destroying them.

When the terrible news was communicated to him, the feelings of Reverend Caldwell can scarce be imagined. At the time, he was with General Lafayette on the heights near Springfield. Seeing smoke ascending from burning houses, he took a spyglass and exclaimed, "Thank God! The fire is not in the direction of my house." He was sadly mistaken and is said to have later overheard some soldiers speaking of the occurrence, and by questioning them, learned the melancholy truth.

Attempts were soon made by the Royalist party to pretend that Mrs. Caldwell had been killed by a chance shot. But the evidence made it clear that the murder was a deliberate act, committed at the instigation of those in authority. Reverend Caldwell wrote in the *Pennsylvania Journal*, 4 October 1780, "Why did the officers not set a sentinel over the corpse, till the neighboring women could be called? They knew she was a lady of amiable character and reputable family, yet she was left half the day stripped in part, and tumbled about by the rude soldiery!" The memory of this American martyr to liberty will long be revered by the inhabitants of the land with whose soil her blood has been mingled.

SUSANNAH FRENCH LIVINGSTON

Susannah Livingston, the wife of the governor of New Jersey, was the daughter of Philip French and the granddaughter of a lieutenant governor of New York Province. Simple and unpretending in manner, she was endowed with a strong intellect and a warm and tender heart. When the British troops made their memorable incursion into New Jersey in 1780, Governor Livingston, learning of the invasion, had absented himself from his family at an early hour to escape capture and suffered intense anxiety on their account. But while the neighboring villages were seen in flames, the enemy respected Liberty Hall, the governor's residence, and treated its inmates with courtesy.

After a day of alarms, with the flames of Connecticut Farms in clear view, and enemy soldiers continually passing the house, the governor's wife and daughters were at a late hour surprised by the entrance of several British officers, who announced their intention to lodge there. With the officers' presence felt to be protection, the ladies retired. About midnight the officers were called away by some intelligence, and not long afterward, a band of intoxicated straggling British soldiers rushed with oaths and threats into the hall. The ladies, crowding together like frightened deer, locked themselves in an upstairs room. Their place of retreat was soon discovered by the ruffians, and afraid of exasperating the intruders by refusing to come out, one of the governor's daughters opened the door.

A drunken soldier seized her by the arm. She grasped the villain's collar, and at that very moment, a flash of lightning illuminated the hall, falling full upon her white dress. The soldier staggered back, exclaiming with an oath, "It's Mrs. Caldwell, that we killed today!" (see HANNAH OGDEN CALDWELL above) The house was eventually cleared of the assassins.

ESTHER de BERDT REED

Esther de Berdt, descended from French Huegenot exiles, was born in London in 1746, the only daughter of Dennis de Berdt, a successful merchant trading with the colonies. His children were educated according to the strictest rules of evangelical piety. Esther's life was adorned by no adventurous heroism but was thickly studded with the brighter beauties of feminine endurance, uncomplaining self-sacrifice, and virtue under trial, of which civil war is so fruitful.

Because of de Berdt's business relations with the colonies, his house in London was home to many young Americans who by pleasure or duty were attracted to the imperial metropolis. Among these visitors in 1763 was twenty-three–year-old Joseph Reed of New Jersey, who had come to London to complete his legal studies at Middle Temple.

To seventeen–year-old Esther de Berdt, Reed projected a sense of education, intelligence, and accomplishment. Their intimacy, thus accidentally begun, soon produced its natural fruits, and an engagement—at first secret, and later avowed—formed between the young English girl and the American stranger, who finished his legal studies in 1765 and returned home to Philadelphia. By then, Esther and Joseph loved long and faithfully—how faithfully the reader will best judge when learning that a separation of five years of deferred hope, with the Atlantic between them, never gave rise to a wandering wish or thought.

Mr. Reed began his practice of law in Trenton, with immediate success. But the distracting element at work in his heart prevented him from looking on his practice with complacency. That his young and gentle mistress should follow him to America was a vision too wild even for a sanguine lover. The love letters exchanged over five long years are filled with plans by which these cherished but delusive wishes were to be consummated.

All this was coincident with that dreary period of British history, when a monarch and his ministers were laboring to tear from its socket and cast away forever the brightest jewel of the imperial crown—the American colonies. This was the interval when Chatham's[6] voice was powerless to arouse the nation, and make Parliament pause when penny-wise politi-

cians—in the happy phrase of the day—"teased America into resistance."
The varied vexations of stamp acts, revenue bills, and tea duties—the congenial fruits of poor statesmanship—were the means by which a great catastrophe was hurried onward.

Mr. de Berdt's house was a place of council for many who sought by moderate and constitutional means to stay the hand of misgovernment and oppression. We may well imagine the alternations of feeling which throbbed
in the bosom of his daughter, as she shared in the consultations of this almost American household, while she estimated the chances of honorable
pacification which would bring her lover home to her.

Esther's letters were filled with allusions to this varying state of things
and remarkable for the sagacious good sense which they develop. She was
becoming, from first to last, a stout American. Describing an April 1776
visit to the House of Commons, her enthusiasm for Mr. Pitt is unbounded,
while she does not disguise her repugnance to George Grenville and Alexander Wedderburn,[7] whom she could not bear, because "they are such enemies to America." Thus was Miss de Berdt receiving the understanding
that, in the end, was to fit her for becoming an American patriot's wife.

Onward, step by step, the monarch and his ministry advanced in their career of tyrannical folly. Remonstrance was in vain.

In 1769 the lovers were reunited, Mr. Reed returning to England on an
uncertain visit. He found everything changed, save Esther's faithful affection. Political disturbance had had its usual train of commercial disasters.
All was ruin and confusion, and Mr. de Berdt had become bankrupt and
sunk into his grave. In May of the following year, Esther de Berdt became an
American wife. In October the young couple sailed for Philadelphia.

On their arrival Reed changed his residence from Trenton to the Pennsylvania capital. In letters to Lord Dartmouth[8] Reed recounts the progress of
colonial discontent. In all the initial measures of peaceful resistance, he
took an active share. In all he did, he had his young wife's ardent sympathies; the English girl had swiftly grown into the American matron.

Philadelphia was then the heart of the nation. That heart beat generously when the news of Lexington and Concord startled the whole land.
When Washington set out for Cambridge in June 1775, Mr. Reed accompanied him. Yielding to the general's solicitation, he became a soldier and
joined the commander in chief's staff as aide and military secretary.

The young mother (for she was then watching by the cradles of two infant children) neither repined nor murmured. Esther remained in Philadelphia during her husband's first tour of duty with the army. In the summer of
1776 while her husband, now Washington's adjutant general, was busy

around New York, Esther took her small family to Burlington,[9] but with the approach of invading British forces, she sought deeper refuge at a little farm-house near Evesham.[10]

Today, we can form little conception of the horrors and desolation of those times of trial. Nowadays imagination can scarcely compass the terrors of that invasion, but then it was rugged reality. The unbridled passions of the mercenary soldiery, hired and paid for their violence and rapine, were let loose on the land. The German troops, as if to inspire terror, were sent in advance to occupy a chain of posts across northern New Jersey to Trenton.

The Reed family at Evesham included Esther, who had recently been confined and was in feeble health; her three children; an aged relative; and a female friend. If the enemy were to make a sudden advance, the group would be thoroughly cut off from the ordinary avenues of escape. A wagon was readied, and if necessary the group would cross the Delaware lower down and push on to the westward settlements; the wives and children of American patriot soldiers thought themselves safer on the perilous edge of the Indian wilderness than in the neighborhood of an army who, com-manded by supposed men of honor like the Howes, Cornwallises, Percys, and Rawdons were sent by a gracious monarch to lay waste this land.

This was among the darkest of the dark stains that disfigure the history of the eighteenth century, and if ever there be a ground for hereditary animos-ity, we have it in the record of the outrages which the military arm of Great Britain committed on this soil. The transplanted sentimentalism which nowadays characterizes George III "a wise and great monarch" is absolute treason to America. There was in the single colony of New Jersey, and in a single year, blood enough shed and misery produced to outweigh all the spu-rious merits which the King's admirers pretend to claim. And let such ever be the judgment of American history.

It is worth a moment's meditation to think of the sharp contrasts in Es-ther's life. The short interval of less than six years had changed her, not merely into womanhood but to womanhood with extraordinary trials. Her youth had been passed in scenes of peaceful prosperity, with no greater anxi-ety than for a distant lover and with all the comforts which social position could supply.

She had crossed the ocean a bride, content to follow the fortunes of her young husband, though she little dreamed what they were to be. She had be-come a mother, and while watching by the cradles of her infants, had seen her household broken up by war in its worst form. She too, let it be remem-bered, was a native-born Englishwoman, with all the royal sentiments that beat by instinct in an Englishwoman's breast—reverence for the throne, the monarch, and for all the complex institutions which hedge that mysterious oracular thing called the British Constitution.

Coming to America, all this was changed; loyalty became a badge of crime; the King's friends were her husband's and her new country's worst enemies. The holiday pageantry of war which she admired in London had become the fearful apparatus of savage hostility. Esther, an Englishwoman, was now a fugitive from the brutality of English soldiers.

The enemy generals, deeply mortified at their discomfiture in New Jersey, resolved on a new and more elaborate attempt on Philadelphia, and in July 1777 set sail from New York with the most completely equipped force they had yet been able to prepare. Mrs. Reed wrote to a friend: "It has become too dangerous for Mr. Reed to be at home more than one day at a time, and that seldom, and uncertain. Indeed, I am easiest when he is away from home, as his being here brings danger with it, there are so many who are disaffected to the cause of their country that they lie in wait for those who are active." Nor were her fears unreasonable; the neighborhood of Philadelphia after it finally fell into the hands of the enemy was infested with gangs of armed Royalists who threatened the safety of every patriot they encountered. Tempted by the hard money that the British promised them, they dared any danger and were willing to commit any enormity. It was these very ruffians, and their wily abettors, for whom afterwards so much false sympathy was invoked.

Mr. Reed and his family, though much exposed, happily escaped all these dangers. During the winter of 1777–1778, one of the worst Americans ever saw, Mr. Reed was in the immediate neighborhood of Valley Forge as one of a committee of Congress, to which body he had some time before been chosen a member, while Mrs. Reed and her little family took refuge in Flemington.[11] She remained there until after the British evacuation of the capital in 1778. While thus separated from her husband, new domestic misfortune fell on her, with the death of one of her children by smallpox.[12]

"Calamity has overcome me," Esther wrote, "and struck the very bottom of my heart. Tell me the work is not yet finished." Nor was it indeed finished, but in a sense different than what Esther apprehended. While her other children were spared, her own short span of life was nearly run. Trial and perplexity and separation from home and husband were doing their sad work. The seat of actual warfare now being forever removed from Philadelphia, Mrs. Reed returned there, to apparent comfort and high social position. Her husband had been elected president—or in the language of our own day, governor—of Pennsylvania. In the liberated city, the suppressed poison of royalism now mingled with the ferocity of ordinary political animosity in a scene discreditable to all concerned. Personal violence was threatened, and gentlemen went armed in the streets. Folly on one hand and fanaticism on the other put in jeopardy the lives of distinguished citizens.

During this time Esther's humble, homely heroism did its good work in helping sustain a spirit that otherwise might have broken. Let those disparage it who have never had the solace that such marital companionship affords—or who never have known the bitter sorrow of its loss.

In May 1780 Mrs. Reed gave birth to another son. He was named George Washington Reed. In the fall of that year, all the ladies of Philadelphia united in a remarkable and generous contribution for the relief of the suffering soldiers by supplying them with clothing. Mrs. Reed was elected to head this association. A letter of the day calls her "the best patriot, the most zealous and active, and the most attached to the interests of her country." Notwithstanding the increasingly feeble state of her health, Mrs. Reed entered upon her duties with great animation.

The work was congenial to her feelings. It was charity in its genuine form and from its purest source—a voluntary outpouring from the heart. The American women met and, seeing the necessity that asked for interposition, relieved it, directly soliciting money and other contributions. They labored with their needles and sacrificed their trinkets and jewelry. The result was remarkable; the aggregate amount of contributions in the city was no less than $7,500 in hard money, at a time of the greatest currency depreciation. All ranks of society seemed to have joined in the liberal effort, from Phyllis, a colored woman, with her humble seven shillings sixpence, to the Marchioness de Lafayette, who contributed one hundred guineas in specie, and the Countess de Luzerne who gave $6,000 in Continental paper.

Mrs. Reed's letters at this time are marked by businesslike intelligence and sound feminine common sense on subjects which, as a secluded woman, she could have had no previous knowledge. It must also be borne in mind that this was a feeble and delicate woman with her husband once more away from her with the army, and her family cares and anxieties daily multiplying. Her body and spirit were alike overtaxed, and alarming disease developed itself and soon ran its fatal course. On 18 September 1780 with her family mourning around her, she breathed her last, at the early age of thirty-four.

When the news was circulated, there was deep and honest sorrow in Philadelphia, stilling for a moment the violence of party spirit, with all classes uniting in a heartfelt tribute to Mrs. Reed's memory.

ANNIS BOUDINOT STOCKTON

Annis Stockton was the wife of Richard Stockton, a signer of the Declaration of Independence, and the mother of six children. Born around 1733, Mrs. Stockton, an accomplished poet, was descended from a family of French Huguenots who fled to America in 1685 after the Revocation of the Edict of Nantes. Elias Boudinot, of Burlington, New Jersey, was her brother.[13]

When the storm of civil war burst on the country, Richard Stockton, at forty-six, had his full share of the peril as well as the honor that awaited those eminent men who had affixed their names to the Declaration. Stockton's beautiful residence at Princeton was directly on the route of the British army on its triumphant march through New Jersey. Warned of the approach of the victorious invaders, Stockton had barely time to move his forty-four–year-old wife Annis and their children to a place of safety.

Their home, left to the mercy of the enemy, was pillaged. The horses and stock were driven away, and the estate was laid waste. The furniture was converted to winter firewood; the old wine stored in the cellar was drunk up, and Stockton's valuable library with all of his papers was committed to the flames. For a time the home served as headquarters for Lord Cornwallis. The family's silver plate and other valuable articles had been packed in three large boxes and buried in the woods at some distance from the mansion. Through treachery, it is said, the place of concealment was discovered by the enemy, and two of the boxes were disinterred and their contents rifled. The remaining box escaped the search and was later restored to the family.

The Stocktons sought refuge at the home of an old friend in nearby Monmouth County. However, Mr. Stockton's retreat was soon discovered by a party of Royalists. They came for him at night, forcibly entering the house and dragging him from his bed. Loading him with indignities, they hurried him off twenty-five miles to Amboy[14] and thence to New York City, where he was thrown into the common gaol and treated with the utmost barbarity. Meanwhile, the suffering of his affectionate wife, unable in any way to alleviate his distresses, was as poignant as his own. At length, through the interposition of Congress, he was exchanged and released, but exposure to the rigorous weather and inhuman treatment laid the foundation for disease from which he never recovered. It now fell to the woman who had shared his brighter fortunes to cheer with tenderness and devotion his declining days, under the further embarrassment of diminished resources. Her husband had once written Annis: "Let me tell you that all the grandeur and elegance that I have yet seen, serves but to increase the pleasure I have for years enjoyed in your society. I see not a sensible, obliging, tender wife, but the image of my dear Emelia[15] is full in view. I see not a haughty, imperious dame, but rejoice that the partner of my life is just the opposite."

Mrs. Stockton wrote a large collection of poems of considerable merit, but she seems to have had a morbid aversion to publishing the effusions of her fancy. This resolution could not have been owing to a lack of praise, for Annis Stockton's friends often alluded to "Emelia's" poetry with much admiration. Among her epistles is one celebrating the death of General Joseph Warren at Bunker Hill, and another was written after the fall of General Richard Montgomery at Quebec. The deeds of Washington also inspired her, and she sent him an address after the Battles of Trenton and Princeton, as well as a pastoral celebrating the surrender of Lord Cornwallis at Yorktown.

How highly Washington esteemed the merit of these complimentary effusions, and how much pleasure their perusal afforded him, may be seen from his letters of acknowledgement. The fifty-year-old commander in chief's playful manner of disclaiming her praise and replying to her pleasant fancies exhibits the Father of His Country in a new light.

As his words to "Emelia" have never been published, they are excerpted here as a literary curiosity. He writes:

Amidst all the compliments which have been made on the occasion [the surrender of Cornwallis], be assured, Madam, that the agreeable manner and very pleasing sentiment in which your compliments are conveyed have affected my mind with the most lively sensations of joy and satisfaction. This address from a person of your refined taste and elegance of expression affords a pleasure beyond my powers of utterance, and I have only to lament that the hero of your Pastoral is not more deserving of your pen.

And at a later date:

You apply to me, my dear Madam, for absolution, as though I was your father confessor, and you had committed a crime. I find myself disposed to be a very indulgent ghostly adviser. You are the most offending soul alive—that is, if it is a crime to write elegant poetry. If you will come and dine with me on Thursday, and go through the proper course of penance which shall be prescribed, I will strive hard to assist you with expiating these poetical trespasses. Without hesitation, I shall venture to recommend your Muse not to be restrained by ill-grounded timidity, but to go on and prosper. You see, Madam, when once the woman has tempted us, and we have tasted the forbidden fruit, there is no such thing as checking our appetite.

Annis Stockton's husband did not live to see the establishment of the independence for which he had done and suffered so much. The commencement of the disease that terminated his life[16] was carefully concealed from his wife for some time. In the fall of 1778 in Philadelphia, he submitted to an operation from which he hoped relief. The cancer could not be extirpated, however, and the patient's lingering sufferings were so great that he could not enjoy the smallest repose without the help of anodynes. Mr. Stockton died at his residence in Princeton in February 1781. His wife lived for another twenty years. As her husband painfully slipped away, she wrote:

> Oh death! thou canker worm of human joy!
> Thou cruel foe to sweet domestic peace,
> He soon shall come, who shall thy shafts destroy,
> And cause thy dreadful ravages to cease.
> Yes, the Redeemer comes to wipe the tears,
> The briny tears from every weeping eye,
> And death, and sin, and doubts, and gloomy fears
> Shall all be lost in endless victory.

MARTHA STEWART WILSON

Martha Stewart was the daughter of Colonel Charles Stewart, a dedicated patriot. She was born at Sidney,[17] where she spent her childhood years. At the age of thirteen, she lost her mother, a woman of strong and polished intellect and taste, said to have been the best-read female of that time in New Jersey. The maternal care which Martha was now called upon to exercise over her younger sisters and brothers cut short her formal schooling away from home, but soon led to the self-cultivation of her inquiring mind and to association at home and in society with the intelligent and the wise, generating a rich store of information and widespread practical knowledge.

When the first breath of the spirit of '76 passed over the land, it kindled within Colonel Stewart's bosom a flame of zeal for the liberty and honor of his country, which no discouragement could dampen, and which neither toil, danger, nor disaster could extinguish. The familiar confidence of the patriot father cherished and strengthened in the bosom of his daughter corresponding sympathies and principles.

In January 1776, at the age of seventeen, Martha Stewart gave her hand in marriage to Robert Wilson, who had several years before emigrated to America and had already amassed a considerable fortune. The first intelligence of the battle at Lexington fired his warm blood to immediate personal action in the cause, and leaving his bride-to-be behind, he was among the volunteers who accompanied General Washington from Philadelphia to the camp at Cambridge. For six months he served at headquarters, honored by the confidence of the commander in chief, and was often a guest at his table. But his health failed, and he was obliged to forego the prospect of a military career and resigned his position. He returned to New Jersey, married Martha Stewart, and moved into a fine country home in Hackettstown,[18] entering into mercantile pursuits in Philadelphia. When he died in 1779, he was only twenty-eight years old. His widow, who was at that time only twenty, gave up her elegant city mansion and returned to Hackettstown. General headquarters being most of the time within twenty or thirty miles of her residence, on a regular route of communication between the northern and southern posts of the army, Mrs. Wilson frequently entertained at her house many military figures. Among these—with numerous others of less distinction—were Washington, Lafayette, Hamilton, Anthony Wayne, Nathanael Greene, Horatio Gates, William Maxwell, Benjamin Lincoln, Henry Lee, Ethan Allen, Count Pulaski, Daniel Morgan, Arthur St. Clair, John Paul Jones, etc.

Martha Wilson was on terms of friendship with General and Mrs. Washington. She had first met him in Philadelphia when he was preparing to join the army at Cambridge, and the commander's wife afterwards visited Mrs. Wilson several times at her Hackettstown home. To one so young, and whose patriotism was so decided, it must have been a pleasure to welcome under her roof so many of the leading spirits of the land.

On one of Washington's visits, a large concourse of people from the adjacent countryside and towns gathered to catch a glimpse of the idolized chief. As it was impossible for the multitude to gain entrance to the house, a strategem was devised by which those outside could gratify themselves without subjecting the General to the annoyance of a mere exhibition of himself.

Knowing Washington's admiration for a fine horse, the hostess had an animal remarkable for its beauty brought into the yard, and the general was invited outside to inspect it. Thus an opportunity was afforded to the whole assemblage to gaze upon and salute him with their cheers.

It was not alone to foreigners and persons of distinction and known rank that Mrs. Wilson opened her home during the Revolution. Such was the liberality of her patriotism that her gate on the public road bore the inscription: "Hospitality within to all American officers, and refreshment for their soldiers."

On one sad occasion, a band of Royalists secreted themselves in a heavily wooded ravine near Mrs. Wilson's home and waited for darkness. The family, visiting together in the cool of the evening on the porch, was startled by a sudden exclamation in a suppressed but authoritative tone, "Surround the house!" A group of twenty or thirty men, disguised with paint and charcoal and armed with various weapons, rushed upon the family. Silence was enjoined, on pain of death, and enquiry was made for Colonel Stewart, Mrs. Wilson's father, who was evidently supposed to be present. His capture, if not his assassination, was obviously the chief object of the Royalist expedition. But the colonel had been summoned away earlier, and in company with General Benjamin Lincoln, had left for Philadelphia. The group's ringleaders then approached the colonel's eldest son Charles—he and the young brother of Mrs. Wilson's late husband were the only gentlemen present—and said, "You are our prisoners," demanding their purses and watches. Mr. Wilson replied, "I would like to know who the h——l you are, first!" He instantly received a severe saber stroke across the forehead, laying open his head from temple to temple.

A pistol was immediately placed at the breast of young Stewart because he hesitated, after delivering his purse, to yield up his watch, the dying gift of his mother. In alarm for her brother, Martha Wilson rushed forward, promising the intruders—if life was spared—all the money and everything valuable in the house. She was ordered with her brother to lead two of the gang to her father's room. Here the captors secured a considerable amount of specie and $4,000 in paper money, but another packet containing a similar amount, being placed under some clothing, escaped notice. In addition to the money, a large amount of silver plate, a quantity of valuable linen, every article of men's apparel, three gold watches, Colonel Stewart's sword, and a pair of superb pistols with heavy mountings of solid silver—a present brought from Europe by Baron von Steuben—were all part of the booty. The leaders of the banditti spent three hours under the guidance forced from Mrs. Wilson and her brother, ransacking the dwelling. The others, relieving each other standing guard outside and over the family, refreshed themselves abundantly from the storerooms and cellars, which the servants were compelled to throw open. Mrs. Wilson at last ventured the request that the raiding party might leave, for her brother-in-law, ill from loss of blood, required her attention.

On their preparing to depart, the Royalists took everyone to an upper room, and extorting a promise from Mrs. Wilson that no one should attempt to leave the chamber within two hours, they fastened the door. The staircases were then barricaded with tables, chairs, and every kind of furniture, and the windows and doors firmly fastened. All lights were extinguished, and the front door locked and the key thrown away amongst the shrubbery in the yard. The jingling of the plate in the bag in which it was carried off could be heard for some time, growing fainter and fainter.

The gentlemen, not regarding Martha Wilson's promise as having any legitimacy, soon forced the door and quickly gave the alarm in the neighborhood. By daybreak some three hundred men were in pursuit of the plunderers. Some were taken on suspicion, but because of the paint and disguises, they could not be fully identified. The ringleaders, who were known as local Royalists, made their escape to New York and were not heard from until the evacuation of that city by the British, at which time they purchased a vessel with the proceeds of the robbery and sailed for Nova Scotia.

NOTES

1. A village on the Delaware River five miles below Trenton.

2. The British raid was reportedly in reprisal for "The Battle of the Kegs," in which hogshead mines—designed by David Bushnell—were floated down the Delaware from Bordentown to explode amidst British shipping at Philadelphia.

3. A waterfront village opposite New York's Staten Island.

4. Present-day Union, New Jersey.

5. In New Jersey on 6 June 1780, General Knyphausen—temporarily commanding the British army in New York and encouraged by reports of mutinous Continentals—led five-thousand troops from Staten Island against the American positions at Springfield, eighteen miles west of New York City. The march of the mercenary German general was successfully blocked at Connecticut Farms by a combined force of Continentals and militia under General Lafayette and Colonel Elias Dayton. Before abandoning the expedition, Knyphausen burned many buildings.

6. By 1764, William Pitt the Elder (later, Earl of Chatham), the great liberal leader in the Parliamentary struggle over British colonial rights, was slipping into his long battle with manic/depressive illness that would effectively keep him out of British politics at a critical period.

7. Two prominent Royalist politicians executing George III's repressive colonial policies. Grenville led the "King's friends" in the House and served as prime minister from 1763 to 1765. Wedderburn, British solicitor general, is best remembered for his infamous examination of colonial agent Benjamin Franklin before Commons in 1774.

8. Lord Privy Seal; liberal in his relations with the Colonies.

9. A New Jersey village twenty miles northeast of Philadelphia.

10. Also in New Jersey, thirteen miles southeast of Philadelphia.

11. A village east of the Delaware River, about twenty miles north of Trenton.

12. Edward Jenner's successful experimentation in combatting smallpox did not begin until two decades later. At one time during the 1776–1777 American

invasion of Canada, almost half of the Continental forces—despite Washington's specific orders against self-inoculation—were incapacitated by the virulent, often fatal disease.

13. Married to Richard Stockton's sister, Boudinot, an extremely wealthy merchant in Philadelphia, was a confidant of Washington's and served for several years as his respected commissary general of prisoners. In 1782 he was elected president of Congress.

14. A bayside village and ferrying point, across Raritan Bay from Staten Island. A dozen years later, President-elect Washington—on his wildly acclaimed inaugural journey from Mount Vernon to New York—would follow the same route.

15. Annis Stockton's poetic nom de plume.

16. A metastatic cancer of the lip.

17. A New Jersey village about forty miles west of New York City.

18. A village eighteen miles northeast of Mrs. Stewart's family home at Sidney, and sixty-five miles from Philadelphia.

CHAPTER SEVEN

PENNSYLVANIA

SARAH FRANKLIN BACHE

Sarah, the only daughter of Benjamin Franklin, was born in Philadelphia 11 September 1744. As an adult, Sarah was rather above middle height and in her later years became quite stout. Her complexion was uncommonly fair, with much color; her hair brown, and her eyes blue—like her father's.

From Benjamin Franklin's appreciation of the importance of education, and the intelligence and information that she displayed through life, we may presume that Sarah's studies were as extensive as were then pursued by females in any of the American colonies.

Strong good sense and a ready flow of wit were among the most striking features of her mind. Her benevolence was great, and her generosity and liberality were eminent. Sarah's friends ever cherished a warm affection for her.

Through life, Sarah took a great interest in political affairs and was a zealous republican. Later in life, having learned that the English lady to whom Sarah's three daughters were sent to study had placed pupils connected with persons in public life—Sarah's children among them— at the upper end of the table, on the grounds that all young ladies of rank should sit together, Sarah sent word that in this country there is no rank—only rank mutton.

A 1764 letter from twenty–year-old Sarah to her father Benjamin Franklin in England, who was acting as provincial agent for Pennsylvania, says: "The subject here is 'Stamp Act,' and nothing else is talked of. The Dutch speak of the 'Stamp tack,' the negroes of 'tamp'; in short, everybody has something to say about it." In a March letter of the following year, the Act is again mentioned: "Heard by a roundabout way that the Stamp Act is repealed. The people seem determined to believe it, though the information came from Ireland to Maryland. The bells rang and we had bonfires. I never heard so much noise in all my life; the very children seemed distracted. I hope and pray the news may be true."

Two years later, in 1767, Sarah married thirty–year-old Richard Bache, a successful merchant of Philadelphia and New York.[1]

The Baches lived for seven years in the Franklin mansion off Market Street in Philadelphia with Sarah's mother, who died suddenly of a stroke in 1774. In December 1776, the approach of the British army through New Jersey induced Mr. Bache to move his family to Chester County,[2] from which place the following letter was addressed by Mrs. Bache to her father, who had been sent to France the previous October by the Congress. He was accompanied overseas by Mrs. Bache's eldest son, who was educated in France and Geneva under the supervision of his grandfather.

"You had not left us long before we were obliged to leave town," Sarah wrote. "I never shall forget, nor forgive, the enemy for turning me out of house and home in the middle of winter. Here we have two comfortable rooms, and are as happily situated as I can be, separated from Mr. Bache, who comes to see us as often as his business will permit. Your library we sent out of town a week before us, well packed in boxes. All the valuable things—mahogany excepted—we brought with us. There was such confusion, it was a hard matter to get out. When we shall get back again, I know not. Things have altered much in our people's favor since I left town; I think I shall never be afraid of staying in it again."

Shortly thereafter, Mrs. Bache returned home with her family, but in the following autumn a fresh approach of the British army after their victory on the Brandywine again drove the Baches from Philadelphia. On 17 September 1777, four days after the birth of her eldest daughter, Sarah Bache left town with her family to take refuge at the home of a friend in Bucks County,[3] and afterwards removed to Manheim in Lancaster County,[4] where they remained until the evacuation of Philadelphia by the British forces in the summer of the following year. This extract is from a letter to Dr. Franklin by his son-in-law after the family's return to the capital:

Once more I have the happiness of addressing you from this dearly beloved city, after having been kept out of it for more than nine months. Upon my return to town, I found your house in much better order than I had reason to expect from the hands of such a rapacious crew, who carried off with them some of your musical instruments. Your harmonica.[5] They took likewise a few books that had been left behind, chief of which were Temple's schoolbooks,[6] and the *History of the Arts and Sciences* in French, which is a great loss. Some of your electric apparatus is also missing. Captain André[7] also took with him the picture of you that hung in the dining room. The rest of the pictures are safe and met with no damage.

Sarah Bache added her own comments on Philadelphia after the occupation:

Everything is so high. If I was to mention the prices of common necessaries of life, it would astonish you. My spirits, which I have kept up during my being driven about from place to place, and are much better than most people's that I meet, have been lowered by the depreciation of the money, which has been amazing lately. I cannot get a common winter cloak and hat, but just decent, under two hundred pounds. I should think it not only a shame, but a sin, to buy it even if I had millions. Money is too cheap, for there are so many people who are not used to having it, nor know the proper use of it, and get so much that they care not whether they give one dollar or a hundred for anything they want. But for those whose every dollar is the same as a silver one—which is our case—it is particularly hard. Mr. Bache could not bear to do business in the manner it has lately been done in this place, which has been almost all by monetizing and forestalling.[8]

The time came when Mrs. Bache's domestics were obliged to take two baskets to market—one empty, to contain the provisions they purchased, and the other full of Continental paper money to pay for them.

In the patriotic effort of the ladies of Philadelphia to furnish the destitute American soldiers with clothing and money, Sarah Bache took a very active part. The duty of completing the collection of contributions devolved on her and four other ladies, as a sort of executive committee. More than two thousand shirts were produced at her home. They bought the linen from their own private purses and took a pleasure in cutting them out and sewing them themselves. On each shirt was the name of the married or unmarried lady who made it.

"I am happy to have it in my power to tell you," Mrs. Bache wrote to a friend in Trenton, "that the sums given by the good women of Philadelphia for the benefit of the army have been much greater than could be expected, and given with so much cheerfulness and so many blessings that it was rather a pleasing than a painful task to call for it." A letter from M. de Marbois[9] to Dr. Franklin in Paris said: "If there are in Europe any women who need a model of attachment to domestic duties and love for their country, Mrs. Bache may be pointed out to them. She has roused the zeal of the Pennsylvania ladies, and on such occasions made happy use of the eloquence which you know she possesses."

After war's end, in September 1785, after an absence of almost seven years at the Court of France, Benjamin Franklin returned to the United States. He spent the last five years of his life with his daughter's family in the Franklin mansion. In 1794 Mr. Bache, having relinquished his commercial pursuits, removed to a farm on the Delaware River sixteen miles above Philadelphia. Here the Baches lived for more than a dozen years, making their residence the scene of generous hospitality. In 1807, Sarah was attacked by cancer. Her disease proved incurable, and on 5 October 1808 she died in the family mansion in Philadelphia; she was sixty-four years old. Both of the Baches are buried beside her parents in the Christ Church burial ground.

REBECCA BIDDLE

Rebecca Biddle was the wife of Colonel Clement Biddle, a Philadelphia merchant who, at the outbreak of war, was among the first to take an active part, resolving to sacrifice everything in the cause of liberty. The Biddles were members of the Society of Friends, and as a consequence of Mr. Biddle taking up arms, he was read out of Meeting by that peace-loving community. In her thirties, Rebecca Biddle, as ardent a patriot in expressing her approval of the war, encouraging her husband in his course of action, was subjected to similar discipline.

In no instance did the enthusiasm and patriotic spirit which animated the heroines of that day shine more brightly than in this high-minded woman. For her part, the purest and most disinterested love of country induced a cheerful submission to all the inconveniences, hardships, and losses rendered inevitable by a protracted conflict.

During the greater part of the war, Mrs. Biddle gave up the comforts of home to join her husband in camp. She formed a lasting friendship with Mrs. Greene and Mrs. Knox (see LUCIA FLUCKER KNOX and CATHERINE LITTLEFIELD GREENE above), who were also with the army, and became an intimate friend to Mrs. Washington, and moreover developed some terms of personal friendship with the commander in chief, for whom she maintained the highest admiration.

In 1777, when the American army was encamped near Brandywine Creek, Rebecca Biddle was informed by an aide to Washington that a large party of British troops was a few miles away and a force of Americans had been ordered to march before daybreak to cut off their retreat.

As a close engagement might be expected, all women were directed to leave the camp. Mrs. Biddle did not consider herself included in the evacuation, and as an opportunity for addressing General Washington presented itself, told him that as his officers would be returning to camp from their expedition hungry and fatigued, she—if allowed to remain—would make provision for their refreshment. The commander gave her permission to remain but recommended to Mrs. Biddle that she should hold herself in readiness to remove at a moment's warning. Rebecca Biddle immediately dispatched servants throughout the neighborhood to collect the necessary provisions, procuring all the food that was cooked in camp that night. The beaten enemy had retreated, and at a very late hour the Americans returned after a fatiguing march. At least a hundred officers gave Mrs. Biddle great pleasure by eating the dinner she had provided, until not a crust remained.

Among her guests on that occasion was the gallant General Lafayette, who on his last visit, paid his respects to Rebecca Biddle in Philadelphia,[10] and reminded her of that evening's repast. The French general also recalled to Mrs. Biddle the suffering condition of the army that winter at Valley Forge, where the want of provisions was at one time supplemented by a flight of wild pigeons, in such vast numbers and so near the ground that they were easily killed with clubs and poles,[11] and afterwards prepared in as many ways as the cooks could devise.

MARGARET COCHRAN CORBIN

Margaret Cochran was twenty-four years old when she met and married John Corbin, a transplanted Virginian living on the Pennsylvania frontier. She was twenty-five when her artilleryman husband died by her side in an outlying redoubt (Fort Tryon) during the British attack on New York City's Fort Washington 16 November 1776. A revolutionary woman of independent spirit and demonstrated courage, Margaret pushed Corbin's body aside to take command of his cannon until she, too, was struck down by enemy grapeshot. Her arm was nearly severed and her left breast badly mangled.

Margaret, captured near her gun, was hospitalized by the British in New York City and convalesced slowly. She never recovered full use of her arm. Her proper status as a combatant prisoner of war confused everyone. She was shipped off to Philadelphia in 1777, where she was paroled, and subsequently assigned to the Continental invalid corps until formally mustered out of the army in 1783.

By her instinctive action, Margaret Cochran Corbin became the first woman in the United States to whom Congress voted (6 July 1779) a military pension—half her dead husband's pay for the twenty-one years remaining in her life. In a further demonstration of government generosity in the middle of a costly war, Congress also voted her a complete set of new clothes.

Margaret's impulsive action was hardly surprising. Born in Franklin County, Pennsylvania, in 1751, she had grown up experienced in the vicissitudes of rugged frontier life and warfare. When Margaret was four years old, her Scotch-Irish immigrant father was killed and scalped by Native Americans striking south into the Upper Delaware River country from the thriving Iroquois settlements in central New York. The Iroquois did not kill enemy women; they carried Margaret's mother off into captivity. Margaret was elsewhere during the raid and was raised by relatives.

After the Revolution, Margaret settled in the Hudson River hamlet of Highland Falls, New York, just below what would become the United States Military Academy at West Point. Now in her mid-forties, she had been transformed into not only a living legend, but into an impossible bibulous harridan, known familiarly among the locals as "Dirty Kate," or "Captain Molly" (which has inevitably led to her confusion with "Molly Pitcher"). Margaret died in 1800. A century later her remains were transferred from Highland Falls to the government cemetery at West Point, and placed beneath a modest memorial.

LYDIA DARRAH

Lydia and her husband William Darrah were members of the Philadelphia Society of Friends. Their religion inculcated meekness and forbearance and forbade them to practice the arts of war. Late in the afternoon of 2 December 1777, a British officer ascended the steps of the Darrah house on Second Street, immediately opposite the headquarters of General Sir William Howe, who had full possession of the city. The Darrahs' house was plain and neat in its exterior. It was a convenient place chosen by the superior officers of the British Army for private conferences.

The redcoated officer knocked at the door, and in the neatly furnished parlor he met the mistress, who spoke to him familiarly, calling him by name. He was Lord Howe's adjutant general, and he appeared in haste to give an order that the Darrah back room upstairs might be prepared to receive himself and others that evening. "But be sure, Lydia," he concluded, "that your family are all in bed at an early hour. And when we are ready to leave the house, I will give notice, so that you may extinguish the candles."

Having delivered this order, the adjutant general departed, and Lydia betook herself to getting things in readiness. But the words she had heard, especially the injunction to retire early, rang in her ears. The evening closed in, and the British officers came to their place of meeting. Lydia had ordered all her family to bed and admitted the guests herself, after which she retired to her room and threw herself upon the bed. Her vague apprehensions gradually assumed a definite shape, till her nervous restlessness amounted to absolute terror. She slid from the bed and, taking off her shoes, passed noiselessly from her chamber and along the hallway, cautiously approaching the back room in which the officers were assembled. Applying her ear to the keyhole, she could only distinguish a word or two amid the murmur of voices. At length there was profound silence, after which a voice was clearly heard reading aloud an order for troops to march from the city on the night of December 4 in a secret attack on the American army, then encamped at Valley Forge and Whitemarsh.[12]

Lydia had heard enough. She retreated softly to her own room and laid herself quietly on the bed. It seemed to her that but a few moments had elapsed when there was a knocking at her door. She knew well what it meant but took no heed. The knock was repeated and more loudly. Still she gave no answer. The knock came again, and this time Lydia rose quickly from her bed and opened the door. It was the adjutant general, informing her they were all about to depart. Lydia locked the front door after them and extinguished the candles.

Again she returned to her chamber and to bed, but for the rest of the night, repose was a stranger. Her mind was disquieted, and she thought of the danger that threatened the lives of thousands of her countrymen and the ruin that impended. Something must be done immediately to avert widespread destruction. To awaken her husband and inform him might place him in special jeopardy by rendering him part of her secret. He might even be less wary and prudent than she. No, come what may, she would encounter the risk alone. After a petition for heavenly guidance, her resolution was formed, and though sleep was impossible, she waited with composure until the dawn of day, when she awakened her husband and informed him that some flour was wanted for the use of the household and that it was necessary that she go through the snow to Frankford[13] to procure it. This was not an uncommon task and Lydia's declining the assistance of the maidservant excited little surprise. Taking a bag with her, she stopped first at British headquarters for a permit to pass their lines, and then set off through the snow. With difficulty she reached Frankford and left her bag at the mill. Then she quietly pressed forward with all haste to reach the outposts of the American army, determined to apprise General Washington of the oncoming danger.

On her way, she met with an American officer on reconnaisance, Lieutenant Colonel Craig of the Light Horse, who immediately recognized her and enquired whither she was going. After having obtained from him a solemn promise not to betray her, since the British might take vengeance on her family, she disclosed her secret. The officer thanked Lydia for her timely warning and directed her to a nearby house where she could get something to eat, but Lydia preferred to return home at once and did so, while the officer made all haste to headquarters, where preparations were immediately made to give the enemy a fitting reception.

With a lightened heart and filled with thankfulness, the intrepid woman pursued her way homeward through the snow, collecting the bag of flour that had served as the ostensible object of her journey. No one suspected the gray and demure Quakeress of having snatched from the British their eagerly anticipated victory. Lydia's demeanor was, as usual, quiet, orderly, and subtle. She attended to the duties of her family with her wonted composure. But her heart beat, as late on the appointed night she watched from her chamber window the departure of the enemy, bound on a secret expedition whose purpose she knew too well.

She listened breathlessly as the sound of footsteps and trampling horses died away in the distance, and silence again reigned throughout the city. Time never appeared to pass so slowly as in the interval between the marching out and return of the British troops. When at last a distant roll of a drum coming nearer and nearer proclaimed their approach, Lydia was watching at the window, when she saw the troops pass in martial order, the agony of anxiety she felt was too much for her strength, and she retreated from her post, never daring to ask a question, or manifest the least curiosity as to the event.

A sudden loud knocking at the front door was not calculated to lessen Lydia's apprehensions. At this critical moment, she knew that the future safety of her family depended on her self-possession. Her visitor was the adjutant general, his face clouded and his expression stern. After a moment of silence, he asked, "Were any of your family up the other night, when I received company in this house?"

"No!" was Lydia's unhesitating reply. "They all retired at eight o'clock." "Very strange," replied the officer. Musing for a few moments, he said, "You, Lydia, I know were asleep; I had to knock on your door three times before you heard me. Yet it is certain that we were betrayed! I am altogether at a loss to conceive who could have given information of our intended attack to General Washington. We found his cannon mounted, his troops under arms, and so prepared at every point to receive us that we have been compelled to march back without injuring our enemy, like a parcel of fools!"

The officer never discovered to whom he was indebted for the disappointment, but the pious Quakeress blessed God for her preservation and rejoiced that it had not become necessary for her to utter an untruth in her own defense.

ELIZABETH GRAHAM FERGUSON

Elizabeth Graham, born in Philadelphia in 1739, was the youngest daughter of Dr. Thomas Graham, a customs collector, and his wife Anne Keith, daughter of a governor of Pennsylvania. The Graham mansion, used as an American hospital during the Revolution, was celebrated before the war for the Graham family's hospitality and for the talents and accomplishments of their daughter Elizabeth, who was the center of the literary coteries of the day. In early life she displayed a mind richly endowed with intellectual gifts, cultivated with care by her excellent and accomplished mother. Elizabeth's verses possessed vigor and talent but were said to lack melody. Her prose indicated both genius and knowledge. She was well read in polemical divinity and a firm believer in the doctrines of Revelation. She is said to have transcribed the whole Bible, to impress its contents more deeply upon her mind and assist the facility with which she selected appropriate passages to illustrate or adorn the subjects of her writing or conversation.

The Grahams spent their summers in Graham Park, a pleasant retreat twenty miles from the city. There, Elizabeth's translation of *Telemachus* into English was undertaken as a relief and diversion from the suffering occasioned by a disappointment in love. The subsequent failure of her health induced her father to send her to England for a year to complete her education. There she was introduced into the best society. Her mental accomplishments attracted the attention of distinguished persons and were particularly noticed by the British monarch. Her mother died while she was in England, and upon Elizabeth's return to Philadelphia, she was welcomed home by a numerous circle of friends who came to condole with her. She soon occupied the place of her mother, managing the house and presiding in the entertainment of visitors. Her brilliant intellect, her extensive and varied knowledge, her vivid fancy, and cultivated taste all offered attractions which were enhanced by the charm of her graceful manners.

It was at one of these assemblies that she first saw Hugh Henry Ferguson, a young gentleman lately arrived from Scotland. They were pleased with each other at the first interview, being congenial in literary tastes and refinement. Their marriage took place in a few months, notwithstanding that Ferguson was ten years younger than the thirty-three–year-old Miss Graham. Not long after this event Dr. Graham died, bequeathing to his daughter the country seat north of the city, where she and her husband, childless, soon elected to reside.

Their happiness was of brief duration. The discontents between Great Britain and America were increasing, and it was soon necessary for Mr. Ferguson to take part on one side or the other. He decided according to the prejudices natural to his birth, espousing the Royal cause. From this time a separation took place betweem him and Mrs. Ferguson. Her husband being engaged in the British service, she was favored by the Royalists, while still being treated with respect by the Americans as a lady who occupied a high social position at Graham Park. There Mrs. Ferguson's desire for the good of her countrymen led to her ardent wish that the daily horrors of civil war with its desolation and misery might cease.

It was not surprising that she was eager to seize any opportunity that offered of being instrumental in helping to end the fratricidal struggle. In June 1778, under a pass granted her by General Washington, Elizabeth came to Philadelphia for the purpose of taking leave of her husband. She was at the house of a friend, which chanced to also be the place appointed for the residence of Governor George Johnstone, one of the members of the Commission sent under Parliamentary authority to try to settle the differences between Great Britain and America.[14]

Mrs. Ferguson was in company with Governor Johnstone three times,[15] the conversation being general on the first two occasions. The Governor's declarations, Mrs. Ferguson said later, were so warm in favor of American interests that she looked upon him as really a friend to her country. He wished—since he could not himself be permitted to pass the American lines—to find some person who would step forward and act a mediatorial part by suggesting something to stop the effusion of blood likely to ensue if the war were carried on.

Mrs. Ferguson said she told the governor repeatedly that the sentiment of the people was in favor of independence. "I am certain," she said in their last conversation, "that nothing short of independence will be acceptable." Yet it does not appear that her own views were averse to some reunion of the two countries.

Governor Johnstone then expressed a particularity for the influence of Colonel Joseph Reed[16] and requested Mrs. Ferguson, if she should see him, to convey the idea that if he could—conformably to his conscience and views of things—exert his influence to settle the dispute, he might command ten thousand guineas,[17] and the best post in the government.

Replying to Mrs. Ferguson's question as to whether Colonel Reed would not look upon such a mode of obtaining his influence as a bribe, Governor Johnstone immediately disclaimed any such idea and said this method of proceeding was common in all negotiations and that one might honorably make it in a man's interest to step forth for such a cause. On her part, Mrs. Ferguson expressed the conviction that if Colonel Reed thought it was right to give up the point of independence, he would say so, without fee or reward. If he were of a different opinion, she said, no pecuniary emolument would lead him to give a contrary vote. Governor Johnstone replied that he did not see the matter in this light.

A day or two after this communication, Mrs. Ferguson sent a note by confidential messenger from the city through the lines to Colonel Reed at headquarters, requesting an hour's conversation and desiring him to fix a place where she could meet without the necessity of entering the camp. She stated that her business could not be committed to writing. The Colonel did not receive this note until three days after the evacuation of Philadelphia by the enemy but immediately sent word that he would wait upon Mrs. Ferguson that evening in the city. At their interview, the conversation treated on Governor Johnstone's desire to settle matters on an amicable footing and his favorable opinions towards Colonel Reed.

The American officer mentioned that he had received a similar letter from Johnstone at headquarters, whereupon Mrs. Ferguson repeated in all its particulars the conversation that had passed between her and the governor. Her repetition of his proposition brought a prompt and noble reply from Colonel Reed: "I am not worth purchasing, such as I am, the King of Great Britain is not rich enough to do it." Thereupon Colonel Reed laid before Congress both the written and verbal communications from Governor Johnstone, withholding the name of the lady, from motives of delicacy and reluctance to draw down popular indignation upon her head.

But his effort was in vain. Suspicion was at once directed to her, and her name was mentioned before the Executive Council of Pennsylvania. Congress issued a declaration condemning "this daring and atrocious attempt to corrupt Colonel Reed's integrity," denouncing it as "incompatible with honor to hold any manner of correspondence with the said George Johnstone."

As soon as Mrs. Ferguson returned to Graham Park and saw the newspaper accounts of the proceedings, she addressed a remonstrance to Colonel Reed, bitterly complaining of having been exhibited merely as an emissary of the peace commissioners, with no note of her own concerns about the struggle. "I find it hard," she wrote, "knowing the uncorruptness of my heart, to be held out to the public as a tool to the Commissioners."

The incident proved of incalculable service in recalling any doubting or irresolute patriots to their proper sense of duty. The story and Reed's noble and famous reply were repeated from mouth to mouth. After the return of Governor Johnstone to England, he ventured to deny the charge proffered in the resolutions of Congress. In a speech in the House of Commons, he boldly asserted the falsehood of the statements made by Colonel Reed, also hinting that all of Mrs. Ferguson's actions were part of her attempt to gain a preferment for Mr. Ferguson in the British army. The Governor's denials no sooner reached America than Mrs. Ferguson published her own narrative of the transaction, confirmed by her oath. "It may be possible," she wrote, "that the multiplicity of ideas which may be supposed to pass through the brain of a politician in the course of a few months may have jostled the whole transaction out of his memory. Insignificant and contemptible as I may appear to him, I believe there are two or three people in Britain who may venture to tell him, in all his plenitude of power, that I would not set my hand to an untruth." Despite her denial, all the consequences that ensued from this incident were severely felt by Mrs. Ferguson, who lived for another twenty-three years, always asserting that her actions had been solely prompted by a disinterested desire for the good of her countrymen.

✦ MARY LUDWIG HAYS

It turned out to be the longest sustained day's action of the Revolution. It also was one of the hottest, where the heat of the day certainly matched the heat of the battle. The desperate struggle against man and the sun raged 28 June 1778 near Monmouth Court House in interior New Jersey. With the temperature at 96° in the shade, thirty-seven Continentals and fifty-nine enemy soldiers died of heat exhaustion.

The full-scale contest between Washington's and Sir Henry Clinton's armies was precipitated by advance units of the fifty-four hundred–man American army, marching eastward with fourteen fieldpieces from Valley Forge, under the detached command of General Charles Lee. The group soon overtook Cornwallis's rear guard of the twelve–mile-long ten thousand–man British column, its progress slowed by three thousand evacuated Philadelphia royalists. The enemy was in slow retreat overland to New York City after leaving Philadelphia ten days earlier.

The ensuing struggle was long and costly to both sides. In the daylong swirl of heat and dust, the British lost 251 dead and 170 wounded. American losses were 119 dead—including the sunstroke victims—and 161 wounded. "I presume everyone has heard of the heat of that day," reminisced Joseph Plumb Martin—"Private Yankee Doodle"—[18] "but none can realize it, that did not feel it." On such a day in such a battle, the need for water on both sides—to drink, and to cool the overheated artillery pieces—was paramount.

Among the many striking events of this last major encounter of the Revolution in the North were Washington's unusually vituperative battle-field sacking of the bungling obstructionist General Lee—and the instant canonization of Mary Ludwig Hays.[19] She was a rowdy, engaging thirty-four-year-old Pennsylvania Dutch woman, known—after the Battle of

Monmouth—to all Americans as "Molly Pitcher." (Later in the war, the name came to be generically applied to any camp woman who carried water to parched or wounded soldiers.)

Mary Hays had gone to Valley Forge to be with her husband John, an artillery private in the seventh Pennsylvania Regiment. On that scorching day at Monmouth, Molly was filling and carrying water buckets—standard gun crew equipment for wetting the large sponge on a staff, used to quench glowing cartridge fragments in the cannon barrel after a discharge.

As in the case of Betsy Ross, the real person was soon obscured by the myth. In the original nineteenth-century version, Mary Hays's husband John falls wounded (or sunstruck) at the side of his overheated cannon, while Molly helps serve the gun—swabbing, loading, ramming, aiming, and firing. But by the middle of the nineteenth-century, revisionist historians were chattering away about her "tarnished reputation," calling Molly an "uneducated woman who drank, chewed tobacco, and swore like a trooper." No wonder a group of Philadelphia society matrons reportedly "thanked their lucky stars when certain contemporary testimony was brought to their attention, and caused them to abandon the idea of erecting a civic monument to Molly's memory."

What probably did her in was a raunchy eyewitness report by Joseph Plumb Martin published in Maine half a century after the battle. In his *Narrative of Some of the Adventures, Dangers, and Sufferings of a Revolutionary Soldier*, the irrepressible "Private Yankee Doodle"—who loved a smoky story—gossips about the events at Monmouth. He recounted:

One little incident in the heat of the cannonade which would be unpardonable not to mention.

A woman attending with her husband at his artillery piece the whole time, and in the act of reaching for a cartridge and having one of her feet as far before the other as she could step, a cannon shot from the enemy passed directly between her legs, without doing any other damage than carrying away all the lower part of her petticoat. Looking down with apparent unconcern, she observed that it was lucky it did not pass a little higher, for in that case it might have carried away something else—and continued her occupation.

It's easy enough to see why this other unsinkable Molly, who lived to be eighty-eight, remains the legendary darling of the United States Artillery, who still toast her memory with a rollicking:

> . . . *beverage stronger and ever richer*
> *Than water poured from Molly's pitcher.*

MARY REDMOND

Mary Redmond was the daughter of a moderately distinguished Philadelphia patriot. Many of her relatives were Royalists, and among them she was playfully called "the little black-eyed rebel." During the enemy's occupation of the city in 1777, Mary, in order to procure and pass along intelligence about what was happening outside, was accustomed to meet with several women whose husbands were in the American service. The dispatches from their friends were usually brought to the city by a boy who came there bringing provisions to market. He carried the messages stitched into the back of his coat.

One October morning when there was reason to fear the boy was suspected, with his movements watched by the British, Mary undertook to get the papers from him in safety. She went to the market as usual, and in a pretended game of romps,[20] she threw her shawl over the boy's head, thus quickly securing the papers. Mary hastened to her anxious friends, and they read them by stealth with shutters carefully closed. When they came to the news of Burgoyne's surrender, and all were secretly rejoicing, the sprightly Mary, not daring to openly give vent to her exultation, put her head up the chimney and gave a shout for General Horatio Gates![21]

ESTHER SKINNER

The name of Wyoming and the history of its early days[22] is well known to the American reader, especially the catastrophic events of July 1778, which converted the fertile and thriving settlement into a field of slaughter and recorded in characters of blood one of the darkest pages in the annals of our race. The pen of the historian, the eloquence of the orator, the imagination of the poet and novelist have by turns illustrated the scene—the realities of which transcend the wildest creations of fiction, and over which hovers the solemn glory that enshrines the resting place of heroes.

The population of the valley had been largely drained to supply the Continental Army; the fury of the Royalists and savages gathered strength until it swept in a tempest of blood and fire over those left to defend their beloved homes. Their gallant deeds and fate have been told in song and story; the wives and daughters of Wyoming deserve to share in the tribute due their unfortunate defenders. The women had cheerfully assumed such a portion of the labor as they could perform. They tilled the ground, planted, mowed hay, gathered the harvest, and assisted in manufacturing ammunition. They, too, were marked out for the enemy's vengeance.

Dreadful was the suspense in which they and their children awaited the event of the battle.[23] When the news was brought in the night, warning that instant flight would be their only means of escape, they fled in terrified confusion without clothes or food, looking back only to behold the light of burning plains, repressing their groans for fear of Indians in ambush.

Two sons of Esther Skinner, in the flower of early manhood, went forth to that day's desperate conflict and were seen no more by their widowed mother. A young man who was among those spared, and who afterwards married Mrs. Skinner's daughter, was pursued to the brink of the Susquehanna River. He plunged into the water for safety and swam to a small island, where, immersed in the river and screened in the darkness of night by some bushes at the water's edge, he happily eluded the search of his bloodthirsty pursuers. Twenty of his companions who had also retreated to the island were all massacred within a few yards of his hiding place, from where he could hear the dismal strokes of the tomahawk and the groans of the dying, every moment expecting to become the next victim. One savage foot trod upon the very bush to which he clung. When the enemy had gone, only a solitary survivor besides himself was left to weep with him over the mangled bodies of their friends.

In the company of other women who had fled the conflagration, forty-seven–year-old Esther Skinner, with her six surviving children—the youngest five years of age—hastened to the water's side, where boats were prepared for their conveyance down the river. The little ones, half destitute of clothing, were ready to cry with the anguish of their bruised and lacerated feet. But the chidings of their weary mother and the dread of being heard by the lurking savages, suppressed their weeping and made them tread their painful way in breathless silence.

With Mrs. Skinner's little property plundered, her home in ashes, her husband long buried, her sons lying mangled on the field of battle, her thoughts turned to the land of her birth. Esther Skinner's journey on foot with six helpless children, without money, clothes, or provisions, was formidable. Much of her way lay through old Dutch settlements, where only by signs could she tell the story of her sufferings or make known her wants. Wyoming's tale of woe, however, swifter in its flight, had spread far and wide, and she received many kindnesses from these people with a strange language. Sometimes, indeed, she was refused admission into their houses, but, she would narrate, "They had nice barns, with clean straw, where my children could lodge very comfortably."

After traveling hundreds of miles by land and water, Mrs. Skinner arrived in safety at the place of her birth in Connecticut. Surviving all her children but one, she died there in 1831 in the one-hundredth year of her age.

FRANCES SLOCUM

Five-year-old Frances Slocum survived the Wyoming Valley raid but was carried off by Indians. No trace of their retreat could be discovered. Her father was murdered, and her widowed mother heard nothing more of her lost child, though peace came in time and prisoners were returned. When intercourse with Canada was resumed, two of Mrs. Slocum's sons, among the most enterprising and intelligent young men in the valley, determined, if she was living, to find their little sister.

They traversed the Indian settlements as far as Niagara, but vain were their inquiries and offered rewards. The conclusion seemed probable that their sister had been killed by her merciless captors. Still the fond mother saw her lost one in her dreams, and her soul clung, as the great and engrossing object of her life, to the hope of recovering her daughter.

At length one young girl was found who had been carried away from the Susquehanna River settlements, and who could not remember her parents. She was brought to Mrs. Slocum's home, but the mysterious sympathy that exists between a mother and her offspring did not appear and draw them together. The mother did not believe the orphan to actually be her own child, and the girl, feeling that she had no claim on a relationship, at length returned to her Indian friends. Time extinguished the last ray of hope, and the bereaved parent, at an advanced age, finally descended into the grave.

Fifty-eight years after the raid on Wyoming, note was made of a white woman living among the Miami tribe of Indians near Logansport, Indiana, who stated she had been brought when very young from the Susquehanna, and that her father's name had been Slocum. Her attachment to Indian life, and fear of being claimed by her kindred, had prevented her in past years from disclosing her name and history, and she did it now from a conviction that her life was drawing to an end. She was a widow, with two daughters, wealthy and bearing an excellent character.

The sensation this information produced throughout Wyoming can scarcely be imagined. Moved by affection, duty, and the known wishes of his deceased mother, Frances's brother Joseph made immediate preparation for the long journey to Indiana. Meeting on the way with his younger brother Isaac, who lived in Ohio, they hastened to Logansport. The lost sister was informed of their arrival and came to the village to meet them, riding a high-spirited horse and accompanied by her two daughters, tastefully dressed in Indian costume.

With a bearing grave and reserved, the woman listened through an interpreter to what the brothers had to say. But doubt, amounting to jealous suspicion, possessed her mind. She returned home, but came to town again the next day, desiring further explanation, ere she would recognize those who claimed such near kinship. At length Joseph mentioned that his little sister, at play with the other children in their father's smithy, once received a blow from a hammer on the middle finger of her hand which crushed the bone, and that his mother had always said the injury would leave a mark that could not be mistaken. This was conviction to the long-separated sister. Her countenance lit up with smiles and tears ran down her cheeks, while she held out the scarred hand.

The welcome recognition, the tender embrace, the earnest enquiries about her parents, all showed the awakening of long-slumbering affection and filled every heart present to overflowing. The events of her life, as Frances detailed them, had been truly remarkable. After her capture, she had been carried to a rocky cave in the mountains, from whence she was taken to the Indian country. She was treated with kindness and brought up as an adopted daughter of their people. When her Indian parents died, she married a young chief of the nation, who removed to the waters of the Ohio. She had been led to regard the whites with a degree of fear and aversion and deemed any return to her kindred a calamity rather than a blessing, so that when prisoners were inquired for, she always earnestly entreated that she not be betrayed.

When her narration was finished, Frances—or "Maconaquah," as she was called—appealed with solemnity to the Great Spirit to bear witness to its truth. The next day her brothers, accompanied by the interpreter, rode out to visit Frances. Everything bore the appearance, not only of plenty, but of rude abundance. Cattle and horses were numerous. The house, though roughly constructed, was better than the Indian wigwams, and the repast of venison, honey, and cakes was excellent. Frances caused her brothers to enter into a formal contract of recognition and affection. The visit was prolonged for several days and was afterward repeated by other members of the Slocum family.

NOTES

1. Bache, like his famous father-in-law, was most active in Revolutionary affairs. He served on many political and military committees, including the influen-

tial Congressional Board of War. He succeeded Franklin as postmaster general, and held the office for six years.

2. About twenty-five miles northwest of Philadelphia.

3. About thirty miles north of Philadelphia.

4. About ninety miles west of Philadelphia. Fleeing the British occupation, Congress made Lancaster a temporary capital of the United States.

5. An instrument invented elsewhere but perfected by Franklin. It consisted of a nested set of tuned glass bowls, rotating on a spindle and resonating to the touch of moistened fingertips. Mozart and Beethoven composed for the harmonica.

6. Temple was Sarah Franklin's eldest son, then residing overseas with his grandfather.

7. Not yet advanced to the rank of major, John André was quartered in the Franklin/Bache mansion during the enemy occupation of the capital. Three years later André was taken, tried, convicted, and hanged for espionage.

8. Monetization is government issuance of paper currency unbacked by gold and silver specie; forestalling is cornering a market. The restoration of American control of Philadelphia also unleashed a wave of unprecedented speculation and corruption, presided over by the military governor of the city, Benedict Arnold.

9. Marquis François de Barbé-Marbois was secretary to the French legation (and later chargé d'affaires) in Philadelphia, 1779–1785. In 1803, as Napoleon's finance minister, he took the lead in negotiating the Louisiana Purchase.

10. In 1824, the Marquis de Lafayette made a nostalgic and triumphal return to the United States.

11. The docile American passenger pigeon was shot or beaten into extinction by 1914.

12. A dozen miles northwest of Philadelphia.

13. A village on the Delaware River eight miles northeast of the capital.

14. Sailing into the port of British-occupied Philadelphia on 6 June 1778, the Carlisle Peace Commission represented a diversionary British maneuver to stave off the impending Congressional approval of the U.S.-French military and trade alliance. The Carlisle Commission offered what it naively considered a peaceful solution to the three-year-old conflict. Parliament was now prepared to grant the former British North American colonies everything they had originally asked for—plus an unsolicited dukedom for George Washington—*except political independence*. The commission was also secretly empowered to cancel fifteen years of repressive colonial trade regulations. The emissaries, who experienced immediate difficulty making contact with anybody on the American side, were a politically unwieldy six-man group that included a brash ex-governor of West Florida (George Johnstone) and the soon-to-be-replaced commander of all the King's troops in America, Sir William Howe. The group was ineffectually led by wealthy and whiggish twenty-nine–year-old Frederick Howard, fifth Earl of Carlisle. Failing to establish any contact at all with the Congress, the commissioners retreated

to New York in July with the withdrawing British army and finally ended their so-called "mission of reconciliation" by sailing back to England in November.

15. As a Royal Navy lieutenant, George Johnstone had been a rabid duellist. Later he served (1763–1767) as governor of British West Florida, where he promoted the scheme for a new channel for the Mississippi River to bypass Spanish-held New Orleans. On his return to England, Johnstone successfully stood for Parliament, becoming one of its more disputatious and illiberal members. At forty-eight, Johnstone had skillfully maneuvered himself into the ranks of the Carlisle Commission.

16. As described above, attorney Joseph Reed of Trenton and Philadelphia was a mainstay of the more moderate revolutionaries in New Jersey and Pennsylvania. Abandoning the concept of reconciliation with Great Britain, he was made president of the Pennsylvania Provincial Congress. With the outbreak of war, Reed moved his family back to New Jersey (see ESTHER de BERDT REED above). A skilled writer, he yielded to Washington's request and became one of his military secretaries. In March 1776, he was promoted to adjutant general of the Continental Army. After much activity around Trenton and Princeton, Reed returned to civilian life early in 1777 to serve in Congress. He subsequently became president of the Pennsylvania State Supreme Executive Council (1778–1781), in which position he led the State's attack on Benedict Arnold's wartime peculations. The British choice of thirty-seven–year-old Colonel Reed as a primary target for Carlisle Commission bribery was a classic and typical piece of enemy miscalculation.

17. About fifty-three thousand (1778) dollars.

18. Martin earned his unique sobriquet by participating in every major campaign of the Revolution.

19. Anglicized from Heis.

20. A child's boisterous, animated horseplay.

21. The American victor at Saratoga. The Revolution did not lack its humorous moments; at Burgoyne's surrender, the portly Gates overheard the epithet "granny"—eighteenth-century slang for "midwife"—floating towards him from the enemy ranks. Turning to British General William Phillips, Gates is said to have remarked, "They may very well call me 'granny'; I have today delivered you of 7,000 men."

22. "Wyoming" was the Delaware Native American name for a twenty-five–mile stretch of rich farmlands above Wilkes-Barre (founded 1769) on the upper Susquehanna River in northeastern Pennsylvania, thirty miles below the New York border. Title to the "back" valley lands, originally settled (1753) by Connecticut pioneers, was not resolved until 1782 by the Pennsylvania and Connecticut legislatures. Bad blood erupted early between Wyoming neighbors of varied origins and different political persuasions. Protective blockhouses were built at Forty-Fort and elsewhere. The outbreak of revolution, with 164 valley men volunteering for the Continental Army, also brought on a bitter struggle against lo-

cal Royalists; dozens were arrested and hastily shipped off—often without trial—to prison mineshafts in Connecticut. In reprisal, on 3–4 July 1778, a combined force of four hundred Royalist Rangers and volunteers—more were recruited en route—and five hundred Senecas and Cayuga Native Americans, all under partisan Major John Butler, marched two hundred miles from Lake Ontario's Fort Niagara to attack the forts and small settlements in the Wyoming Valley. The precipitate and inept American leadership by Colonel Zebulon Butler (no relation) led to an unprecedented and shocking military defeat and subsequent Seneca/Cayuga depredation. The Wyoming disaster was immediately put to wide propaganda use throughout the states.

23. In a poorly planned action near Fort Wintermoot on 3 July, more than 80 percent of the attacking American force was killed; only sixty soldiers and officers managed to flee. Enemy losses were three killed and eight wounded. The Senecas carried away 227 trophy scalps. Many of the American corpses lay unburied for four months.

CHAPTER EIGHT

MARYLAND

ANNE FRISBY FITZHUGH

Anne Frisby, born in 1727, was the daughter of Peregrine Frisby of Cecil County. After the death of her first husband, she married in 1759 William Fitzhugh, a colonel distinguished in the British service. At the commencement of the difficulties between the colonies and the mother country, the Fitzhughs were living on a large estate at the mouth of Maryland's Patuxent River.[1]

By the time discontent had ripened into rebellion, Colonel Fitzhugh was advanced in years, in feeble health, and had almost entirely lost his sight. But neither the infirmities of age nor any advantage to be derived from adherence to the government prevented his taking an open and active part with the patriots. He resigned his British army commission and declared for the land that had given him birth. Unable himself to bear arms, he furnished his two sons for the Continental service and sent them off with a command to be true to the interests of their country.

Colonel Fitzhugh took his seat in the Executive Council of Maryland, giving his vote and influence to the debates till the political opinions of that body were no longer wavering. He traveled from place to place through the countryside, haranguing the people with stump speeches, devoting all his energies to the task of rousing them to fight for their rights. This act of zeal for American freedom, of course did not fail to render the venerable patriot obnoxious to the Royalists. He was often apprised of danger from British emnity. But no risk could deter him.

At one time, when he had disregarded a warning from some unknown bands, Mrs. Fitzhugh was surprised during the colonel's absence from home by news of the near approach of a party of British soldiers. She instantly decided on her course of action in the emergency and collected the slaves, furnishing them with such arms as could be found. Taking a quantity of cartridges in her apron, she led the way to meet the enemy, resolved that they should at least have a round of shots by way of welcome. Finding preparations for resistance where they probably expected none, the British party retired from the grounds without doing any damage.

Another time, the Fitzhughs received information of a design on the enemy's part to attack the house at night and take the colonel prisoner, carrying off what plunder could be found and laying waste the premises. Colonel Fitzhugh was persuaded by his anxious family from making any attempt at defense. He reluctantly consented to leave the place. The next morning nothing remained of the Fitzhugh mansion but a heap of smoking ruins.

The Fitzhughs then removed to Upper Marlboro, about fifty miles up-river, where they continued to reside until the close of the war. In the fall of 1782, a shore party of British soldiers, having landed on the banks of the Patuxent River, marched to the Fitzhugh house. About midnight, the family was aroused from sleep by a loud knocking at the door. The colonel raised the window and called out to know who was there. The reply was, "Friends." He asked, "Friends to whom?" "Friends to King George," was the shouted answer, with the peremptory order to open the door.

Knowing well that remonstrance or resistance would be useless and that delay would but irritate the intruders into acts of violence, the colonel assured them that he being blind, his wife would immediately descend and admit them to the house. Mrs. Fitzhugh did not hesitate, though not small was her dismay and terror when, parting the curtains, she saw the courtyard was filled with soldiers. It was cloudy and a drizzling rain was falling, but their bayonets could be distinctly seen in the faint light. Hastily lighting a candle and putting on her slippers, the fifty-five–year-old woman went downstairs, stopping only to give her two sons, who happened to be staying at the house, their pistols. She warned them they must lose no time in making their escape, and they left the house by the back door as their mother, with unusual difficulty, turned the ponderous key which secured the front door.

The intruders instantly rushed in, touching Mrs. Fitzhugh's nightdress with their bayonets. But she walked calmly before them into the parlor. Addressing the officer in charge, Mrs. Fitzhugh said she hoped they intended no harm to the inmates of the house. The officer replied that they did not but must see Colonel Fitzhugh at once. Then, his attention being attracted by some articles of military dress, he demanded, "What officers have you in the house, Madam?" "There is no one here but our own family," Mrs. Fitzhugh answered. The question was repeated, to which the same calm reply was given. With a smile, the officer said, "Then we must take these," pointing to the empty pistol holsters.

In obedience to the order that her husband must come down, Mrs. Fitzhugh went to assist him in dressing and soon returned with him, unmindful that in her anxiety she had taken no time to dress herself. The officer informed Colonel Fitzhugh that he was a prisoner and must go with the British by ship to New York, then still in the possession of the enemy. The colonel replied that his age and want of sight made it scarcely worth their while or time to take him there. He said he could do neither harm nor service, being unable to take care of himself.

Such arguments availed nothing, and the colonel was about to be hurried off, his captors apparently fearing some local surprise. Although Mrs. Fitzhugh had made no provision for a journey, she had too much character and courage to hesitate a moment. She simply took her husband's arm, and when the enemy officer endeavored to persuade her to remain behind—saying she would suffer from exposure—she answered that her husband was not able to take care of himself, and that even if he were able, she would not be separated from him. The officer then picked up a cloak and threw it over Mrs. Fitzhugh's shoulders. With only this slight protection from the cold and rain, she left the house with the rest.

The enemy's boat lay a half-mile away, and Mrs. Fitzhugh had to walk through the mud along the shore in her slippers. But the matron's resolute spirit did not fail her. The party had already reached the boat when an alarm was caused by the accidental discharge of a gun, which the soldiers took to be a signal for some gathering of neighborhood patriots. The British quickly consented to permit Colonel Fitzhugh to remain on his parole,[2] which was hastily prepared and signed. Leaving their prisoner and his wife on shore, the British pushed off rapidly. On their return to the house, the Fitzhughs were much surprised to find all their negroes gone, except one little girl who had hidden in the garret. A few of them later returned.

NOTES

1. An area of Chesapeake Bay fifty miles southeast of present-day Washington D.C.

2. Usually a written oath not to again take up arms against an enemy until formally exchanged.

CHAPTER NINE

DELAWARE

HANNAH ERWIN ISRAEL

Israel Israel was a Delaware cattle farmer who formerly traded with the West Indian islands, and who was now living a few miles from Wilmington. Late in 1777 he was returning home from a surreptitious trip to visit his worried mother behind British lines in Philadelphia, when he was betrayed to the enemy by the same vindictive Royalist neighbor who had actually supplied him with the necessary password and countersign. Israel and his brother-in-law were immediately arrested and carried aboard the frigate *Roebuck* lying in the Delaware River directly opposite his farm, to be tried as spies.

As a member of the local Committee of Safety, the position of Mr. Israel under an accusation of espionage for passing British lines to visit Philadelphia for any reason, was extremely critical. Awaiting trial on board the warship he was treated with the utmost severity. His watch, silver shoe buckles, and various articles of clothing were taken from him; his bed was a coil of rope on deck, with no covering from the bitter night air.

To all appearances Mr. Israel's fate was already decided. The testimony of his Royalist neighbors would be strong against him. Several stood ready to swear that while the royal population had willingly furnished their share of provisions needed by the British ships of war, Mr. Israel had been heard to say repeatedly that he "would sooner drive his cattle as a present to General Washington, than receive enemy gold for them." Thus informed, the naval commander gave orders to a detachment of soldiers to drive the rebel's cattle—then grazing in full view in a meadow—down to the river and slaughter them in the face of the prisoner.

What must have been the feelings of nineteen–year-old Mrs. Israel, herself about to become a mother, when her husband and brother were led away? Mrs. Israel, born in Wilmington of highly respectable Quaker parents, is described as of middle height, of slight but symmetrical figure with the finest turned foot and ankle in the world, of fair complexion with clear blue eyes and dark hair. Her manner was modest and retiring; she was devoted to her family and domestic concerns. It needed the trying scenes by which she was surrounded to develop the heroism which, in times more peaceful, might have been unnoticed by those who knew her most intimately.

The Israel farm was a mile or more from the river, but there was nothing to interrupt the view of the meadow, sloping down to the water. From her position, Hannah Israel saw the soldiers land from the ships, shoulder their arms, and advance towards the cattle in the meadow. In an instant, Hannah divined their purpose, and her resolution was taken.

With the help of Joseph—a boy only eight years old, whom she bade follow her at his utmost speed—Hannah started off, determined at the peril of her life to baffle the enemy and save the cattle. Down went the fence bars and, followed by the little boy, Hannah ran to drive the herd to the opening.

The soldiers called out repeatedly to Hannah to desist and threatened, if she did not, to fire upon her. "Fire away!" cried the heroic woman. They fired, and the musket balls flew thick around her, and the frightened cattle ran in every direction over the field. "This way, Joe!" she called to the boy, "Head them there, Joe! Stop them! Do not let even one escape!" And not one did.

The bullets fired by the cowardly British soldiers continued to whistle around Hannah. The little boy, paralyzed by terror, dropped to the ground. She seized him by the arms and lifted him over the fence, and by herself drove the cattle into the barnyard. The assailants, baffled by the courage of the woman, and probably not daring, for fear of the neighbors, to invade the farmhouse retraced their steps and returned disappointed to their ships.

All this scene passed in sight of the officers of the *Roebuck*, as well as the two prisoners. The agony of suspense and fear endured by Hannah Israel's husband and brother, when they saw the danger to which she exposed herself, may be better imagined than described. It may also be conceived how much they exulted in her triumph.

The trial of the two prisoners was held aboard the *Roebuck*, and it was evident that their lives were in great danger. But discovering that several of the British officers in charge of his trial were, like himself, Freemasons, Mr. Israel acknowledged many of the charges against him. Watching his opportunity, he made to the commanding officer the secret sign of the Masonic brotherhood. Its effect was instantly observable; a change of opinion among the judges became evident. The Royalist witnesses were rebuked for bringing espionage charges against an honorable man, bound on a mission of love and duty to his aged Philadelphia mother. The acquitted prisoners were dismissed and loaded with hard-to-find housekeeping articles like pins and handkerchiefs for the intrepid wife.

PART THREE

THE WAR IN THE SOUTH

IN THE SOUTHERN states more than in any other area of the emerging nation, the War of the Revolution quickly became a bitter internecine struggle. After an initial naval repulse off Charleston at the very beginning of the war, the British concentrated all their military effort in the northeastern and middle states, counting on the strong royalist faction in the South to hold the Revolutionary forces in check. Powerful American defenses in the North, like the massive iron chain that closed the Hudson River at West Point, put an end to Britain's dream of cutting the United States in two.

By the end of 1778 the enemy had refocused its attention on the South, but bitter hostilities in the region had been going on for years. Brother was pitted against brother, cousin against cousin, as kidnapping, arson, looting and killing rose to a fever pitch. On the western frontiers, British-supplied natives carried on a brutal conflict in which settlers' wives and older children played a significant role.

In 1778 General Gates—the hero of Saratoga—was dispatched by Congress to raise his standard at Camden, South Carolina, and rally all the militiamen, guerillas, partisans, and a small number of Continental regulars into some sort of a unified army. Gates moved precipitately; the result was disaster. Gates personally ran away.

With Savannah and Charleston now securely in enemy hands, Washington sent General Greene, a Rhode Islander, to counter the British campaign under Cornwallis. Cornwallis's poorly planned foray was sweeping up through the South in a broad swath of devastation and civilian harassment that would eventually lead him to Virginia and the Yorktown peninsula. The battles fought along the way by one of Washington's ablest generals and his subordinates are legendary—Cowpens, King's Mountain, and Guilford Court House (where the British actually fired into their own troops).

For some of the 438,000 African Americans held in bondage in the South, there was a moment of intense rejoicing as they fled the abandoned tidewater plantations of their masters and mistresses for the supposed freedom and safety of the British lines around Charleston and Savannah. But their liberation was short-lived. They were quickly auctioned off by the enemy for renewed servitude in the canefields of the West Indies. An identical fate befell soldiers of the all-black 1st Rhode Island Regiment captured by the British north of New York City in the spring of 1781.

Meanwhile Cornwallis slogged resolutely on in pursuit of the elusive Greene, never realizing he was leading his shrinking army into a Franco-American trap of Washington's devising.

The complete loss of this second British army in North America brought down the wrath of the merchants and traders of Bristol and other major English commercial cities, whose fleets were now being punished mercilessly by swarming American privateers. Their wrath was vented upon the "King's Friends" in Parliament. It took another two years to turn the de facto victory of the United States at Yorktown into the de jure Treaty of Paris, while skirmishes continued along much of the seaboard and on the western frontier.

But the new nation was independent and free to work out its own destiny.

—LINCOLN DIAMANT

CHAPTER TEN

VIRGINIA
(AND KENTUCKY)

MRS. DAVIES

Among the exploits of the pioneers of Kentucky, there are many tales of women's fortitude, intrepidity, and heroism. Dwelling in the frontier area of east central Kentucky, Mrs. Davies had abundant opportunity to demonstrate her presence of mind and cool deliberate courage. It brought about the deliverance of herself and her family from the savages.

Early one morning, after her husband left the cabin to carry the alarm of Indians in the neighborhood, four of the savages rushed into the cabin. Mrs. Davies was still in bed with her four children. By signs, the Indians ordered her to rise immediately, and one enquired how far it was to the next cabin. Mrs. Davies comprehended that it was important to make the distance appear as great as possible, to detain them until her husband might have time to bring back assistance. Counting on her fingers, Mrs. Davies made the Indians understand that the nearest cabin was eight miles distant. It—and help—was actually much closer.

She then rose and slowly dressed herself, after which she showed the savages various articles of her clothing, donning one after another. Their pleased examination delayed their departure nearly two hours.

Another Indian who had been pursuing her husband now entered the cabin and held up his hands stained with pokeberry juice, using violent gestures and brandishing his tomahawk to persuade Mrs. Davies that the fugitive husband had been slain. Her quick eye discovered the deception, and she rejoiced in this evidence that he had indeed escaped, and endured.

The cabin was now plundered of everything that could be carried away, and the savages set out, taking with them as prisoners Mrs. Davies and her children, with the two oldest carrying the two younger ones. Mrs. Davies well knew that death would be the penalty for any failure of strength or speed. The Indians watched closely that no twig or weed was broken off as they passed along to mark the course they had taken. The length of Mrs. Davies's dress interfering, as the Indians thought, with their rapid movement, one of them drew a knife and cut some inches off her skirt.

All the time, this courageous woman was revolving plans in her mind to accomplish her deliverance, determining that if she was not rescued during the course of the day, she would make a desperate attempt to escape at night, when the Indians were asleep, by possessing herself of their arms, killing as many as she could, and inducing the belief of a night attack to frighten the others.

To such extremity was female resolution driven in those times. Friends who knew Mrs. Davies had little doubt that her enterprise would have succeeded. But she was prevented from the perilous attempt by being overtaken and rescued at nine o'clock that evening by her husband and a party of neighbors.

"JOHN'S WIFE"

It was at Blue Lick Springs in northeastern Kentucky that a bloody battle was fought with the Indians that shrouded the area in mourning.[1]

In the annals of savage warfare, it is second only to Braddock's defeat.[2]

A romantic incident occurred after that fatal action. Among the unfortunate ones who survived the ordeal of the gauntlet, painted jet black by the savages, was an excellent husband and father from Garrard County. By some unaccountable freak of clemency, his life was spared when all his fellow prisoners were butchered. For almost a year his friends believed him numbered with the slain of that disastrous day.

His wife was soon wooed by another but continued to hope against hope that her husband still lived and would return to her. At length, persuaded by the expostulations of others that her affectionate instincts were a delusion, she reluctantly yielded consent to the second nuptials—which, however, she postponed several times, declaring that it was impossible to divest herself of the belief that her husband still lived.

Finally submitting to the judgment of her friends, she allowed the day of her marriage to be appointed. Just before dawn on that day, when we may suppose she was wakeful with reflection, the crack of a rifle was heard near her lonely cabin. Startled by the familiar sound, she leaped up like a liberated fawn, exclaiming as she sprang toward the door, "That's John's gun!" In an instant, she was clasped in the arms of her lost husband.

In poetic justice to the disappointed suitor, it should be mentioned that nine years afterwards, the same husband was killed at St. Clair's defeat,[3] and that in proper time, the once-rejected suitor obtained the hand of the fair widow.

MRS. JOHN MERRILL

An Indian attack on the Merrill family's cabin in Lincoln County provided an unusual instance of female heroism. Alarmed at midnight by the barking of his dog, Merrill opened the front door and was immediately fired upon by several Indians. He fell back wounded, while his wife instantly closed the door.

An Amazon in both strength and courage, Mrs. Merrill stood on guard with an axe and killed or wounded four of the attackers as they attempted to enter the cabin through a breach in the wall. Other savages then climbed onto the cabin roof, to try to come down the chimney, but Mrs. Merrill hastily ripped up a feather bed[4] and threw it on the fire. The blaze and smoke brought two Indians tumbling down onto the hearth, where Mrs. Merrill quickly dispatched them, while she also wounded another who had meanwhile assailed the front door. He fled with a loud yell, and afterwards gave an exaggerated account of the fierceness of the young white squaw.

MRS. JOHN WALKER

In June of 1781, Tarleton led his cavalry Legion[5] on a secret forced march from Cornwallis's main army to Charlottesville, in an attempt to capture Governor Thomas Jefferson and his Virginia legislature. Several of the legislators chanced to be staying at the house of Colonel John Walker, twelve miles distant from the town. The Walker home was directly on Tarleton's line of march, and the first intimation the family had of the enemy approach was the appearance of Tarleton's Legion at their front door.

Colonel Walker was at that time with the army in lower Virginia. Having made prisoners of one or two laggard members of the legislature, Colonel Tarleton ordered breakfast for himself and his men. Mrs. Walker was a staunch Whig and knew well that the design of her unwelcome guest was to proceed quickly to Charlottesville and plunder and destroy the public stores collected there. So she delayed as long as she could her preparations for breakfast, to enable the legislators who had escaped to reach the town and remove and secrete such portions of the stores as could be saved.

Mrs. Walker's patriotic stratagem gained the necessary time. Tarleton lingered fruitlessly a day or two at Charlottesville and then hurried back to rejoin the main army under Cornwallis.

MARTHA DANDRIDGE (CUSTIS) WASHINGTON

No one interested in the history of George Washington can fail to desire some knowledge of the woman who shared his thoughts and plans, and who was intimately associated with him in the great events of his life. Those who read the record of the great worth of Mrs. Washington may dwell with interest on the loveliness of her character. To a superior mind, she joined those amiable qualities and Christian virtues which best adorn the female sex. She possessed a gentle dignity that inspired respect without ever creating enmity.

Few women have been called upon to move amid scenes so varied and imposing. Fewer still have sustained their part with so much dignity and discretion. In the gloom of adversity, Martha Washington walked at the side of the commander in chief, ascending with him the difficult path that Heaven had opened.

The life of Mrs. Washington was a changeable one, with a full measure of sorrow and joy, endurance and self-sacrifice. Martha Dandridge was descended from a family that had migrated early to the colony of Virginia, where she was born in New Kent County in May 1732. Her education was only a domestic one, such as was given to females in those days, when there were few seminaries of instruction, and private teachers were generally employed.

Martha's beauty and fascinating manners, with her admirable qualities of character, gave her distinction among the ladies who gathered at Williamsburg, then the seat of government. When but seventeen, Miss Dandridge was married to Colonel Daniel Parke Custis, a successful Virginia planter. Their residence was on the Pamunkey, a branch of the York River. Neither of the two Custis children survived their mother, who lived until 1802. Mrs. Custis was early left a widow, in the full bloom of beauty and splendidly endowed with worldly benefits.[6] As sole executrix, she managed the extensive business of the Custis estate with great ability. Surrounded as she was by advantages of fortune and position and possessing such charms of person, it is easy to see why suitors for Martha Custis's hand and heart were many and pressing.

On a morning in 1758, a Virginia militia officer crossed the Pamunkey at Williams's ferry. When the boat touched the New Kent shore, the soldier's progress was arrested by one of those personages who was the beau ideal of the Virginia gentry—the very soul of hospitality. He would hear of no excuse on the officer's part for declining the invitation to stop at his home. In vain the twenty-six–year-old militia colonel pleaded important business at Williamsburg; host Chamberlayne insisted that his friend must at the very least dine with him. As a temptation, he also promised to introduce Colonel Washington to a charming widow his own age, who chanced to be staying at his house.

The soldier surrendered, resolving, however, to pursue his journey that same evening. The two men proceeded to the mansion, where the host presented the colonel to his guests, among whom was Mrs. Custis.

Tradition says that the two were favorably impressed with each other. The day passed quickly, and the sun was sinking on the horizon when Mr. Chamberlayne insisted that no guest ever left his house after sunset; without much difficulty, his visitor was persuaded to remain.

The next day was far advanced before the now enamored soldier was on the road to Williamsburg. Once his business there was concluded, he hastened back to the captivating widow. A short time after their marriage, which took place early in 1759, Colonel and Mrs. Washington fixed their residence at Mount Vernon on the Potomac. Their mansion was at that time a very small building. It did not receive many additions before Washington left home to attend the Continental Congress, and thereafter to become commander in chief of the armies of his country. He was accompanied to Cambridge by his wife, who remained some time and witnessed the siege and evacuation of Boston. She then returned to Virginia.

During the journey, so prevalent was the Royalist disaffection in Philadelphia that few of the ladies of that city called upon her. She usually passed the winters with her husband; it was the habit of the commander to dispatch an aide-de-camp at the close of each campaign to escort Mrs. Washington to headquarters, and her arrival was a much anticipated event. She brought a cheering influence which relieved the general gloom in seasons of disaster and despair. Martha Washington's example was followed by the wives of other general officers (see LUCIA FLUCKER KNOX and CATHERINE LITTLEFIELD GREENE above).

Lady Washington, as she was always called in the army, usually remained at headquarters until the opening of the succeeding campaign, when she returned to Mount Vernon. After the war, she often said that it was her fortune to have heard the first and last cannon of every campaign of the Revolution. Her equanimity and cheerfulness were preserved throughout the sternest periods of the struggle, as testified to in many military journals. Her conversation is described as agreeable, and her manner simple, easy, and dignified.

She was at Valley Forge during that dreadful winter of 1777–1778;[7] her presence and submission to privation strengthened the fortitude of those who might otherwise have complained and gave hope and confidence to the despondent. Mrs. Washington soothed the distresses of many sufferers, seeking out the afflicted with benevolent kindness and extending relief wherever it was in her power to do so, while residing with graceful deportment in the chief's humble dwelling. Here, forgetful of herself, the patriot wife anxiously watched the aspect of affairs and was happy when the political horizon brightened.

For Mrs. Washington, a heavy cloud of sorrow hung over the conclusion of the campaign of 1781. Her surviving child was seized with the fever while attending to his duty during the siege of Yorktown. He lived to behold the surrender of the British army and then expired in his mother's arms, mourned by Washington as his own son.

MRS. WOODS

A singular adventure occurred one morning at the Woods family's Lincoln County, Kentucky cabin. Mr. Woods had gone to the station [fort] and did not expect to return until nightfall. He left his family, consisting of his wife and young daughter and a lame negro manservant.

Mrs. Woods was a short distance from the cabin when she saw several Indians approaching. Screaming to give the alarm, she ran to reach the cabin ahead of the savages. Before she could close the front door, one of the Indians pushed his way into the cabin.

The Indian was instantly grappled by the negro. A scuffle ensued, and both of them fell to the floor, with the black man underneath. Mrs. Woods could render no assistance, having to exert all her strength to keep the door closed against the party without. But the lame domestic, holding the Indian tightly in his arms, called out to the daughter to take an axe lying under the bed and dispatch the savage with a blow to the head. Self-preservation demanded instant obedience—after one misstroke she succeeded, and the Indian was killed.

The negro then proposed to his mistress that she let in another of those still trying to force open the door, in order to dispose of them singly in the same manner. Mrs. Woods thought the experiment too dangerous.

Shortly thereafter some men from the station discovered the situation of the family and soon scattered the cabin's besiegers.

ELIZABETH ZANE

Fort Henry stood on the left bank of the Ohio River, a little way above the mouth of Wheeling Creek. It covered three-quarters of an acre, with a blockhouse at each corner and eight-foot palisades between them. The fort was near the foot of a hill that rose abruptly from the bottomland along the river.

On the cleared land between the fort and the base of the hill was a rude village of some twenty or thirty log houses which, although then of little importance, was the germ of one of the fairest cities that now grace the domain of Virginia.[8] Within the fort were several cabins for the temporary use of local families, with a gate opening on the straggling village without.

May and June 1777 saw a number of savage forays upon the Kentucky settlements. As the summer advanced, these depredations became bolder and more frequent. So imminent was the danger that people threw aside their private pursuits; the militia was constantly in service, and civil jurisdiction gave way to martial law. By September it became plain that a large Indian force, under the direction of the notorious white renegade and Royalist, Simon Girty,[9] was concentrating on the Sandusky River. This savage host, numbering from three hundred to five hundred warriors, was eventually brought before the walls of Fort Henry. The inhabitants of the village and several other families in the neighborhood quickly betook themselves to the fort for safety.

At the next sunrise, a man dispatched from the fort to bring in some horses was killed. A party of fourteen soldiers was sent to dislodge the savages from a cornfield near the fort; they found themselves unexpectedly and furiously assailed, and only two survived. Others pushing forward to their relief fell into an ambuscade, and two-thirds of their number perished.

The Indians then advanced with loud whoops to take their positions before the fort. The garrison of fighting men, which had at first numbered forty-two, was now reduced to twelve, including boys. This little band had a sacred charge to protect their mothers, sisters, wives, and children. They resolved to fight to the last extremity, trusting in Heaven for a successful issue.

For many hours, the bullets of the Indians were met by a well-directed fire from the tiny garrison, composed of excellent marksmen. The courageous women in the fort molded bullets, prepared gun patches, and by their presence at every point where they could perform useful service, inspired the soldiers.

But the stock of gunpowder in the fort was nearly exhausted. A temporary cessation of hostile fire offered an opportunity to procure a keg of powder hidden in the cabin of Ebenezer Zane, about sixty yards from the gate of the fort. The officer commanding the garrison explained the matter to his men, but he was unwilling to order any of them upon an enterprise so desperate. He asked for volunteers for the perilous service. Three or four young men promptly offered to undertake the mission. Their commander answered that only one man could be spared and left it to the volunteers to decide who it should be.

While they disputed, every moment of time was precious, with the danger of a renewed attack before the powder could be procured. The sudden interposition of a young girl put an end to their contention. Elizabeth Zane, the sister of Ebenezer, had just returned to the frontier from a school in Philadelphia. She came forward and requested that she be permitted to go for the powder. Her proposal was at first met with peremptory refusal, but she renewed her petition with steadfast earnestness; she would not be dissuaded from her heroic purpose by either the commander or her anxious relatives.

Elizabeth argued that the danger of the undertaking was the reason for her offer to perform the service. Her loss would not be felt, while not a single soldier could be spared from the already badly weakened garrison. That argument prevailed, and Elizabeth's request was granted.

When she had divested herself of such articles of clothing as might impede her speed, the fort gate was opened for her to pass out. The opening of the gate arrested the attention of Indian stragglers in the village, and their eyes were upon Elizabeth as she crossed the open space, striding as rapidly as possible to reach her brother's cabin. The surprised savages permitted her to somehow pass without molestation.

In a few moments she reappeared, carrying the keg of powder in her arms—one account says she tied the powder in a tablecloth fastened around her waist—walking at utmost speed towards the fort. This time the Indians suspected the nature of Elizabeth's burden; they raised their firelocks and discharged a leaden storm around her. But she kept on as the musket balls whistled harmlessly past her, and the intrepid girl with her prize reached the fort in safety.

When fate seemed against them, the noble act of Elizabeth Zane inspired the soldiers, sustaining their resistance with new courage, until military relief finally arrived.

NOTES

1. Exactly eight months before the end of the Revolution, on 19 August 1782, a raiding party of 240 Native Americans and Royalists, operating near Lexington, drew a hastily assembled body of 182 Kentucky frontier militiamen into a one-sided engagement near lower Blue Lick Springs on the middle fork of the Licking River. Ignoring Colonel Daniel Boone's advice to wait for reinforcements, the Americans launched a disorganized attack across a deep Licking River ford. In a matter of minutes, the militiamen were completely routed, at a cost of seventy-seven killed, twelve wounded and eight captured (including "John"). Disproportionate enemy losses were seven killed and ten wounded. The debacle shook the entire frontier.

2. The 1755 ambush in the forests of Western Pennsylvania, during the French and Indian Wars.

3. Major General Arthur St. Clair—former Revolutionary field commander and 1787 President of Congress—was heading the United States Army when he was disastrously defeated 4 November 1791 in the old Northwest Territory by Little Turtle and his Miami Nation.

4. Always a valued household possession.

5. Five months earlier, British Lieutenant Colonel Banastre Tarleton's awesome reputation for military invincibility suffered a severe setback at the Battle of Cowpens in South Carolina, where his cavalrymen were shattered by General Daniel Morgan.

6. Martha Custis was reputedly the wealthiest relict in British North America.

7. By most accounts, the privation and suffering Martha Washington witnessed in the Continental army huts at Jockey Hollow near Morristown, New Jersey, during the cruel winter of 1779–1780 surpassed the previous year's terrible hardships at Valley Forge.

8. Wheeling, now situated in what became West Virginia during the Civil War.

9. Ellet errs—as do many Revolutionary historians. The thirty-six–year-old Girty, son of an Irish emigrant to Pennsylvania, was in his youth a captive of the Senecas. But in the fall of 1777, Girty was still serving the Americans as an Indian interpreter; he did not desert to the British until the following year.

CHAPTER ELEVEN

NORTH CAROLINA
(AND TENNESSEE)

MARTHA POLK BREVARD

It was in Charlotte, the seat of Mecklenburg County, that the bold idea of national independence was first proclaimed to the world. In May 1775 an immense concourse of people assembled in this frontier settlement, all agitated by the excitement that had plunged the whole land into commotion. It was on the day that the first intelligence of the commencement of hostilities at Lexington, and when the convention of the people was addressed, that the universal cry was, "Let us declare our independence, and protect it with our lives and fortunes."[1]

Resolutions drawn up by Dr. Ephraim Brevard were discussed and unanimously adopted the following day by the approving multitude. The citizens of Mecklenburg County declared themselves a free and independent people.

Due honor is awarded to the doctor who took part in that memorable transaction. But where is the tribute that should be paid to the mother who sowed the seeds implanted in her seven sons' minds? One son, Captain Alexander Brevard, took part in nine battles. The youngest was, at seventeen, first lieutenant of a company of horse.

When the southern states became the arena of war, Dr. Brevard entered the army as a surgeon and was taken prisoner at the surrender of Charleston.[2] In that city he was seized with a fatal disease, to which he fell victim after being set at liberty and placed under the care of friends.

The deplorable suffering of the unfortunate prisoners in Charleston moved the sympathy of the inhabitants of western Carolina. News came that many of them were perishing in captivity of want and disease. Men could not go and visit their captured friends and relatives without insuring their own destruction. But women like Martha Brevard gathered clothing, medicines, and provisions and traveled long journeys, encountering dangers as well as hardships, to minister to those who so sorely needed their succor. Much relief was brought to the sufferers by these visits of mercy although the lives preserved were sometimes saved at the sacrifice of those of the noble benefactors.

During Cornwallis's pursuit of Generals Nathanael Greene and Daniel Morgan, the British burned the property of the widowed Mrs. Brevard at Centre congregation. The reason given by the officer for permitting her house to be burned and her farm plundered was that she had too many sons in the rebel army.

RACHEL CRAIGHEAD CALDWELL

Rachel Craighead, third daughter of the Reverend Alexander Craighead, was born in western North Carolina in 1739. She was regarded by all who knew her as a woman of remarkable character and influence and is still remembered with high respect.

In early life, Rachel had her share in many of the perils and hardships of the Indian war, the inroads of the savages being frequent and murderous, with her home in an exposed situation. Describing these incursions, she often said that as the family would escape out of one door, the Indians would come in at another.

When Braddock's defeat[3] left the Virginia frontier at the mercy of the savages, Reverend Craighead fled with some of his people—including young Rachel—back across the Blue Ridge to the more quiet regions of North Carolina, where he remained till the close of his life.

In 1766, twenty-seven–year-old Rachel married the Reverend David Caldwell, fifteen years her senior. For almost sixty years, Rachel's husband was the pastor of the two oldest and largest Presbyterian congregations in Guilford County. He also kept a celebrated classical school, for a long time the only one of note in the area. The influence of Rachel Caldwell in the school was great and beneficial, increasing the respect of the students towards her husband. They bore uniform testimony to her intelligence and zeal, and to the value of her counsel, while her kindness won their regard and confidence.

The success with which Mrs. Caldwell labored to inculcate the lessons of practical piety gave currency to the saying throughout the area, "Dr. Caldwell makes the scholars, and Mrs. Caldwell makes the preachers." Not only was David Caldwell thus the father of education in North Carolina, but before and during the Revolutionary struggle he exerted a strong influence in favor of national independence and bore an active part in the prominent events of the period.

Sometime in the fall of 1780, a stranger, faint and worn with fatigue, stopped at the Caldwell home and asked supper and lodging for the night. He announced himself as an express rider bearing dispatches from General Washington to General Greene. He had imagined that he would be free from danger under the roof of a minister of the gospel, but Rachel Caldwell soon undeceived him on this point. She was alone and could not tell the day or hour when an attack might be expected. Should the local Royalists chance to hear of the traveler and learn that he had important papers in his possession, he would certainly be robbed before morning. She said that he should have something to eat immediately but advised him to seek safer shelter for the night. This alarmed the stranger, and but a short time passed before voices were heard without, with cries of, "Surround the house!" And the dwelling was presently assailed by a body of Royalists.

With admirable calm, Rachel Caldwell bade the stranger follow her and led him out a back door. A large locust tree stood close by, and the night was so dark that no object could be discerned. Amid its clustering foliage, she bade him climb the tree, thorny as it was, and conceal himself till the men should be engaged in plundering the house. He could then descend and trust to flight for his safety.

The house was pillaged as Mrs. Caldwell had expected, but the express rider made good his escape, remembering with gratitude the woman whose prudence had saved him with the loss of her property.

For some days before the battle at Guilford Court House,[4] Cornwallis's army was encamped within the bounds of Dr. Caldwell's congregations and most of the local men being with General Greene, distress fell on their defenseless women and children.

In the detail of spoliation and outrage, the Caldwells had been repeatedly harassed by the British and local Royalists who bore them special enmity. A price had been set upon Dr. Caldwell's head. On the eleventh of March, while he was in Greene's camp, the British army marched to his plantation and encamped there, the officers taking possession of his house.

Mrs. Caldwell was at home with her children when they arrived. They at first announced themselves as Americans and asked to see the landlady. But a female domestic had ascertained, by standing on a fence and seeing red coats at a distance, that the men belonged to Cornwallis's army. She quickly communicated her discovery to her mistress.

Excusing herself by saying that she must attend to her child, Mrs. Caldwell retired into the house and immediately gave warning to two neighbors who happened to be there that they should escape through the back door and conceal themselves. She then returned to the gate.

The party in front, when charged with being British soldiers, avowed themselves and said they must have the use of the dwelling for a day or two. They immediately established themselves in their quarters, turning out Mrs. Caldwell and her children into the smokehouse, where she was frequently insulted by brutal and profane language. To a young officer who came to the door for the purpose of taunting the helpless mother by ridiculing her countrymen, whom he termed "rebels and cowards," Rachel Caldwell replied, "Wait and see what the Lord will do for us." "If He intends to do anything," pertly rejoined the military fop, "it's time he had begun."

In reply to Mrs. Caldwell's application to one of the soldiers for protection, she was told she could expect no favors, for the women were as great rebels as the men. After remaining two days, the army took their departure from the ravaged plantation on which they had destroyed everything. Before leaving the Caldwell house, the officer in command gave orders that Dr. Caldwell's library and papers should be burned. A fire was kindled in the yard, and valuable books and manuscripts were carried out by the soldiers, armful after armful, and ruthlessly committed to the flames. Not even the family bible was spared.

On the fifteenth was heard the roar of the battle that soon achieved the deliverance of North Carolina. The women of Dr. Caldwell's congregation met and, while the conflict was raging fiercely between man and man, wrestled in earnest prayer for their defenders. After the cold, wet night which succeeded the action at Guilford, the women wandered over the field of battle to search for their friends, administer the last sad rites to the dead, and bear away the wounded and expiring.

One American officer, who had lain thirty hours undiscovered, was found in the woods by an old lady, who had him carried to his house, where he survived long enough to relate how a Royalist of his aquaintance had passed him the day after the battle, had recognized him, and bestowed a blow and execration, instead of the water he craved to quench his consuming thirst. Conscience, however, sometimes avenges the insulted rights of nature; the man who had refused the dying request of a fellow creature was found after the officer's death, suspended on a tree before his own front door.

The venerable Reverend Caldwell survived the Revolution and died in 1824, at the age of one hundred. Rachel Caldwell died a year later, aged eighty-six.

MARGARET SHARPE GASTON

Margaret Sharpe was born about 1755 in the county of Cumberland, England. Her parents, desiring her to have every advantage of education in the Catholic faith, to which they were attached, sent her to France when young to be brought up in a convent. She often referred in after life to happy days passed there.

Margaret's two brothers were extensively engaged in commerce in America, and she came out to visit. It was during her sojourn in North Carolina that she met Dr. Alexander Gaston, a native of Ireland, of Huguenot ancestry, to whom she was married at New Bern,[5] in the twentieth year of her age. As a surgeon in the British army, Dr. Gaston had served with the expedition that captured Havana[6] but, being attacked by fever and suffering from the exhaustion of the warm climate, had resigned his post to make his home in the North American provinces.

The happy married life of these two young persons was destined to be of short duration. Dr. Gaston was one of the most zealous patriots in North Carolina, being a member of the New Bern Committee of Safety, and served in the army at various periods of the war. His devotion to the cause of freedom, while it secured the confidence of the Whigs, gave him the implacable enmity of the opposite party.

On the twentieth of August 1781, a body of Royalists entered New Bern, some miles in advance of the British regular troops, with the view of taking possession of the town. The Americans, taken by surprise, were forced, after an ineffectual resistance, to give way. Dr. Gaston, unwilling to surrender to the foe, hurried his wife and children from their home, hoping to escape across the Trent River and thus retire to a plantation eight or ten miles distant. He reached the wharf with his family and seized a light scow for the purpose of crossing the river. But before his wife and children could step on board, the Royalists, eager for his blood, came galloping in pursuit. There was no recourse for the husband and father but to push off from the shore where his wife and little ones stood—the wife alarmed only for him against whom the rage of their enemies was directed.

Throwing herself in agony at the Royalists' feet, Mrs. Gaston implored his life, but in vain. Their cruelty sacrificed him in the midst of her cries for mercy; the ball that found his heart was from a musket leveled over her shoulder.

Even the indulgence of grief was denied to the bereaved wife, for she was compelled to exert herself to protect the remains of her murdered husband. Loud were the threats of the inhuman Royalists that the "rebel should not have even the rest of the grave." In her lonely dwelling, she kept watch beside her beloved's lifeless form until it was deposited in the earth.

Margaret Gaston was now left alone in a foreign land, her two brothers having died earlier. Her son William, three years of age,[7] and infant daughter remained the sole object of her care and love. Many women possessing her acute sensibility would have been overwhelmed in such a situation, but trials served only to develop the admirable energy of her character. Though still young when left a widow, she never laid aside the habiliments of sorrow, and the anniversary of her husband's murder was kept as a day of fasting and prayer.

MARY HOOKS SLOCUMB

In February 1776, at a time when the whole country was aroused by the march of Royalists in the Cape Fear area, old General Donald McDonald raised the Royal standard and issued his Proclamation at Cross Creek. But the patriots of New Bern and Wilmington[8] were not idle.

The gallant Colonel Richard Caswell hastily called his neighbors together, and they came as readily as the clans of the Scotch mountains used to muster at the signal of the burning cross. The whole county rose en masse; the militia regiments encountered McDonald at Moore's Creek,[9] where, on the twenty-seventh, was fought one of the most important battles of the Revolution. Colonel Ezekiel Slocumb was accustomed to dwell but lightly on the gallant part borne by him in that memorable action, but he gave abundant praise to his associates. And he would say, "My wife, Mary was there."

She was indeed, but her story is best told in her own words:

"The men all left on Sunday morning; more than eighty left this house with my husband. I could see that every man had mischief in him. I know a coward whenever I set eyes upon one. The Royalists more than once tried to frighten me, but they always showed coward at the bare insinuation that our troops were about.

"Well, they got off in high spirits, every man stepping quick and light. I slept soundly and quietly that night, and worked hard the next day, but I kept thinking where the men had gone and how far, and how many of the Regulars and Royalists they would meet. I could not keep myself from thinking about them. I went to bed at the usual time, but still continued to think.

"As I lay, whether waking or sleeping I know not, I had a dream, yet it was not all a dream. I distinctly saw a body wrapped in my husband's guard cloak, bloody dead; and others dead and wounded on the ground about him. I saw them plainly and distinctly.

"I uttered a cry and sprang out of bed. I gazed in every direction to catch another glimpse of the scene, but everything was still and quiet. My child was sleeping but my woman was awakened by my crying out and jumping to the floor. If ever I felt fear, it was at that moment. Seated on the bed, I reflected a little and said aloud, 'I must go to him!'

"I told my woman I could not sleep, and would ride down the road a bit. I told her to lock the door after me, and look after my child. I dressed, went to the stable, saddled my mare, and in a minute we were tearing down the road. After a mile or two, the cool night seemed to bring reflection. I asked myself where I was going, and for what purpose. Again and again, I was tempted to turn back, but I was soon ten miles from home.

"My mind became stronger every mile I rode. That I should find my husband dead or dying was my firm presentiment. When day broke, I was some thirty miles from home. I knew the general route our little army had expected to take, and followed it without hesitation.

"About sunrise I came upon a group of women and children standing and sitting by the roadside. Each one of them showed the same anxiety of mind that I felt. Stopping for a few moments, I inquired if the battle had already been fought. They knew nothing, and had assembled on the road to gather intelligence. They thought Colonel Caswell had taken the road to Cape Fear.

"Again I was skimming over the ground through a country thinly settled, and very poor and swampy, but neither my own spirits nor my nag's failed in the least. I followed the trail of the troops, and the sun must have been well up when I heard a sound like thunder, which I knew must be cannon.

"It was the first time I ever heard a cannon. I stopped still, when presently the cannon thundered again. The battle was then fighting. What a fool! My husband could not be dead last night, and the battle only fighting now. Away I went again, faster than ever, and I soon found from the noise of guns that I was near the fight. Again I stopped. I could hear muskets, I could hear rifles, and I could hear shouting. I spoke to my mare, and dashed on in the direction of the firing and the shouts, now louder than ever.

"The path I was following brought me into the Wilmington road a few hundred feet below Moore's Creek Bridge. A few yards from the road, under a cluster of trees, were lying perhaps twenty men. They were the American and Royalist wounded. I knew the spot; the very trees and the position of the men I knew as if I had seen it a thousand times! In an instant my whole soul was centered in one spot, for there, wrapped in his bloody guard cloak, was my husband's body. I remember uncovering his head and seeing a face covered with gore from a dreadful wound across the temple. I put my hand to the bloody face; 'twas still warm, and an unknown voice begged for water! I brought it, poured some in his mouth, washed his face, and behold—it was Frank Cogdell.

"He soon revived, and could speak. I was washing the wound in his head, when he said, 'It is not that. It is the hole in my leg that is killing me!' A puddle of blood was on the ground around his feet. I took his knife, cut away his trousers and stocking, and found the blood came from a shot-hole, through and through the fleshy part of his leg. I could see nothing that looked as if it would do for dressing wounds, but some leaves.

"I gathered a handful and bound them tight to the holes, and the bleeding soon stopped. I then went to the others. I had not inquired for my husband, but while I was busy dressing wounds, Colonel Caswell came up, and appeared very much surprised to see me. With his hat in hand, he was about to pay me some compliment, when I interrupted by asking, 'Where is my husband?' 'Where he ought to be, Madam, in pursuit of the enemy,' said he. 'But how came you here?' 'Oh,' said I, 'I thought you would need nurses, as well as soldiers. And here is one,' going to Frank Cogdell, lifting him up with my arm under his head so that he could drink some more water, 'who would have died before any of you men could have helped him.' 'I believe you,' said Frank.

"Just then I looked up and saw my husband, as bloody as a butcher and muddy as a ditcher, standing before me. 'Why, Mary,' he exclaimed. 'What are you doing there, hugging Frank Cogdell, the greatest reprobate in the army?'

" 'I don't care,' I cried. 'Frank's a brave fellow, a good soldier and a friend to Congress.' 'True! true! You are right, Madam,' said Colonel Caswell with the lowest possible bow.

"I did not tell my husband what brought me to the scene of battle. I knew he was surprised, but he was not displeased with me. I was so happy, and so were all. It was a glorious victory. Many prisoners were brought in, and among them some very obnoxious, but the worst of the royalists were never taken prisoner. They were, for the most part, left in the woods and swamps wherever they were overtaken.

"I begged for some of the poor prisoners, and Caswell readily told me none should be hurt but such as have been guilty of murder, and houseburnings. In the middle of the night, I again mounted my mare and started for home. Caswell and my husband wanted me to stay till morning, when they would send a party with me, but no, I wanted to see my child, and I told them they could send no party that could keep up with me. What a happy ride I had back, and with what joy did I embrace my child as he ran to meet me."

NOTES

1. Historians traditionally believed that the phraseology of the twenty–point Revolutionary "Mecklenburg Resolves" of 31 May 1775 inspired similar wording in the Declaration of Independence a year later. Thomas Jefferson always denied this, and recent research has proven him correct.

2. 12 May 1780.

3. 9 July 1755.

4. This obstinate, bloody struggle between the British led by Earl Cornwallis and the Americans commanded by Nathanael Greene took place 15 March 1781, after three weeks of maneuvering in central North Carolina. General Greene's 4,449 regular troops and militiamen outnumbered the enemy by more than two to one. But almost three thousand of the Americans had never seen combat before, while the opposing soldiers were seasoned veterans. Greene placed his men in three successive lines, inviting Cornwallis to attack. The relatively short seesaw struggle ended in an orderly American retreat. The British suffered more than six hundred casualties—one-third of their army, while Greene's losses numbered 261, with many militiamen simply running away.

5. Coastal port city north of Wilmington; one-time capital of North Carolina.

6. In 1762 during the French and Indian wars, the Spanish capital of Cuba was besieged and captured by an Anglo-American expedition.

7. In adult life a distinguished liberal North Carolina legislator and jurist. He died in 1844.

8. See Note 5, above.

9. Forced to take sides by the news from Lexington and Concord, many North Carolinians chose the Royal cause. But the Revolutionaries were better organized and successfully kept their enemies from linking up with British army units on the coast near Cape Fear. On 27 February 1776, over one thousand hastily gathered patriot militiamen under Colonel Richard Caswell cut off and destroyed a twelve-hundred–man Royalist force rallying around Colonel Donald McLeod, at the greased stringers of strategic Moore's Creek Bridge on the Cape Fear River, twenty miles above Wilmington. Only thirty Royalists were killed or wounded, but 850 were taken prisoner. One American militiaman was killed and one wounded.

CHAPTER TWELVE

SOUTH CAROLINA

MARTHA BRATTON

Before Charleston fell to the British,[1] when effectual American resistance throughout the state was in a great measure rendered impossible by the want of ammunition, the governor sent a supply to all the patriots to enable them to harass the invaders.

In the back country, many of these supplies were secured by secreting them in hollow trees and the like. The portion given to Colonel William Bratton was, in his absence from home, confided to the care of his wife Martha. Some Royalists who heard of this informed the British officer commanding the nearest post, and an enemy detachment was immediately sent out to secure the valuable prize.

Mrs. Bratton, informed of their approach, was aware that there was no chance of saving her charge and resolved that the enemy should have no advantage of it. She immediately laid a train of powder from the ammunition to a spot where she stood, and when the enemy came in sight, set it afire. The explosion that greeted the ears of the foe informed them that the object of their expedition was frustrated.

The officer in command, irritated to fury, demanded to know who had dared to perpetrate such an act and threatened severe justice upon the culprit. The woman to whom he owed his disappointment answered, "It was I who did it. Let the consequence be what it will. I glory in having prevented the mischief contemplated by the cruel enemies of my country."

A little later in the war, during a dark year for the patriots of South Carolina, the Bratton homestead again figured in a dramatic incident that related to the subsequent engagement at Hanging Rock.[2]

A month earlier, a small British force led by Captain Christian Huck visited the Bratton house. Entering rudely, Huck demanded to know where Martha Bratton's husband was. "In Sumter's army,"[3] was her undaunted reply. The officer then tried persuasion and proposed that Mr. Bratton come in and join the royalists, promising that he should have a commission. Martha Bratton answered that she would rather see her husband remain true to his duty to his country, even if he perished with Sumter's army. Mrs. Bratton's son John remembers that Captain Huck was caressing him while speaking to his mother. On receiving her answer, he pushed the boy off his knee so suddenly that the child's face was bruised by the fall.

One of Huck's soldiers, infuriated at Mrs. Bratton's boldness, seized a reaping hook that hung nearby on the piazza and brought it to her throat. She still refused to give any information that might endanger her husband.

But Captain Huck's second in command intervened and compelled the soldier to release her.

The captain then ordered Mrs. Bratton to prepare supper for him and his troops. It may be conceived with what feeling she saw her home occupied by the enemies of her husband and her country, while she found herself compelled to minister to their wants. The desperate idea occurred to her of playing a Roman's part, by mingling poison, which she had in the house, with the food they were to eat, thus delivering her neighbors from impending danger. But her nature shrank from such an expedient, even to punish the invaders of her home.

After dinner, Captain Huck and his men moved up the road and encamped at a neighboring plantation and were sleeping when they were suddenly attacked by an American force under Colonel Bratton. Roused by the roar of the guns, Huck mounted his horse and attempted to rally his men, but his efforts were unavailing. The spirit and bravery of the patriots carried all before them.[4] When Captain Huck fell, his men threw down their arms and tried to flee. Some were killed or mortally wounded. The rest escaped into the woods or were made prisoners.

In the pursuit, the conflict raged around the Bratton house, and Mrs. Bratton and her children, anxious to look out, were in some danger from the shooting. Much against his will, she made her son John sit inside the chimney.

When the firing ceased, Mrs. Bratton ventured out, fearful of finding her nearest and dearest relatives among the dead and wounded lying around her dwelling. But none of her loved ones had fallen. Her house was soon open alike to the wounded on both sides, as she humanely attended all the sufferers. Thus her lofty spirit was displayed no less by her humanity to the vanquished than by her courage and resolution in the hour of danger.

At the death of Captain Huck, the officer next in command became the leader of his troop. He was among the prisoners who surrendered to the Whigs, and they were determined to put him to death. He entreated, as a last favor, to be conducted to Mrs. Bratton, who instantly recognized him as the officer who had interfered in her behalf the previous evening and possibly saved her life. Gratitude prompted her now to intercede for him. She pleaded with an eloquence which, considering the share she had borne in the common stress and danger, could not be withstood. Her petition was granted and she procured the officer's deliverance from the death that awaited him and kindly entertained him until he was exchanged.

MRS. DILLARD

In the summer of 1780, Major Patrick Ferguson was in the vicinity of Green Spring, actively recruiting Royalist cavalrymen. A party of American militia under Colonel Elijah Clarke, operating in the same area, had stopped briefly for refreshment at the home of a Captain Dillard, who was also serving with the group. After a lunch of milk and potatoes—the simple fare which those hardy soldiers often found it hard to obtain, the Americans had gone into camp near Green Spring, some distance away.

That same evening, Major Ferguson, with Major James Dunlap and a large party of mounted royalists, arrived at the Dillard house, and inquired of Dillard's wife as to whether Colonel Clarke and his men had been there, at what time they had departed, and what were their numbers.

Mrs. Dillard answered that the militia had indeed been at the house, but they had been gone a long time. The officers then ordered her to prepare their supper with all possible dispatch. Mrs. Dillard set about preparing supper, and in going backwards and forwards from the kitchen outside, she overheard much of the conversation. The officers probably apprehended no danger from disclosing their plans in the presence of a lone woman. Mrs. Dillard ascertained that the British had determined to surprise Colonel Clarke and his party and intended to pursue him as soon as they had finished their meal. She also overheard an officer telling Major Ferguson that the rebels under Clarke were now encamped for the night at Green Spring. It was resolved to attack them there before daylight.

Mrs. Dillard hurried with supper, and as soon as it was placed upon the table and the officers sat down, she slipped out the back door into the darkness, determined to go herself to apprise Colonel Clarke and his men of their danger. She hoped to be in time for Clarke to make a safe retreat, for she believed the enemy was too numerous to justify a battle. She went to the stable and, without a saddle, quietly mounted and rode at all possible speed to the place the British officer had described.

Half an hour before daybreak, she came in full gallop to one of the American videttes,[5] by whom she was immediately conducted to Colonel Clarke. In eagerness and haste, she called to the Colonel to be in readiness to either fight or run: "The enemy will be upon you immediately, and they are strong!" In an instant, every man in the camp was up, and no time was lost in preparing for action.

Mrs. Dillard's intelligence came just in time to put the Whigs in readiness. Major Ferguson had detached two-hundred mounted men under Major Dunlap to ride ahead and engage the Americans and keep them employed until he arrived with the rest of his British force. Dunlap charged the American camp, but the surprise was on his part. The British were met hand to hand, with a firmness they had not anticipated. Their confusion was increased by the darkness, which rendered it hard to distinguish friend from foe.

The battle was warm for fifteen or twenty minutes, when the Royalists gave way. They were pursued nearly a mile but not overtaken. Major Ferguson arrived too late for the frolic.[6] Colonel Clarke and his little band soon returned to North Carolina for rest and refreshment.

ISABELLA BARBER FERGUSON

Shortly before the fall of Charleston in 1780, Samuel Ferguson had looked upon the face of Isabella Barber and found it fair. They were soon married and went to live with her father; her brothers, also having married, fixed their homes on the opposite hill. The brothers were in the field with General Thomas Sumter while Samuel was enjoying a protracted honeymoon. Samuel, too, had two brothers, who were rampant royalists and were with the British force at Rocky Mount.[7]

Samuel's brother James held a colonel's commission in the British army, and Samuel and Isabella often discussed the war and the difference of opinion between her brothers and his own. Samuel was never strong in argument, not being highly gifted in mental endowment, whereas Isabella had sat under the preaching of a learned minister and had been regularly catechised and indoctrinated in both the Scriptures and the political creed of her people. Her husband was thus constrained to acknowledge that to her beautiful countenance she added a good understanding, and it usually happened that she had the best of every discussion.

Samuel's brother, Colonel James Ferguson, having raised 150 or more royalists, was not a little proud of his new command and his fine British uniform. He was a man of impressive appearance, and the honors heaped on him were very gratifying to his other Royalist brother who, like the colonel, anticipated nothing but honors and riches in a military career. But what was to be done about Samuel and his Irish wife, whose counsels had so far prevailed with him against all their solicitations to join the King's party?

At this time Colonel Ferguson was preparing to accompany Captain Huck on his expedition (see MARTHA BRATTON above). With his command, he left Rocky Mount one morning, dressed in full uniform and mounted on a noble charger, with drum and fife sounding, and the colors of Old England flying. He could not help thinking that if his young sister-in-law could see him thus in the pomp of war, she would no longer detain her husband from the chance of a like promotion.

It was not much out of his way to take the road by the Barber home, where his martial appearance might have a proper effect on that nest of Covenanters![8] James pleased himself with imagining Isabella's surprise when she should see how much better her brother-in-law looked in a splendid uniform than in tow trousers and a hunting shirt.

In the afternoon of the first day's march, the colonel's cavalcade of British regulars and South Carolina Royalists approached the house of old Barber. A messenger was dispatched to say that Colonel Ferguson of His Majesty's army wished to speak to Samuel. Samuel presently made his appearance, looking rather awkward. His brother formally invited him to join his force, saying that he had come for that special purpose. "It may be," he urged, "that I may become a lord. How then shall I feel on hearing it said that my brother was a rebel?"

Isabella was within hearing while the colonel was endeavoring to persuade her husband and came forward at his last words. "I am a rebel," she said proudly, "glorying in the name. My brothers are rebels, and the dog Trip is a rebel, too. Now, James, I would rather see you with a sheep on your back, than tricked out in all those fine clothes! Rebel and be free that is my creed!" Then turning to her husband, "We have often talked it over, Samuel," she said, "and you could never justify their unhallowed practice of coming here to make slaves of us, who would die first. Now, in the presence of the British army, I tell you, if you go with them you may stay with them, for I will no longer be your wife."

Samuel was unable to withstand this determination of his bonnie Isabella, whom he loved the better for her spirit. He requested his brother to excuse his going at this time, despite the fact that he might be reported as a true subject of the King. His wife being rather on the wrong side, he would content himself with doing what he could at home to serve His Majesty and bring back the rebels to their proper duty. "Could Isabella but be convinced," he said, "she might be able to turn the whole lot of Covenanters, for she is never afraid to speak her mind." Thus Samuel spoke, but in his heart he felt sure that his wife would stand firm and doubted if after all she were not in the right. His brother shook hands and bade him be faithful and have courage, and he would no doubt obtain a commission for him.

In the subsequent action at Williamson's,[9] James Ferguson was to be seen everywhere, endeavoring to rally the scattered British force. A fatal shot brought him from his horse, his head striking the ground. Once Samuel Ferguson heard of his brother's death, he could never look again on the bonnie face of Isabella without a feeling of thankfulness that he had escaped a similar fate.

EMILY GEIGER

At the time General Nathanael Greene retreated before Lord Francis Rawdon from Ninety-Six,[10] he was then desirous to send an order to General Thomas Sumter on the Wateree River to join him, that they might attack Rawdon, who had divided his force. But the country to be passed through was for many miles full of bloodthirsty Royalists, and it was a difficult matter to find a man willing to undertake so dangerous a mission.

At length a young girl, Emily Geiger, presented herself to General Greene, proposing to act as his messenger. The general, both surprised and delighted, agreed to her proposal and accordingly wrote a letter and gave it to her, at the same time communicating the contents verbally, to be told to General Sumter in case of accident.

Emily was soon off, mounted sidesaddle, but on the second day of her journey, she was intercepted by a party of Lord Rawdon's scouts. Coming from the direction of Greene's army and not being able to tell an untruth without blushing, she was shut up, and the officer in command, having the modesty not to search her, sent for an older Royalist matron as more fitting for the purpose. Emily was not wanting in expediency, and as soon as the door was closed, she ate up the letter piece by piece.

After a while the matron arrived. Upon searching carefully, the matron found nothing about the prisoner to be of an unusual nature, and she disclosed nothing. Suspicion being thus allayed, the officer commanding the scouts suffered Emily to depart whither she said she was bound. She took a route somewhat circuitous to avoid further detection and soon after struck into the road to Sumter's camp, where she arrived in safety.

She recounted her adventure, and verbally delivered Greene's message. In consequence Sumter soon joined the main army at Orangeburg.[11]

NANCY STINSON (ANDERSON) GREEN

Nancy Stinson, of Scots Covenanter descent, was born in the County of Antrim, Ireland, in 1750. She had no inconsiderable share of beauty of that striking order which suited her rather tall and robust figure, and though mild and amiable, she possessed great energy and firmness. In 1773, the congregation to which she belonged emigrated to America and took up their abode on the banks of Rocky Creek, a branch of the Catawba River.

Shortly before their ship sailed from Ireland, Nancy married William Anderson. Thus her wedded life began with a voluntary renunciation of home and the society of her early friends to seek a new country, encountering unforeseen privations and difficulties. The family was accompanied by Anderson's orphaned niece Lizzie Craig.

During their seven years' settlement in the woods, the Andersons enjoyed a life in which nothing of earthly comfort was wanting. Every Sabbath morning, the parents in their Sunday clothes with their three neatly dressed and well-behaved children might be seen at the log church, their pocket Bibles in their hands. Thus their simple, trustful piety caused the wilderness to rejoice.

But this happiness could not be lasting. The rumor of war had gone over the land, heard even in this remote section. The desolation that ravaged the North ere long took its way southward.

On a certain Sabbath in June 1780, William Anderson, on his way home from meeting, was unusually silent, as if some weighty matter had engaged all his thoughts. His wife, too, had been reflecting and spoke first, "I think little Lizzie and I can finish the crop, and gather it in if need be, as well as take care of the stock." "I am glad of that," came William's reply. "Tomorrow morning I leave home. The way is now clear. The word of God approves. It shall never be said that the Covenanters, the followers of the reformers of Scotland, would not lend a helping hand to the renewers of the Covenant in the land of America."

Early on Monday morning, the plow stood still in the furrow; the best horse, saddled and bridled, was at the door. Mrs. Anderson had been up since a little after midnight, making cornmeal cakes on the hoe,[12] and corn dodgers[13] in the oven. While cooking meats, she was busily plying the needle, running up sacks and bags to hold provisions for man and horse on a long journey. As soon as he had taken his breakfast, William Anderson, bidding his wife farewell, mounted and rode off.

In about two hours, Nancy heard the firing of horsemen's pistols from the direction of the militia muster ground, and soon William made his appearance, riding as fast as his horse could carry him. Passing around the house, he crossed the creek at the cow ford. Some British dragoons, who had been in close pursuit, failed to overtake him, and then gave vent to their rage by plundering the Anderson home of its most valuable articles of furniture, insulting Nancy Anderson with gross and indecent language.

Their visit also brought the smallpox, and the poor mother's attention was soon entirely absorbed by the sufferings of her children, leaving little time for distress on other accounts. The brief glimpse that she had of her husband as he fled from the British turned out to be her last. William Anderson never again came home. He fought in the battle at Williamson's[14] and was killed two months thereafter. Such was the end of the brave man whose name deserves honor from his adopted state.

Meanwhile Nancy had only the assistance of Lizzie in nursing the three little ones and was often compelled to leave them in order to plow the cornfield and finish working the crops. Before the return of the next Sabbath, the livestock had been driven off by the enemy, and the log meeting house had been burned to the ground. Stripped now of most everything both indoors and without, she had no resource but to roast the ears of green corn, or dry the corn in the mill and grate it on the rough stone into coarse meal of which she made mush for herself and the sick children.

Mrs. Anderson was now a widow in peculiar circumstances of desolation. With the militia gone, the neighborhood was left to the depredations of the royalists. As the season for harvest approached, the widows of those who were slain were obliged to cut and gather in the corn for the use of their families. But what certainty had they, exposed to cruel marauders, that they would ever have a bushel of the grain for bread? It was truly a dismal prospect. They had little to expect but nakedness and starvation.

At the proper season, Mrs. Anderson pulled her flax, watered and put it through the break, then scuttled it with the hand scuttle, and hackled it on the coarse and fine hackle. Day after day, and at night too, the humming of her busy little wheel might be heard, as she spun the flax. She now had no livestock to attend, except an old sorrel mare and a colt.

During the winter, she was confined and delivered a boy, who died in infancy of the scarlet fever. From time to time, soldiers returning to visit the neighborhood would call to inquire after the Widow Anderson and assist her by doing little turns of service, such as cutting wood and the like. But a great part of the fuel she used she gathered herself and carried it home on her shoulders with the help of Lizzie. The food on which Mrs. Anderson and her children subsisted during the winter was chiefly bread, though occasionally a little meat was brought to her by patrolling militia men. Often was she heard to say that her life was not an unhappy one, though she suffered many privations. Incessant occupation kept her thoughts from dwelling on past sorrows or anticipating future distress. Her trust was placed in Him who has said to the faithful, "I will never leave thee, or forsake thee."

About the time she began preparation for putting in a new crop of corn, an occurrence took place which influenced her future life. One April morning in 1781, Mrs. Anderson was confronted by a stranger who had been living in extreme poverty down the road from the burned meeting house and who had been grubbing a nearby neighbor's fields. The stranger's poverty was a complaint which the ravages of war rendered too common to be disreputable. He was so reduced that he owned not a hunting shirt, except one much the worse for wear, but he was willing to work, and readily engaged to do a certain quantity of field labor for the neighbor, for a new one. Having finished the work, he set off to fulfill a resolution he had now formed to take the first horse he could find and make for the army under General Greene. He walked through the surrounding fields till near noon without seeing a horse grazing or hearing the bell commonly worn by animals at liberty. At last he heard the sound of a distant bell and followed it up a small stream that bordered a cultivated field.

In the midst of the field he saw a log cabin, with two or three little children playing on the sunny side of the house. Coming nearer, he perceived a very young girl letting down some fence bars to give entrance to a sorrel mare, followed by a colt and a woman of comely appearance. By this time she had noticed the approaching stranger and was looking anxiously towards him, as if doubtful whether he was friend or foe.

As soon as he saw her, he walked directly up and asked if she had seen any other horse in the area besides her own. Mrs. Anderson replied in the negative and courteously invited the stranger to enter the cabin. The invitation was accepted, and in the conversation that ensued, the visitor learned that she was a widow, the mother of the children he had seen, and the young girl was an orphan she had undertaken to bring up, and that she had suffered not a little from the depredators infesting the country.

The stranger told her on his part that he had resolved to join Greene's army. At the widow's hospitable solicitation, he sat down to dinner with the family, relinquishing, for that day at least, his project of securing a horse. Of course he could not think of taking the only one belonging to a poor woman.

Parting from his new acquaintance, he took his course back to his own dwelling, much more thoughtful than he had come. The image of the sociable woman went with him, her fair face and handsome features set off by soft light hair of the hue poets call golden. Her lot in life was like his own. She lived alone, with means sadly diminished by the troubles of war, and her little family depended on her labor for their day-to-day subsistence.

That night it may be supposed he slept but little, having much food for reflection. His conclusion was to return to the cabin, trusting for his welcome to fortune and the woman's kindly nature. It was not long before he was at the fair widow's house, and to all appearance, on a comfortable footing. When at length he ventured to question, "I suppose, Madam, you may think well of a stranger of whom you know but little?" Mrs. Anderson's frank answer was, "I do. My own dear Willie died the death of a soldier." "Then you would remarry a soldier?" "I have not thought about that, but if I ever should marry, if I think as I do now, none but a soldier would I have."

What turn the discourse took after this avowal, tradition does not exactly inform us, nor how the round, unvarnished tale which the soldier—for he, too, had earlier fought in the war, in the North—told concerning himself was received by his gentle auditor. But it is certain that some three or four days after this conversation, the stranger had borrowed a horse and, accompanied by Nancy Anderson mounted on the sorrel mare, was riding along the road on the way to the old Justice John Gaston. After a short ceremony the justice pronounced them man and wife and received the fee of one dollar, all the money which the newly made husband, Daniel Green, possessed in the world.

The sudden conversion of Mrs. Anderson into Mrs. Green gave no small offense to many of her Covenanter friends, who fancied they had an undoubted right to control her in a step involving her future prospects. They were especially scandalized that she had thought proper to dispense with formalities prescribed by the church, and the custom of their fathers, which required an intended marriage to be published by the minister on three successive sabbaths.

It was impossible for her to comply with this requisition, there being no meeting for public religious service in those days of desolation, but the over-strict deemed this no sufficient excuse. Nancy, however, did not suffer herself to be rendered uncomfortable by their disapprobation of her choice or their censure of her hasty nuptials. She considered herself the most competent judge in the matter and had decided that circumstances may modify cases to such an extent as to render proper a course which, at a different time, might have been ill-advised and unbecoming.

She thought also that Daniel Green and herself had probably become better acquainted with each other's disposition and character in the five days preceding their marriage than many whose course of love is projected for years. Knowing what it was to be alone and destitute, it was something to find one who could take care of her little property, aid in the maintenance of her family, and defend her in case of need. Both she and her soldier had been tried in the crucible of the Revolution and came forth like gold refined.

MRS. THOMAS HEYWARD

Following the enemy victory over General Greene at Guilford Court House,[15] the British in occupied Charleston ordered a general illumination of the city. It was remarked that the house occupied by Mrs. Heyward and her sister showed no lights. A British officer called to demand the reason for this mark of disrespect.

In reply, Mrs. Heyward asked how could she be expected to join in celebrating the victory claimed by the British army while her husband was a prisoner at St. Augustine.[16]

The answer was a peremptory command to illuminate the house. "Not a single light," said Mrs. Heyward, "shall with my consent be placed in any window in the house." To the threat that her home would be destroyed before midnight, she answered with the same expression of resolute determination.

On the first anniversary of the battle of Charleston,[17] another illumination was ordered in testimony of joy for that event. Mrs. Heyward again refused compliance. Her sister was lying in the last stage of a wasting disease, while the indignation of the Royalist mob was vented in assaults upon the house, with brickbats and other missiles. In the midst of the clamor and shouting, the invalid expired.

The town officials later expressed regret for the indignities and requested Mrs. Heyward's permission to repair damage that had been done. She thanked them but refused, on the ground that the authorities could not thus cause insults to be forgotten which they should not have permitted to be offered in the first place.

ELIZABETH HUTCHINSON JACKSON

After Colonel Banastre Tarleton routed Colonel Abraham Buford's retreating troops at Waxhaw Creek,[18] local women and children fled from the ravages of the merciless enemy. Mrs. Elizabeth Jackson,[19] with her children, quitted her home in the Waxhaws, the Carolina border settlement where she had earlier buried her husband, and found a place of refuge at Sugar Creek Congregation, where she remained during part of the summer of 1780.

Like other widowed mothers of North Carolina, she trained her sons to become zealous patriots amd efficient statesmen. Returning to the Waxhaws after a journey to Charleston to carry clothing and other necessaries to some friends on board the prison ship, Mrs. Jackson was seized with the prison fever. She died in a tent in the midst of a wide sandy wilderness of pines. Were the spot known, her lonely grave by the roadside would speak mournfully of woman's self-immolating heroism.

SARAH WAYNE McCALLA

Sarah Wayne, a relative of General Anthony Wayne, was born in eastern Pennsylvania. She was a very shrewd and independent person, and although remarkable for self-control, she often expressed by the rapid play of her features the emotion called up at the moment which she did not deem it prudent to utter in words. With a strong will and steadfast purpose, she had great quickness of perception, and her measures were always proportioned to the difficulties to be overcome. Though firm of resolution as a rock, her heart was full of all gentle and generous impulses; the sight of distress was sufficient to melt her at once into sympathy, and she would hesitate at no sacrifice of her own interest nor endurance of privation to afford relief to the sufferer.

In the first year of the Revolution she married Thomas McCalla, who was soon called to militia service and saw action in the heavy fighting around New York and Philadelphia. When Thomas had served out the time for which the militia had been summoned, he and Sarah removed to South Carolina. As new dwellers in an almost wild region, they lived in a log cabin, cultivating the ground for their daily bread and trusting to Divine protection from the evils surrounding them incident to a primitive state of society and from the more appalling dangers rapidly approaching with the desolating footsteps of civil strife.

During the severe campaign of 1780, the struggle in the south between the Whigs and the British, aided by gangs of Royalist outlaws, was carried on amid scenes of bloody contest and deeds of unprecedented cruelty. It was no time for a patriot to remain a mere spectator. McCalla did not hesitate to cast his lot with the few brave spirits who scorned security purchased by submission. He joined the fighting men and was in every engagement from the beginning of Sumter's operations against the royal forces.

Returning from a leave of absence, McCalla was taken prisoner by a British patrol and carried to Camden, where he was thrown into jail and threatened every day with hanging, having been found in arms against the royal government after what the British chose to consider the submission of the state of South Carolina. While this brave man was languishing in prison, expecting death from day to day, his wife remained in the most unhappy state of suspense. For about a month she was unable to obtain any tidings of him.

She visited the place where he presumably had been seized, and sought for some trace of him, but without success. No one could give her the least information. In the midst of Mrs. McCalla's distress, she was called to another claim on her anxiety; her children took the smallpox. One son was very ill for nine days with the disease, and his mother thought every day would be his last. During this terrible season of alarm, while her mind was distracted by cares, she had to depend altogether on herself. All the families in the vicinity were visited with the disease, and to many it proved fatal.

As soon as her children were out of danger, Mrs. McCalla made preparations to go to Camden, clinging to the hope that she might there learn something of her husband or even find him among the patriot prisoners. Setting her house in order, she was in the saddle long before day, taking the old Charleston road leading down the west side of the Catawba River. As the sun rose, she passed the mountain gap on Wateree Creek, and by two o'clock she had crossed the ferry, passing the guard there stationed, and entered Camden. Pressing on with fearless determination, she desired to be conducted to the presence of Lord Rawdon and was escorted by Major Welbore Doyle to the headquarters of the commander.[20]

Into the presence of this haughty nobleman, Mrs. McCalla was conducted by the British major. Being desired to explain the object of her visit, she pleaded her cause with the eloquence of nature and feeling, making known the distressed situation of her family at home. From Major Doyle she had already learned that her husband was being held a prisoner by His Lordship's orders. She had therefore come to entreat mercy for him and to pray that he might be released and permitted to go home with her.

This appeal to compassion she made with all the address in her power. Lord Rawdon heard her to the end. His reply was characteristic: "I would rather hang such damned rebels than eat my breakfast." This insulting speech was addressed to his suppliant, while her eyes were fixed on him in the agony of entreaty, and the tears were streaming down her cheeks.

His words dried up the fountains at once, and the spirit of an American matron was roused. "Would you!" was her answer, while she turned on him the look of deepest scorn. A moment after, with a struggle to control her feelings, for she knew well how much depended on it, she said, "I crave your Lordship's permission to see my husband."

The haughty chief felt the look of scorn his cruel language had called up on her face, but pride forbade his yielding to dictates of better feeling. "You should consider, Madam, in whose presence you now stand. Your husband is a damned rebel!"

Mrs. McCalla was about to reply, but the major gave her a look that warned her to be silent, feeling in truth that the words that sprang to her lips would have ill-pleased the commander. Rawdon then said to his visitor, with a stately coldness, "I will give Major Doyle my permission to let you go into the prison, for ten minutes only." So saying, he bowed to her, intimating that the business was ended, and she was dismissed.

What had been granted seemed to Mrs. McCalla a mockery, rather than an alleviation of her sorrow. Ten minutes with a husband from whom she had been parted so many weeks, and that, too, in the presence of a royal officer—a brief time in which to inquire into his wants and learn what she must do for him. "Other Whig women who have come down to see their friends," Major Doyle observed, "have shown a more submissive disposition. None have dared reply to His Lordship so angrily, or give him scornful looks."

The sight of the prison pen almost overcame the fortitude of the resolute wife—an enclosure like that constructed for animals, guarded by soldiers, was the habitation of the unfortunate prisoners, who sat within on the bare earth, many of them suffering with the prevalant distemper and stretched helpless on the ground with no shelter from the burning September sun. "Is it possible," cried Mrs. McCalla, turning to Major Doyle, "that you shut up men in this manner, as you would a parcel of hogs?"

She was admitted into the jail, and welcome indeed was the face of her McCalla. The time allotted for the interview was too short to be wasted in condolement or complaint. She told him she must depart in a few minutes and informed him of the state of his family, inquiring carefully what were his wants, and promised speedy relief.

When the ten minutes had expired, Mrs. McCalla shook hands with her husband, assuring him she would shortly return with clothes for his use and what provisions she could bring. Then, turning, she walked away with a firm step, only stopping to shake hands with other captives she recognized. As she bade the prisoners adieu, she said, "Have no fear. The women are doing their part in the service."

"I admire your spirit, Madam," Major Doyle said to her, "but must request you to be a little more cautious."

From this time she made her journey about once a month to Camden, carrying clean clothes and provisions, often accompanied by other women bound on a similar errand, conveying supplies to their captive fathers, husbands, or brothers. They rode without escort, fearless of peril along the way and regardless of fatigue, although the journey was usually performed in haste and under the pressure of anxiety for those at home, as well as those to whose relief they were going.[21]

ELIZABETH MARSHALL MARTIN

Elizabeth Marshall was born in Virginia and moved with her husband, Abram Martin, to a settlement on the borders of the Cherokee Nation at

Ninety-Six[22] in South Carolina. The country at that time was sparsely settled, mostly by pioneers from Virginia. In the time of the Revolution,
Ninety-Six was among the foremost in sending into the field its quota of
hardy and enterprising troops to oppose the British and their savage allies.

By the commencement of the contest, Mrs. Martin had nine children,
seven of whom were sons old enough to bear arms. These young men, under
the tuition and example of their parents, had grown up in attachment to
their country and were ardently devoted to its service. They were ready on
every occasion to encounter the dangers of border warfare, and when the
first call for volunteers sounded through the land, Mrs. Martin encouraged
their patriotic zeal.

"Go, boys," she said, "Fight for your country. Fight till death, if you must,
but never let your country be dishonored! Were I a man, I would go with
you."

At one time, several British officers stopped at her house for refreshment,
and one asked how many sons she had. She answered, "Eight," and to the
question, "Where are they all?" She promptly replied, "In the service of
their country." "Really, Madam," observed an officer sneeringly, "you have
enough of them." "No, sir," said the matron proudly. "I wish I had fifty."

Mrs. Martin's only daughter, Letitia, had married Captain Edmund Wade
of Virginia, who fell with his commander, General Richard Montgomery, at
the 1775 siege of Quebec.

During the absence of Mrs. Martin's sons, the wives of the two eldest, Rachel and Grace, remained with their mother-in-law. One evening, intelligence came to all of them that a courier, conveying dispatches to one of the
upper British posts, was to pass that night along the road, guided by two enemy officers. The two young women determined to waylay the party and, at
the risk of their lives, obtain possession of the papers.

For this purpose, Rachel and Grace disguised themselves in their husband's clothes and, being well provided with arms, took their station at a
point on the road which they knew the escort must pass. It was already late,
and they had not waited long before the tramp of horses was heard in the
distance.

It may be imagined with what anxious expectation the heroines awaited
the approach of the critical moment on which so much depended. The forest solitude around them, the silence of night and the darkness must have
added to the terror conjured up by busy fancy. Presently the courier appeared with his attendant guards. As they came close to the spot, the disguised women leaped from their covert in the bushes, presented their pistols

at the officers, and demanded the instant surrender of the party and their dispatches.

The men were taken completely by surprise, and in their alarm at the sudden attack, yielded a prompt submission. The seeming soldiers put them on their parole,[23] and having taken possession of the papers, hastened home by a shortcut through the woods. No time was lost in sending the important documents by a trusty messenger to General Nathanael Greene.

The adventure had a singular termination. The paroled officers, thwarted in their mission, returned by the same road they had taken, and stopping at the home of Mrs. Martin, asked accommodation for the night as weary travelers. The hostess inquired the reason for their returning so soon after they had passed; they replied by showing their paroles, saying they had been taken prisoner by two rebel lads. All the ladies rallied them upon their want of intrepidity. "Had you no arms?" they asked. The officers answered that they had arms, but had been suddenly taken off their guard and were allowed no time to use their weapons.

They departed the next morning, having no suspicion that they owed their capture to the very women whose hospitality they had claimed.

MRS. RICHARD SHUBRICK

An American soldier near Charleston, flying from British pursuit, sought the protection of Mrs. Richard Shubrick. The enemy who followed him insisted with threats that he be delivered into their hands. While the other ladies in Mrs. Shubrick's house were too much frightened to offer remonstrance, the young and fragile woman withstood the enemy. With a delicacy of frame that bespoke feeble health, she still possessed a spirit strong in the hour of trial. Her pale cheek could flush, and her eyes sparkle with scorn for the oppressor.

She resolutely placed herself at the door of the room in which the fugitive had taken refuge, declaring her determination to defend it with her life. "To men of honor," she said, "the chamber of a lady should be sacred as a sanctuary." The officer in charge, struck with admiration for her intrepidity, immediately ordered his men to retire.

On another occasion, when a party of Tarleton's dragoons was plundering the house of one of her friends, a sergeant followed the overseer of the plantation into the room where the ladies were assembled. The old man refused to tell him where the silver plate was hidden, and the soldier struck him with his saber. Whereupon, Mrs. Shubrick, starting up, threw herself between them and rebuked the ruffian for his barbarity. She bade him strike her, if he gave another blow, for she would protect the aged servant. Her interposition saved him from further injury.

MRS. JOHN SIMPSON

The Reverend John Simpson was among the band of heroes who defeated the enemy at Mobley's,[24] and the Royalists determined his punishment should be speedy. On Sabbath morning, 11 June 1780, a Royalist party took their way to Reverend Simpson's church, where they expected to find the pastor with his assembled congregation, intending to burn both church and people by way of a warning to other disturbers of the King's peace. But the previous Friday, Reverend Simpson had shouldered his rifle and marched off to the field, taking his place in the ranks and performing the duties of a private soldier, submitting to the rigorous discipline of the camp.

At the church, some negroes overheard the destroyers declare their intention to go to Reverend Simpson's house and "burn the rascal out!" The negroes hastened to carry this information to Mrs. Simpson—who was eight months pregnant—urging her to save herself and her family by immediate flight.

Looking out the window, Mrs. Simpson saw a body of men coming down the lane. Stopping only to gather a set of silver teaspoons, a gift from her mother, Mrs. Simpson went out the back door with her four children and hid in the orchard.

The Royalists rifled the house of everything valuable and took out four feather beds, ripping them open in the yard. They collected all the clothing, from which they selected such articles as they fancied for their own keeping and, having exhausted their invention in devising mischief, finally set fire to the house, which soon burned to the ground. Just as the Royalists were going away, they noticed an outbuilding that was usually occupied by Reverend Simpson as a study and contained a valuable library. This was soon also in flames.

The party now left the premises. As soon as they were out of sight, Mrs. Simpson hastened to the little building and carried out two aprons full of books. She could save no more, and in doing this, was much burned. The feathers in the yard had also taken fire, but she succeeded in saving enough for one bed. She then went to a neighbor's house, where she remained till after her confinement. As soon as she recovered, she returned to her own place and took up her residence in another small outbuilding which had escaped the enemy's vengeance. Here she contrived to live with her five children but not yet free from depredation and danger.

At one time, when she had procured some cloth to make clothing for her children, a company of Royalists came by and plundered her again. Some of the gang were dressed in Reverend Simpson's clothes and, strutting before her, tauntingly asked if they were not better looking than her husband, telling her at the same time that they would one day make her a present of his scalp.

MRS. STRONG

In the summer of 1780, on the first incursion of royal troops into remote parts of South Carolina, many outrages were committed upon helpless families where they passed. On Sunday morning, June 11, British troops under Captain Christian Huck (see MARTHA BRATTON above) arrived at the Strong house near Fishing Creek Church.

They immediately entered and plundered the house of everything, also carrying away the corn and wheat. Some of the grain being accidentally scattered in the yard, a tame pigeon flew down to pick it up. The brutal captain struck the bird, cutting off its head with a blow of his sword. Turning to Mrs. Strong, he said, "Madam, I have cut off the head of the Holy Ghost." She replied with indignation, "You will never die in your bed, nor will your death be that of the righteous!" The prediction thus uttered was in a month signally fulfilled.

After this insult and blasphemy, some of Huck's men went to the barn where William, Mrs. Strong's son, had gone shortly before their arrival. He had taken his Bible with him and was engaged in reading the sacred volume. They shot him dead upon the spot and dragged his body out of the barn. The officers then began to cut and hack the dead body with their broadswords. Mrs. Strong rushed from the house, pleading with all a mother's anguish that the officers would spare the corpse of her son. But they heeded not her agonized entreaties, till she threw herself upon his bleeding and mangled body, resolving to perish, as he had done, at the cruel hands of her enemies, rather than see her child cut to pieces before her eyes.

Such outrages were of common occurrence, and the example set by officers of the Royal Army in the slaughter of boys of too tender an age to become soldiers and in the plundering of houses defended only by women and aged men, gave encouragement to the Royalists who followed their banner, to practice similar cruelties. Robbery, spoliation, and murder were the order of the day.

ESTHER GASTON WALKER

Esther Gaston's Protestant ancestors fled from France and sought refuge in Ireland after the Revocation of the Edict of Nantes in 1685. Her father emigrated to Pennsylvania around 1730 and shortly thereafter married Esther's mother, Esther Waugh. Twenty years later he left that colony for South Carolina, settling with some other famlies near Fishing Creek on the Catawba River. Esther Gaston was born there in 1761, the eleventh child in a family consisting of nine sons and two daughters.

When the separation took place between the colonies and the imperial government, Mr. Gaston urged his patriotic band of sons to a vigorous defense of their rights. In the darkest period of the war for the South, when South Carolina was claimed by the British as a conquered province and when the people were prostrated and compelled almost everywhere to accept protection by professing allegiance to the Crown, the zeal of the patriots was not extinguished.

At the end of May 1780, a messenger brought the distressing intelligence to the Gaston home that Tarleton with his cavalry had pursued and overtaken Colonel Buford near the Waxhaws and, refusing quarter, had slaughtered his men without mercy.[25] The wounded had been carried to Waxhaw Church as a hospital.

Esther Gaston was at this time about eighteen years of age, tall, stout, and erect in person and possessed of great mental as well as physical energy. Determined to bear her part in the work that was to be done, Esther lost no time in repairing to Waxhaw Church. The temporary hospital presented a scene of misery. The floor was strewn with wounded and dying Americans, men suffering for want of aid—for men dared not come to minister to them. It was left to woman, like the angel of mercy, to bring relief to the helpless and perishing.

Day and night Esther was busy aiding the surgeon to dress their wounds and in preparing food for those who needed it. Nor did she regard fatigue or exposure, going from place to place about the neighborhood to procure such articles as were desirable to alleviate the pain or add to the comfort of those to whom she ministered.

Two months later, on the night of July 30, American soldiers under General Thomas Sumter marched near Esther Gaston's home. She was informed by one of them, her lover Alexander Walker whom she later married, that they were advancing against the enemy's position at Rocky Mount. By the morning she was in readiness to follow, and riding about two miles to the house of her brother, John Gaston, she urged her sister-in-law

Jane to come with her to the scene of action. The two were soon mounted and making their way at a gallop down the road. Firing could be distinctly heard.

While these brave women were approaching the spot, they were met by two or three men hastening from the ground, with faces paler than became heroes. Esther stopped the fugitives, upbraided them for their cowardice, and entreated them to return to their duty. While they wavered, she advanced and, seizing one of their guns, cried, "Give us your guns, then, and we will stand in your place." As the most cowardly of men must have been moved by such a taunt, the runaway soldiers were covered with confusion and for very shame dared not refuse to go back. Wheeling about, they returned to the fight in company with the two heroines.

During the action, Esther and Jane were not merely spectators but busied themselves diligently rendering whatever services were required, assisting in dressing the wounds of the soldiers and carrying water to allay their burning thirst. A Catawba Indian ally, severely wounded, was succored by them, and his last looks were turned in gratitude on those who had soothed his pain and supplied his wants. In these services, the training Esther had received at the Waxhaw Church enabled her to do her part skillfully, and while she gave comfort to the dying, her animating words encouraged the living to persevere. Esther's heart was wrung by the suffering she witnessed in those she knew as neighbors. She spared herself no exertion nor fatigue in helping the surgeon, who was her cousin, and remained for a considerable time in the hospital, and afterwards went with the wounded to Charlotte where she continued her care of the sufferers.

ELIZA YONGE WILKINSON

Eliza Yonge's father was a wealthy Welsh immigrant who lived on Yonge's Island, thirty miles south of Charleston. Mr. Yonge suffered much rough treatment from the British, from whom he refused to take a protection. Both his sons served in the American army.

All this happened at the time of General Benjamin Lincoln's approach to relieve Charleston from occupation by British General Augustine Prevost and the engagement at Stono River Ferry.[26] Mr. Yonge's daughter had been married only six months when her husband died. At this period of the war, she was a young and fascinating widow, quick at repartee and full of cheerfulness and good humor.

Eliza bore her part in many Revolutionary privations and frequently suffered from British cruelty. The surrounding country had been waiting in a distressed condition for the coming of General Lincoln, to whom the people looked for deliverance. Many painful days of suspense passed before the glad tidings were received. All trifling discourse was laid aside as the ladies gathered in knots, talking only of political affairs. American troops at last arrived from Charleston and, as always, were received by Mrs. Wilkinson with friendly hospitality. "The poorest soldier," she wrote in one of her frequent letters, "who would call at any time for a drink of water, I would take a pleasure in giving it to him myself. Many a dirty, ragged fellow have I attended with a bowl of water or milk. They really merit everything, who will fight for principle alone. From what I could learn, these poor creatures had nothing to protect themselves, and seldom got their pay. Yet with what alacrity will they encounter danger and hardships of every kind."

Of one British raid, Mrs. Wilkinson wrote: "I heard the horses of the inhuman Britons coming in such a furious manner that they seemed to tear up the earth. The riders were bellowing out the most horrid curses imaginable, with imprecations that chilled my whole frame. Surely, thought I, such horrid language connotes nothing less than death. But I had no time for thought; they were up to the house, entering with drawn swords and pistols in their hands. They rushed in in the most furious manner, crying out, 'Where are these women rebels!' That was their first salutation.

"But it is not in my power to describe the scene; it was terrible to the last degree. What augmented it—they had several armed negroes, who threatened and abused us greatly. They then began to plunder the house of everything they thought valuable or worth taking. Our trunks were split to pieces, and each mean, pitiful wretch crammed his bosom with the contents. I ventured to speak to the inhuman monster who had my clothes. I represented to him that the times were such that we could not replace what had been taken from us, and begged him to spare me only a suit or two. I got nothing but a hearty curse for my pains. So far was his callous heart from relenting, that casting his eyes towards my shoes, 'I want them,' said he, and immediately knelt at my feet to take them off.

"While he was busy doing this, a brother villain, whose enormous mouth extended from ear to ear, bawled out, 'Shares, there. I say, shares!' So they divided my buckles between them. The other wretches were employed in the same manner. They took Miss Samuel's earrings from her ears, and demanded her ring from her finger. She pleaded for it, telling them it was her wedding ring, and begged they would let her keep it. But they still demanded it, and presenting a pistol at her, swore that if she did not deliver it immediately, they would fire. She gave it to them.

"After drinking all the wine, rum &c. they could find, and inviting the negroes they had with them, who were very insolent, to do the same, they went to their horses. After such unwelcome visitors, it is not surprising that unprotected women could not eat or sleep in peace, but lay in their clothes every night, alarmed by the least noise, while the days were spent in anxiety and melancholy.

"After bundling up all their booty, they mounted their horses. But such despicable figures, each wretch's bosom stuffed so full, they all appeared to be afflicted with some dropsical disorder. Had a party of rebels, as they call us, appeared we should have seen their circumference lessen. They took care to tell us, when they were going away, that they had favored us a great deal; that we might thank our stars it was no worse.

"I had forgot to tell you that upon their first entering the house, one of them gave my arm such a violent grasp that he left the print of his thumb and three fingers black and blue, which was to be seen plainly for several days afterwards. I showed it to one of our officers who dined with us, as a specimen of British cruelty. After they were gone, I began to be sensible of the danger I had been in, and the thought of the vile men seemed worse, if possible. When I had time to consider, I trembled so I could not support myself."

The subsequent siege and capitulation of Charleston[27] brought the evils under which the land suffered to their height. The hardships endured by those within the beleaguered city brought a gloomy resignation of hope and submission to inevitable misfortune.

After the surrender, Mrs. Wilkinson visited the city, went on board the prison ship, and drank coffee with the prisoners awaiting an exchange. She saw the departure of her friends who were driven into exile in Florida,[28] and indulged herself occasionally in provoking her enemies by sarcastic sallies.

"Once," she writes, "I was asked by a British officer to play the guitar. 'I cannot play, I am very dull.' 'How long do you intend to continue so, Mrs, Wilkinson?' 'Until my countrymen return, sir.' 'Return as what, Madam, prisoners or subjects?' 'As conquerers, sir!' He affected a laugh. 'You will never see that, Madam.' 'I live in hope, sir, of seeing the thirteen stripes hoisted once more upon the bastions of this garrison.' I have often wondered since, that I was not packed off to the provost, for I was very saucy and never disguised my sentiments."

Like many others, Mrs. Wilkinson refused to join in the amusements of the city while it was in possession of the British but gave her energies to the relief of her friends. Many and ingenious were the contrivances they adopted to carry supplies from the British garrison, which might be useful to the defenders of their country. Sometimes cloth for a military coat, fashioned into an appendage of female attire, would be borne away unsuspected by the vigilant guards whose business it was to prevent smuggling and afterwards converted into regimental form. Boots, a world too wide for the delicate wearer, were often transferred to the partisan who could not procure them for himself. A horseman's helmet was concealed under a well-arranged headdress and epaulettes delivered from the folds of a matron's simple cap. Other articles in demand for military use, more easily conveyed, were regularly brought away by some stratagem or other.

It was after the return of Mrs. Wilkinson to Yonge's Island, in the fall of 1781, that news was received of the glorious victory of Washington over Cornwallis. A last letter from Mrs. Wilkinson of any public interest contains her congratulations on this event.

ELEANOR WILSON

On 14 October 1780, learning of Major Patrick Ferguson's disastrous defeat at King's Mountain, Lord Cornwallis slowly withdrew southward from Charlotte, North Carolina, to Winnsboro.[29]

During this march the British army halted for the night at Robert Wilson's plantation near Steel Creek. The commander and his staff occupied the house and required Mrs. Wilson to provide for them. Drawing her out in conversation, Lord Cornwallis determined the principal items of her family history and found he was occupying the house of a noted Whig leader, with several sons who were active soldiers—two of whom were already His Lordship's prisoners in the Camden jail. Cornwallis artfully attempted to enlist Mrs. Wilson in the King's cause. He began by observing that he deeply regretted being compelled to wage a war in which many of its worst calamities fell upon women. He was constrained to believe that in this instance, as well as many others, many were the men who were at heart good subjects of the King but had been seduced from their duty by the delusive promises of aspiring and unprincipled leaders.

"Madam," he continued, "it seems that your husband and two of your sons are now my prisoners. The fortunes of war may soon place all your sons[30] and kinsmen in my power. Your sons are young, aspiring and brave. In a good cause, fighting for a generous and powerful king such as George III, they might hope for rank, honor, and wealth.

"If you could but induce your husband and sons to leave the rebels, and take up arms for their lawful sovereign, I would almost pledge myself that they shall have rank and consideration. If you, Madam, will pledge yourself to do so, I will immediately order your husband and son discharged."

To this artful appeal, Eleanor Wilson replied that her husband and children were indeed dear to her and that she had felt, as a woman must, the trial and troubles which the war had brought upon her. She felt proud of her sons and would do anything she thought right to advance their real and permanent interests but in this instance they had embarked in the holy cause of liberty—had already fought and struggled for it five years, never faltering for a moment, while others had fled from the contest and yielded up their hopes at the first obstacle. "I have seven sons who are now, or have been, bearing arms," Mrs. Wilson continued. "Indeed, my seventh son, Zaccheus, who is only 15 years old, I yesterday assisted to go and join his brothers with Sumter. Sooner than see one of my family turn back from this glorious enterprise, I would take these young boys," pointing to her youngsters, "and would them with myself, enlist under Sumter's standard, and show my husband and older sons how to fight. And if necessary, to die for their country."

"Ah, General," interrupted the coldhearted Tarleton, "I think you've got into a hornets' nest."

"Never mind," Cornwallis replied. "When we get to Camden, I'll take good care that old Robert Wilson never comes back again."

NOTES

1. On 12 May 1780, General Benjamin Lincoln surrendered the port city to Sir Henry Clinton.

2. At Hanging Rock 6 August 1780, General Thomas Sumter led one thousand militiamen against five hundred encamped Royalists, killing or wounding two hundred and dispersing the rest. American losses were twelve killed and forty-one wounded.

3. Forty-six-year-old General of Militia Thomas Sumter, the "Carolina Gamecock," was a contentious partisan leader who succeeded in keeping the British—and frequently the astonished Americans—off balance. When the war moved south in 1780, and his own plantation was burned by Tarleton's cavalry, Sumter swiftly rallied a large force of militia with their local colonels along the border between the Carolinas, thus giving the lie to Cornwallis's proclamation that the South had been subdued. Sumter was soon named a senior brigadier general of militia and continued to struggle with his men, not always propitiously, alongside the regular army in the Camden campaign and thereafter. He lived to be ninety-eight, the oldest surviving general of the Revolution.

4. This action at Williamson's Plantation pitted 250 American militia under Colonel Bratton against Captain Huck's 115 men, with lopsided results.

The surprised enemy suffered thirty-five killed and twenty-nine captured; the Americans lost only one killed and one wounded.

5. Picket guards.

6. The engagement at Green Spring 1 August 1780 was Major Patrick Ferguson's first surprise on the long road that led two months later to his defeat and death at King's Mountain.

7. British outpost protecting Camden, South Carolina. It was unsuccessfully attacked by General Thomas Sumter 1 August 1780.

8. Stubbornly anti-Anglican Scots Presbyterians.

9. See Note 4 above.

10. Before the Revolution, Ninety-Six—named for a (mistaken) mileage designation—was a stockaded settlement on the road from Charleston to the western Cherokee country. It became a scene of bitter conflict between local Royalists and outnumbered patriots and was soon made an important, heavily fortified back country British post. General Greene unsuccessfully besieged the position for twenty-eight days in the summer of 1780 before retreating to Charlotte, North Carolina.

11. A British outpost fifty miles south of today's Columbia, South Carolina. It was easily captured by Sumter 11 May 1781.

12. A flat-bladed fireplace cooking tool.

13. Small cornmeal rolls.

14. See Note 4 above.

15. On 15 March 1781.

16. British stronghold in East Florida, a haven for Royalists from the Carolinas.

17. General Lincoln surrendered the city 12 May 1780, after a six-week British siege.

18. The battle was fought 29 May 1780 after the fall of Charleston. The British slaughter of wounded Americans under Colonel Abraham Buford earned the enemy commander the sobriquet "Bloody Tarleton" and brought the phrase "Tarleton's Quarter"—no quarter at all—into military usage.

19. Mother of the seventh president of the United States.

20. Lieutenant Colonel Francis, Lord Rawdon—twenty-six years old at the time of Sarah McCalla's visit—was, along with Tarleton, an *enfant terrible* of the British army. Irish-born and Oxford-educated, he initially distinguished himself in the debacle at Bunker Hill where he took over the command of a wounded superior officer. Rawdon has achieved some measure of immortality for a paragraph he wrote home in August 1776: "The fair nymphs here are in wonderful tribulation, as the fresh meat our men have gotten has made them as riotous as satyrs. A girl cannot step into the bushes to pluck a rose without running the most imminent risk of being ravished, and they are so little accustomed to these vigorous methods, that they don't bear them with the proper resignation, and of consequence we have most entertaining courts martial every day." In 1780 Rawdon was ordered south where he participated brilliantly in the campaign that destroyed

the American army under General Horatio Gates 16 August 1780. When Cornwallis marched north to Virginia in 1781, Rawdon was left behind to defend the scattered British posts in South Carolina and Georgia. He returned to England in July 1781, before the defeat of Cornwallis at Yorktown, and entered the House of Commons. From 1813 to 1826 Rawdon served as governor general and commander in chief in India.

21. Thomas McCalla was eventually freed by General Cornwallis in an exchange of prisoners with General Sumter.

22. See Note 10 above.

23. The usual promise not to further participate in the war until exchanged.

24. A party of militia led by Colonel William Bratton (see MARTHA BRATTON above) scattered a Royalist force at Mobley's Meeting House near Winnsboro, 29 May 1780.

25. See Note 18 above.

26. Maneuvering south of Charleston 20 June 1779, American troops under General William Moultrie failed to support an attack by General Benjamin Lincoln on a British and German force led by Lieutenant Colonel John Maitland, who later retreated.

27. After a month-long struggle, General Lincoln surrendered the city to Sir Henry Clinton on 12 May 1780.

28. See Note 16 above.

29. Thirty miles north of today's Columbia, South Carolina.

30. Eleanor Wilson had eleven children.

CHAPTER THIRTEEN

GEORGIA

NANCY HART

At the commencement of hostilities, so great a majority of the people of Wilkes County, named in honor of the distinguished English politician,[1] espoused the Whig cause that the area received from the Royalists the name of "the hornet's nest." In a part of this district flowed a stream known as "War-Woman's Creek," a name derived from the character of an individual who lived near the entrance of the stream into the Broad River.

This person was Nancy Hart, a woman entirely uneducated and ignorant of all the conventional civilities of life, but a zealous lover of liberty and the "Liberty Boys"—as she called the Whigs. She had a husband whom she denominated a "poor stick" because he did not take a decided and active part with the defenders of his country, although she could not conscionably charge him with partiality to the Royalists.

This vulgar and illiterate, but hospitable and valorous, female patriot could boast no share of beauty, a fact she would have herself readily acknowledged if she ever enjoyed the opportunity of looking in a mirror. She was cross-eyed, with a broad, angular mouth, ungainly in figure, rude in speech, and awkward in manners—but a tigress to the enemies of her country.

She was well known to the Royalists, who stood somewhat in fear of her vengeance or grievance towards an aggressive act, though they let pass no opportunity of teasing or annoying her, when they could do so with impunity. On the occasion of an excursion from the British camp at Augusta, a party of Royalists penetrated into the interior and, after savagely massacring Colonel John Dooly in his bed, proceeded up the country with the design of further atrocities.

On their way, a detachment of five diverged to the east and crossed Broad River to examine the neighborhood and pay a visit to their old acquaintance, Nancy Hart. Arriving at her cabin, they unceremoniously entered, though receiving from her no welcome but a scowl. They informed her they had come to learn the truth of a story in circulation that she had secreted a noted rebel from a company of King's men who were pursuing him, and who, but for her interference, would have caught and hanged him.

Nancy undauntedly avowed her agency in the fugitive's escape. She had, she said, first heard the tramp of a horse and saw a man on horseback approaching her cabin with the utmost speed. As soon as she recognized him to be a Whig, flying from pursuit, she let down the fence bars in front of her cabin and motioned him to ride through both doors, front and rear of her one-room cabin, and to take to the swamp to secure himself as well as he could. This he did without loss of time. Nancy put the bars back up, entered the cabin, closed the doors, and went about her usual employments.

Presently the pursuing Royalists rode up to the fence, calling vociferously for Nancy. She muffled up her head and face, and opening the door, inquired why they disturbed a sick, lone woman? They said they had traced a man they wanted to catch to near her house and asked if anyone on horseback had passed that way. Nancy answered, "No"—but she had seen someone on a sorrel horse turn out of the path into the woods, three hundred yards back. "That must be the fellow," cried a Royalist, and they all turned about and went off, well fooled. "Had they not been so lofty," Nancy said, "and had looked on the ground inside the fence, they would have seen his horse's tracks up to the door, as plain as you can see, and the tracks on this here floor and out of t'other door down the path to the swamp."

This bold story did not much please Nancy's new visitors, but they did not wreak revenge upon the woman who so unscrupulously avowed the check she had put upon the pursuers of a rebel. They contented themselves with ordering her to prepare something to eat. She replied that she never fed traitors or King's men if she could help it, the villains having put it out of her power to feed even her own family and friends by stealing and killing all her poultry and pigs "except that one old gobbler you can see in the yard."

"Well, then," said the leader of the party, "that's what you shall cook for us," and raising his musket, shot down the turkey and brought it into the house to be cleaned and cooked. She stormed and swore a while, for Nancy occasionally swore, but seeming at last disposed to make a merit of necessity, began with alacrity the arrangements for cooking.

She was assisted by her daughter, a little girl ten or twelve years old, and sometimes by one of the party with whom she seemed in a tolerably good humor, now and then exchanging rude jests with him. The Royalists, pleased with her freedom, invited her to partake of the liquor they had brought with them, an invitation that was accepted with jocose thanks.

The Harts' spring, of which every settlement had one nearby, was by the edge of the swamp, and a short distance within the swamp was hid among the trees a high snag-topped stump, on which was placed a conch shell. This rude trumpet was used by the family to convey information by variations in its notes to Mr. Hart or his neighbors, who might be at work in the fields, to let them know that the British or Royalists were about.

Pending the operation for cooking the turkey, Nancy had sent her daughter to the spring for water, with directions to blow the conch for her father, to inform him that there were Royalists in the cabin, and he was to stay close with his three neighbors.

The party soon became merry over their jug and sat down to feast upon the slaughtered gobbler. They had cautiously stacked their arms where they were in view and within reach. Mrs. Hart, assiduous in her attention upon the table and her guests, occasionally passed between the men and their muskets. Water was called for and our heroine, having contrived that there was none left in the cabin, she despatched her daughter for the second time to the spring, with instructions to blow such a signal upon the conch as to call out Mr. Hart and his neighbors immediately.

Meanwhile, Nancy had managed, by slipping out one of the pieces of pine from the chinking between the logs of the cabin, to open a space through which she was able to pass to the outside two of the five guns. She was detected in the act of putting out the third, and the whole party sprang to its feet. Quick as thought, Nancy put the gun she held to her shoulder, declaring she would kill the first man who approached her. All were terror-struck, for Nancy's obliquity of sight caused each to imagine himself her destined victim. At length, one of them made a movement to advance upon her, and true to her threat, she fired and shot him dead.

Seizing another musket, she leveled it instantly, keeping the other Royalists at bay. By this time her daughter had returned from the spring, and taking up the remaining gun, she carried it out of the house, saying to her mother, "Daddy and them will soon be here!" This information much increased the alarm of the Royalists, who perceived the importance of recovering their arms immediately, but each one hesitated in the confident belief that Mrs. Hart had at least one eye on him for a target. They proposed a general rush, but no time was lost by the bold woman. She fired again, and brought down another of the enemy. Her daughter had a fresh musket ready, which her mother took, and posting herself in the doorway, called upon the Royalists to surrender to her. Her spirit being up to boiling heat, she swore that, "shooting is too good for you." This hint was enough. When her husband and the neighbors arrived, the dead Royalist was dragged out of the house, and the wounded man and the others were bound, taken beyond the fence, and hanged.

The tree upon which they were suspended was later shown by one who lived in those bloody times, and who also pointed out the spot once occupied by Mrs. Hart's cabin, accompanying the mention of her name with the emphatic remark, "Poor Nancy! She was a honey of a patriot, but the devil of a wife."

NOTE

1. John Wilkes was a firm supporter of English political liberty and colonial rights. He attacked the policies of George III in print and spent time in jail.

CHAPTER 14

SLEEPING WITH THE ENEMY

IN ADDITION TO a specified number of noncom and private soldier's mates, the wives (or mistresses) of many high-ranking officers in the British army were permitted to accompany their men overseas. More than a few mothers also brought young children and even joined in the campaigns. The dedication of a handful of these women in caring for their wounded spouses (and other soldiers)—particularly during Burgoyne's luckless invasion from Canada—became legend. Some women like Jane McCrea or the long-suffering Baroness Riedesel found themselves sadly enmeshed in a chain of military circumstances. Others like sharp-tongued Rebecca Franks (who eventually wed a British general) asserted an indulgent social position floating far above the fray, from which she unhesitatingly flayed both friend and foe. Still other women stood in forthright opposition to the new republic; they often included wives and daughters of wealthy Royalists who helped lead the loyal one-third of the colonial population against the Revolution. Such women either made an eventual shaky peace with the new American government or fled with their families from their victorious and vengeful neighbors to the safety of Canada or England. Before they fled, however, some of these young women—like Peggy Shippen Arnold—proved perfectly willing to participate in nefarious plots to bring down the entire Revolutionary structure.

—LINCOLN DIAMANT

LADY HARRIET ACLAND

Lady Harriet, daughter of the Earl of Ilchester, was the wife of Major John Dyke Acland, an officer with General John Burgoyne's invading army. She accompanied her husband to Canada in 1776 and was with him in the following year's disastrous campaign from Montreal to Saratoga. Beautiful and admired as she was and accustomed to all the luxuries and refinements incident to rank and fortune, Lady Harriet's delicate frame was ill-calculated to sustain the various hardships to be undergone. Yet she shrank not from her husband's perils and privations in traversing the dreary wilderness.

When Major Acland lay ill in a miserable hut at Chambly,[1] her attentions were assiduous, in defiance of fatigue and discomfort. Later, when her husband was wounded at Hubbardton,[2] Lady Harriet hastened from Montreal, where she had been persuaded to remain, and crossed Lake Champlain—resolved to leave her husband no more. Her vehicle of conveyance was a small two-wheeled tumbril, drawn by a single horse over almost impassable roads.

Women with Burgoyne's army usually followed in the rear with the artillery and baggage but heard all the uproar in encounters with the Americans. After the advance to Fort Edward, the tent in which Lady Acland lodged took fire, the light being pushed over by a pet Newfoundland dog; she and her husband made their escape with the utmost difficulty.

But no hazard dissuaded Lady Harriet from her purpose; she was not only a ministering angel to him she loved so devotedly but also won the admiration of the rest of the army by her amiable deportment. She continually made little presents to the officers belonging to her husband's corps, whenever she had anything among her stores worth acceptance. She received in return every kind attention which could mitigate the hardships she had daily to encounter.

In the decisive action of October 7,[3] Lady Acland was again in the tumult of battle. During the heat of the conflict, tortured by anxiety, she took refuge among the wounded and dying. Her husband, commanding the grenadiers, was in the most exposed part of the battle, and she awaited his fate in awful suspense. The Baroness Riedesel (see BARONESS FRIEDERIKE VON RIEDESEL below) and the wives of two other field officers were her companions in apprehension. One of the officers was brought in wounded, and the death of the other was announced.

In the midst of the heartrending scenes that followed, intelligence came that the British army was defeated and that Major Acland was desperately wounded and a prisoner. The unhappy lady, sustained by the counsel of her friend, the Baroness, determined to join her wounded husband in the American camp. She sent a message to General Burgoyne through his aide-de-camp, asking permission to depart. The British commander was astonished at this application; he was ready to believe that patience and fortitude were most brightly displayed in the female character, but he could hardly understand the courage of a woman who, after suffering so long the agitation of suspense—exhausted by want of rest and want of food—was yet ready to brave for many hours the darkness of night and the drenching rain, and deliver herself up to the enemy, uncertain into what hands she might fall.

"The assistance I was able to give," Burgoyne says, "was small indeed. I had not even a cup of wine to offer her. All I could furnish was an open boat and a few lines written to General [Horatio] Gates[4] on dirty and wet paper—recommending her to his protection."

Hastening to her husband's aid, Lady Acland first obtained the refreshment of a little spirits and water and then set out down the Hudson River at night with her maid in an open boat, through a violent storm of wind and rain, arriving at the American outpost after suffering much from the wet and cold. The sentinel of the advance guard, hearing the sound of oars, hailed the boat. What must have been his surprise to see that a woman had braved the storm on such an errand! He sent for the officer of the guard, Major Henry Dearborn,[5] before he would permit the passengers to land. Major Dearborn invited Lady Acland to his guardhouse, offered her a cup of tea, and every other accommodation in his power. He also gave her the welcome intelligence of her husband's safety. In the morning, she experienced the kindness of General Gates, who treated her with the tenderness of a parent, bestowing every attention which her sex and circumstances required. She was soon conveyed with a suitable escort to the quarters of General Enoch Poor on Bemis Heights and remained there with her wounded husband until he was taken to Albany. Lady Harriet's resolution and devotion to him touched the feelings of the Americans and won the admiration of all who heard her story. The benevolent and conciliating efforts by which this heroine endeavored to settle differences between the captive British soldiers and their conquerors, at the time Burgoyne's troops were quartered in Cambridge after his surrender, are well known (see HANNAH WINTHROP above, and BARONESS FRIEDERIKE VON RIEDESEL below). It is also related that Major Acland, while later in New York City on parole, showed his sense of the generous treatment he had received, by doing all in his power to alleviate the condition of American prisoners of distinction.

MARGARET SHIPPEN ARNOLD

The wife of Benedict Arnold was Margaret Shippen of Philadelphia, daughter of Edward Shippen, chief justice of Pennsylvania. His family, of Quaker descent, was distinguished among the aristocracy of the day and, after the commencement of the Revolution, remained prominent among those in Philadelphia known to cherish Royalist principles. His daughters were educated in these beliefs and had constant associations and sympathies with those who were opposed to American independence.

Margaret, the youngest daughter, was—at the age of eighteen—beautiful, brilliant, and fascinating, full of spirit and gaiety, the toast of British officers when their army occupied Philadelphia. She was a woman of beauty and accomplishment and a leader of what was called "fashion" by the aristocracy of her native city. Her connections were all thorough and sincere Royalists.

Eventually Miss Peggy Shippen became the object of General Benedict Arnold's admiration. She had been "one of the brightest of the belles of the Mischianza."[6] This gay and volatile young creature, accustomed to homage paid to beauty and high station, was not one to resist the lure of ambition, and her girlish fancy was soon captivated by the splendor of General Arnold's equipment and his military ostentation.[7] These also appear to have had an effect upon Peggy's relatives, one of whom wrote in a letter, "General Arnold, a fine gentleman, lays close siege to Peggy," thus noticing Arnold's brilliant and imposing exterior, without a word of information or inquiry as to his character or principles.

A February 1779 letter from Arnold to Miss Shippen, not long before their marriage, shows the discontent and rancor of his heart, in his allusions to the president and council of Pennsylvania (see ESTHER DE BERDT REED above). These feelings were expressed freely, as it was Arnold's pleasure to complain openly of injury and persecution; while the darker designs of which no one suspected him—till the whole community was startled by the news of his treason—were buried in his own bosom.

Some writers have taken delight in representing Mrs. Arnold as another Lady Macbeth—an unscrupulous and artful seductress whose inordinate vanity and ambition were the cause of her husband's crime. But there seems no foundation for the supposition that she was acquainted with General Arnold's purpose of betraying his trust.

With his marriage to Peggy, General Arnold won his way into a circle generally exclusive and intolerant, mainly because of his known disaffection and especially by his insolence to the local authorities, particularly to Joseph Reed as the chief executive of Pennsylvania. The aristocratic beauty smiled kindly on a lover who felt the same antipathy she had been taught to cherish. Peggy was soon communing with her husband in all his hatreds and discontents. He probably did not trust her with the whole of the perilous stuff that was fermenting in his heart, for it was not necessary or safe to do so. But he knew her nature and habits of thought well enough to be sure that if success crowned his plans, and if honors and rewards were earned, his wife would not frown, or reject them because they had been won by treachery. Arnold played his game out boldly and resolutely.

Probably Mrs. Arnold was not the being the General would have chosen as the bearer of a secret so perilous, nor was the dissimulation afterward attributed to her in any way consistent with her character.[8]

Arnold's marriage, it is true, brought him more continually into familiar association with the enemies of American liberty and strengthened distrust of the general in the minds of those who had already seen enough to condemn in his previous conduct. It is likely that his propensity for extravagance was encouraged by his wife's taste for luxury and display, while exerting no saving influence over him. In the words of one biographer, "She had no domestic security for doing right; no fireside guardianship to protect him from the tempter." Utterly rejecting, as we do, the theory that Mrs. Arnold was the instigator of her husband's crime—all common principles of human action being opposed to it—we still believe there was nothing in her influence or associations to countervail the persuasions to which the general ultimately yielded.

Margaret Arnold was young, gay, and frivolous, fond of display and admiration, utterly unfit for the duties and privations of a poor man's wife. As a Royalist's daughter taught to mourn the disappearance of even the poor pageantry of colonial rank and authority, Mrs. Arnold could only recollect with pleasure the pomp of those brief days of enjoyment when military men of noble station were her admirers. Arnold had no counselor on his pillow to urge him to the imitation of homely republican virtue, or to stimulate him to follow the rugged path of a Revolutionary patriot. He fell, and though his wife did not tempt or counsel him to his ruin, there is no reason to think that Mrs. Arnold ever uttered a word, or made a sign to deter him.

Her instrumentality in the evil intercourse, carried on while the iniquitous plan was maturing, was in all probability an unconscious one. Major John André had been an intimate of her father's family while General Howe was in possession of Philadelphia. André wrote to her in August 1779 to solicit her remembrance, and offer his services in securing supplies, should she require any in the millinery department—in which, he says playfully, "the Mischianza had given him skill and experience."[9]

This missive, sent more than a year after Major André had parted from the fair young woman, for whom he now professed such a lively regard—and the singularity of the letter itself—justified the suspicion which became general after its seizure by the Pennsylvania Council. Its offer of service in the details of obtaining cap-wire, needles, and gauze seemed to cover a meaning deep and dangerous. Still, it is not conclusive evidence of Mrs. Arnold's participation in the design or knowledge of the treason, the consummation of which was as yet more than a year distant.

It was after the plot was far advanced towards its denouement and only two days before General Washington commenced his tour to Hartford,[10] that Mrs. Arnold came to West Point, traveling by short stages in her own carriage, to join her husband. She passed the last night at Smith's house,[11] where she was met by the general and proceeded up the [Hudson] river in his barge to headquarters.

When Washington and his officers sent from Fishkill[12] to announce their coming, the commander in chief was about to turn his horse into an alternate road leading to the river. Lafayette reminded him that Mrs. Arnold would be waiting breakfast, to which Washington sportively answered, "Ah! You young men are all in love with Mrs. Arnold, and wish to get where she is as soon as possible. Go, breakfast with her and do not wait for me."

Mrs. Arnold was at breakfast with her husband and his aides-de-camp—Washington and the other officers not having yet come—when a letter arrived which bore to the traitor the first intelligence of André's capture. Arnold left the room immediately, went to his wife's chamber, sent for her, and informed her of the necessity of his instant flight to the enemy.

This was probably the first intelligence she received of what had been so long going on. The news overwhelmed her, and when Arnold quitted the chamber, he left her lying in a swoon on the floor. Her almost frantic condition, plunged into the depths of distress, is described with sympathy by Colonel [Alexander] Hamilton, who soon arrived with Washington: "The General went to see her; she upbraided him with being in a plot to murder her child, raved, shed tears, and lamented the fate of the infant. All the sweetness of beauty, all the loveliness of innocence, all the tenderness of a wife, all the fondness of a mother, showed themselves in her appearance and conduct." Hamilton expressed his conviction that she had no knowledge of Arnold's plan, till his announcement to her that he must banish himself from his country forever.

The opinion of other persons qualified to judge without prejudice acquitted her of the charge of having participated in the treason. From Madrid, John Jay wrote: "All the world here are cursing Arnold, and pitying his wife." Robert Morris wrote: "Poor Mrs. Arnold!! Was there ever such an infernal villain!"

Mrs. Arnold went from West Point to her father's house—but was not long permitted to remain in Philadelphia. The traitor's papers having been seized by the authorities, the correspondence with André was brought to light. Suspicion rested on Mrs. Arnold, and by an order of the Council, she was soon required to leave the state, to return no more during the continuance of the war. She accordingly departed to join her husband in New York.

When she stopped en route in a village about to burn Arnold in effigy, all popular exhibition of indignation was suspended, as if in respectful pity for the grief and shame Mrs. Arnold suffered. The people put off their bonfire until the following night.

The fugitive wife of an American traitor soon fled from her native soil. She died unnoticed, dishonored by her husband's crime and lost in his traitorous ignominy. Such was then and such will ever be the fate of all who so baselessly betray a public and a patriot trust.

REBECCA FRANKS

Rebecca Franks was the daughter—and youngest of five children—of David Franks, a Jewish merchant of Philadelphia, who married an Englishwoman before coming to this country around 1750. Rebecca was widely known for her pointed wit, which spared neither friend nor foe, chastising presumption and folly. Her information was extensive, and few were qualified to enter the lists with her. Many anecdotes of her quick wit and sarcastic speech have been preserved. Admired in fashionable circles and courted for the charm of her conversation, she found many opportunities to exercise her feminine privilege of humbling the arrogance of those whose military success would render them indifferent to the feelings of others.

Though a decided Royalist—during the "Mischianza," Miss Franks had appeared as one of the several princesses—her satire did not spare even those whose opinions she favored. At one splendid ball given by British army officers in New York (which she was allowed to visit), during an interval in the dancing, General Sir Henry Clinton, engaged in conversation with Miss Franks, called out to the musicians, "Give us 'Britons, Strike Home!'" "The commander in chief," exclaimed Miss Franks, "has made a mistake. He meant to say, 'Britons, Go Home!' "

The keenness of her irony was not less promptly shown in sharp tilting with the American officers. In Philadelphia after the British evacuation, Lieutenant Colonel Jack Stewart of Maryland, dressed in a fine new scarlet uniform, took an early occasion to pay his compliments to Miss Franks, gallantly saying, "I have adopted your colors, my Princess—better to secure a courteous reception." To this covert "Mischianza taunt," Miss Franks made no reply, but turned to the company surrounding her and exclaimed, "How the ass does glory in the lion's skin!"

General Charles Lee seriously angered Miss Franks with a humorous let-ter alluding to a "jeu d'esprit"—calling her "a lady who has had every human and divine advantage."

MRS. MARY HARVEY

Simon Kenton, who rose to the rank of militia brigadier general in the Revolution, was one of the frontier's most celebrated pioneers and was hon-ored by having his name given to one of the counties in Kentucky. In 1779, on an expedition to seize horses from the Indians, he was captured and for eight months suffered incredible cruelties.

At length, after being assigned to help a Canadian trader, he was deliv-ered to the British commander at Detroit. Here, while he worked for the garrison, his hard lot excited the commiseration of Mrs. Mary Harvey, the wife of another trader. Kenton's exterior was calculated to interest the gen-tle and enthusiastic sex in his fate. He was twenty-four years of age, and ac-cording to one who served with him, was fine-looking, with dignified and manly deportment, with a soft, pleasing voice.

Wherever Kenton went he was a favorite among the ladies. He soon ap-pealed to Mrs. Harvey for assistance to aid him and two other Kentuckian prisoners in their escape. She promised to help by procuring rifles and am-munition, which were indispensible for the journey through the wilderness.

It was not long before Mrs. Harvey found the opportunity to execute her benevolent design. A large concourse of Indians was assembled at Detroit to "take a spree." Before indulging in their potations, several stacked their guns near Mrs. Harvey's house. As soon as it was dark, she stole out noise-lessly and selected three of the best-looking guns and quickly hid them in a patch of peas in her garden.

Carefully avoiding observation, she hastened to Kenton's lodging to in-form him of her success. She directed him to come at midnight to the back of her garden, where he would find a ladder, by means of which he could climb the fence and get the guns. She had previously collected such articles of ammunition, food, and clothing as would be necessary for their journey. With Kenton's knowledge, she had hidden them in a hollow tree some dis-tance from the town.

No time was lost by the prisoners in their secret preparations for flight. At the hour appointed, they came to the back of Mrs. Harvey's garden. The ladder was there. Kenton climbed over and saw Mrs. Harvey waiting for him, seated by the place where she had concealed the guns.

No woman ever appeared so beautiful in the eyes of the grateful young hunter. His thanks were expressed with the eloquence of true feeling, but Mrs. Harvey would not suffer the fugitive to waste a moment. The night was far advanced, and the shouting of the Indians in their drunken revelry could be heard all around them. A few hours would reveal their escape with the stolen guns; instant pursuit would be made.

Mrs. Harvey bade Kenton to be gone, and with a brief farewell, he made haste to join his companions. Hastening away from Detroit, they traveled swiftly towards the safety of the prairie of the Wabash. Until his death fifty-seven years later, Kenton never ceased to acknowledge, in language glowing with gratitude and admiration, the kindness of the trader's wife.

A thousand times in his reveries, Kenton said, he had seen Mary Harvey as he had last beheld her, sitting by the guns in the garden.

JANE McCREA

Jane McCrea, a beautiful young woman twenty-three years old, resided with her brother on the western bank of the Hudson River about four miles from Fort Edward.[13]

She had blonde hair, blue eyes, and a fresh complexion. Her father, Reverend James McCrea, was an Episcopal clergyman from New Jersey, who had died before the Revolution. In the solitude of the wild, Jane had formed an intimacy with a young man named David Jones, who took the side of the British, going off to Canada and being made captain of a company serving with Burgoyne's Provincials. The headquarters of the division of the American army commanded by Benedict Arnold was at that time between Moses Creek and Fort Edward.

The lovers had kept up a correspondence, and Jones was informed that his affianced bride would be visiting Mrs. McNeil, a widowed lady whose home stood about a third of a mile north of Fort Edward. The post was then in the possession of a guard of one hundred Americans, but Miss McCrea felt no assurance of her own safety and was alarmed by rumors of the approach of advance parties of General Burgoyne's Indians. She had been counseled by her lover not to leave her friend's house until the arrival of the British troops should enable her, in company with Mrs. McNeil, to join him. The woods being filled with American scouting parties, it would have been dangerous for the Royalist captain to attempt to visit Jane; if taken prisoner, he could expect no mercy at the hands of his countrymen.

The catastrophe took place at the end of July 1777. Jane and her friend were first alarmed by seeing a party of Indians advancing toward the house.

The savages had been a terror to all that part of the country, and the tales told of their unsparing cruelties were fresh in the remembrances of the two women, whose first impulse was to endeavor to escape. But the Indians made signs of pacific intent; one of them held up a letter, intimating that it would explain their business.

The letter proved to be from Captain Jones, who now entreated Jane and her friend not to remain where they were but to put themselves under the protection of the Indians, who would escort them to the British camp, where they would be safe from the inevitable hostilities. The two women lost no time in preparation and set off under the guidance of the savages.

But it happened that another party of Indians, commanded by an independent chief, had come forth on some enterprise. After their successful attack on the picket guard near the fort, the two savage parties met. A violent altercation arose between them regarding the division of rewards to be received for their respective services. The group to whom the peaceful mission had been entrusted were apparently unaware of Miss McCrea's position in relation to their employer. They looked upon her rather as a prisoner, whom they feared to lose. The quarrel became furious; violent words and blows ensued. In the midst of the fray, one of the chiefs fired at the girl. The shot entered her breast; she sank to the ground, and instantly expired.

The Indian grasped her long flowing locks, drew his knife, and took off her scalp. Leaping from the ground with a yell of savage exultation, he brandished his trophy in the air, and tossed it into the face of the other chief. The murder terminated the quarrel, and the Indians, fearful of pursuit from the fort, where the alarm had been given, hurried away with Mrs. McNeil towards General Simon Fraser's[14] encampment on the road to Fort Anne. The body of the murdered girl was left behind, gashed in several places by a tomahawk or scalping knife. A messenger was immediately dispatched with the dreadful tidings to her brother, who soon arrived and took charge of his sister's corpse. Miss McCrea was buried on the east side of the river about three miles below Fort Edward.

Revealing the horrible truth, the bloody trophy was presented to the anguished Captain Jones. He experienced deep bereavement over the innocent girl who had fallen victim to confidence in her lover. The officer lived but a few more years and went to the grave heartbroken.

General Gates reproached Burgoyne for the murder, and the frightful story of this sacrifice of youth and innocence spread rapidly over the country. Edmund Burke gave a glowing description of the crime in one of his most celebrated speeches to the House of Commons, rendering it familiar throughout Europe, where it gave the British cause little benefit.

FLORA McDONALD

The residence of this world-celebrated heroine on the banks of the Cape Fear River, and the part she took in the American Revolution, link her name as inseparably with the history of North Carolina, as it is with that of her native Scotland. As a young maiden, Flora McDonald first made her appearance during those events that followed the unsuccessful Jacobite uprising in favor of the Young Pretender, Charles Edward Stuart,[15] that failed rebellion in 1745, in which the power of the Highland lairds was broken at the Battle of Culloden Moor.[16] The defeat led to the emigration of many Highlander families who settled amid the sandy forests of Cape Fear.

After many suggestions for the escape of the Prince from Scotland had been proposed and rejected, it was agreed that he be dressed in female attire as a spinning maid and passed off as "Betsy Burke." The twenty-four–year-old Flora had never seen the Prince, but agreed at once to assist in his eventful escape. At their final meeting, the Prince kissed Flora and said, "Gentle, faithful maiden, I hope we shall yet meet in the Palace Royal." But the youthful heroine never again met the Prince who owed so much to a woman's tenderness.

Flora McDonald was arrested and imprisoned in the Tower of London. The public took up the cause of the beautiful, high-spirited girl who had demonstrated such romantic devotion to the cause of royalty. Even the heir apparent (George III) visited her in prison and soon obtained her release. She was presented to George II, and when asked how she dared render assistance to the enemy of his Crown, she answered with modest simplicity, "It was no more than I would have done for Your Majesty, had you been in a like situation."

In 1750, four years after her return to Scotland, the twenty-eight–year-old Flora married a kinsman, Allen McDonald, son of the Laird of Kingsburg, and thus became mistress of the mansion in which the Prince had passed his first night of flight on the Isle of Skye. In 1773, Flora, though by now a matron and a mother, still blooming and graceful, and full of the enthusiasm of her youth, contemplated with her husband a removal to America, on account of pecuniary embarrassments.

Allen McDonald, with his family and some friends, landed in North Carolina, so long a place of refuge for distressed Scottish families. They stopped first at Cross Creek, the present town of Fayetteville,[17] the rallying place of the Highland clans. The town was surrounded by swampy, barren country, sprinkled with lofty pines. The new American home of Flora McDonald's family stood in the midst of this waste. It was a stormy period, and those who came to the New World to seek peace and security found instead disturbance and civil war.

The colonial governor summoned the Highland emigrants to support the Royal cause. General Donald McDonald, another kinsman of Flora's, erected his standard at Cross Creek. On 1 February 1776 he sent forth a proclamation calling on all loyal countrymen to join him. Flora herself espoused the cause of the English monarch with the same spirit and enthusiasm she had shown thirty years before in the cause of the prince she saved.

Flora accompanied her husband when he went to join the army. There is no doubt that her influence went far to inspire the assembled clansmen with a zeal kindred to her own. The celebrated battle at Moore's Creek Bridge proved another Culloden to the brave but unfortunate Highlanders.[18]

The unhappy General McDonald, who was prevented by illness from commanding his troops in the encounter, was found when the engagement was over sitting alone on a stump near his tent. As the American officers advanced toward him, he waved in the air the parchment scroll containing his British commission and surrendered it into their hands.

Flora's husband was among the prisoners of that day and was sent north towards Virginia. The fifty-four–year-old Flora found herself once more in the condition of a fugitive and outlaw. The McDonalds, like other Highlanders, suffered from the plundering and confiscation to which the Royalists were exposed. Flora's house was pillaged and her plantation ravaged. Her husband, after his release, finding his prospects unpropitious, determined to return with his family to their native land and soon embarked in a sloop of war.

Flora was accustomed afterwards to say pleasantly that she had hazarded her life for both the House of Stuart and the House of Hanover but could not perceive how she had greatly profited by either exertion. At her death on the Isle of Skye, in 1790, several thousand persons attended her funeral. According to her wish long previously expressed, her shroud was made of the sheets in which the Prince had slept the night he lodged in her house. She had carried them with her through all her migrations.

MARGARET MONCRIEFF

In the early part of the war, a gentleman named Wood resided about seven miles from Peekskill.[19] He was of American birth and a zealous patriot, married to an Englishwoman whose associations and tastes were not such as disposed her to be content with the new republican state of society.

The family circle was suddenly enlarged by the arrival in the household, with her maidservant, of Margaret Moncrieff, a relative of Mrs. Wood's, who came up from British-held New York City to pay a long visit. Margaret was the twenty–year-old daughter of Major James Moncrieff of the Royal Engineers, a brigade officer under Lord Cornwallis. By all accounts Margaret was surpassingly beautiful, with dark and glossy hair and eyes full of witchery. She possessed a complexion of dazzling fairness, with a rich tint of roses on her cheeks.

Like many women of that day, Miss Moncrieff was a capital equestrienne and could manage the most spirited horse for her favorite exercise on the roads along the Hudson and through the wooded hills in the vicinity. Almost every day she rode out alone on horseback. The riding habit she was accustomed to wear on these excursions was the subject of much comment among the country people. They censured the girl for her defiance of "public opinion" by "exhibiting herself in men's clothes"—which was of course the formal equestrienne style of that period.

The luggage she brought from the city was of unusual quantity and even more than could conveniently be placed in the room she occupied. Her extensive wardrobe was not composed of ordinary materials. The interest of the female population in matters of dress being proverbial, the care Miss Moncrieff lavished on the decoration of her person soon called forth remarks of the curious.

It may be well to give a description of her habit. The material was of deep blue cloth. A very long skirt was set upon a sort of coat or jacket, fitting close to her figure and edged with narrow gold lace. This coat was worn open in front, displaying a buff vest fashioned exactly like a man's waistcoat and decorated with plain but brilliant buttons of the finest gold. The upper portion of this vest stood open, exhibiting an immaculate shirt bosom with neatly plaited ruffles; and a white lawn neck handkerchief, the ends of which were long and garnished with lace. Her hat was of white beaver, three-cornered, and adorned with a rosette in front.

Small heed was paid by the fair horsewoman to the opinions of the neighborhood, or to the circumstance that everyone who chanced to meet her inquired who it was that wore a dress so conspicuous. Margaret was not unwilling to become celebrated, feeling confident in her power to charm all who curiosity might attract to seek her acquaintance. The result might have been anticipated; numbers heard of—and were ardently desirous of knowing—the beautiful and spirited girl, and Mrs. Wood's parlor was soon thronged.

Among the visitors who came from far and near to pay their respects were generally a number of young officers of the American army. It will not be thought surprising that most of these speedily became enslaved to the charms of Miss Moncrieff, who delighted in seeing how easily she could—with winning words and glances—captivate the brave but susceptible hearts that were so adamant to British allurements or threats. With apparently warm interest, she entered into the discussions overheard around the hearth and table of her hostess and softly sympathized with the feelings of her admirers, expressing friendship for the patriot cause and a generous indignation against its oppressors. The officers, fascinated by her grace and beauty, were enchanted to hear such expressions of patriotism from her lips and felt no restraint in conversing with her on the state and prospects of the country, the occurrences of the day, and the plans and movements by which they expected to circumvent the enemy. From time to time, confidential disclosures were made to her by visitors, and none imagined Miss Moncrieff could have either inclination or opportunity to divulge the information she extracted—sometimes by teasing or by pertinacious questioning.

One morning Miss Moncrieff took her accustomed ride without, as she preferred, any companion. She had not ridden far when, on passing a farmhouse, the barking of a dog that suddenly sprang into the road frightened her horse. She was thrown to the ground, and so severely stunned as to render her entirely insensible. The women in the house ran out, lifted her up, carried her inside, and laid her on a bed. Using all the means in their power for her restoration, one of them unbuttoned her vest to allow her to breathe more freely. A letter dropped out, which was put upon the table.

It was not long before Margaret began to recover consciousness, just as the man who lived in the farmhouse came home. In a few moments she was restored to her senses. Then, suddenly starting, and seizing the opened flaps of her vest, she sprang up as if struck by a fearful thought.

"Who unbuttoned my waistcoat? Where is the letter! Ah, I am lost—lost!" she exclaimed, in tones that betrayed the utmost agitation and alarm. One of the women took up the letter and was about to hand it to her, when the man, suspecting from Margaret's strange behavior that something was wrong, reached forward and seized the letter. Perceiving that it was directed to New York City, he refused to give it up. In extreme agitation, Margaret begged him to restore the letter. But he felt convinced that there was more in the affair than the girl was willing to admit; her entreaties only made him more determined to have the affair sifted.

There was no recourse left for the young lady but to adjust her dress and ride back to Mr. Wood's house. Fear of the consequences of detection now pointed her course; no time could be lost in returning to the city, while it was still possible to do so with safety. She immediately commenced to pack her things, but before she could get ready, information had been carried to the proper quarter. A party of soldiers rode up and entered the house. The officer announced to Miss Moncrieff that she was their prisoner, and she was conveyed across the Hudson, where a guard was placed over her.

It was ascertained that the letter in question contained information respecting intended movement of the Continental forces. It came out upon examination that the young lady had been sending her British friends the information she obtained from the American officers who, not suspecting any sinister motive, confided their plans to her. When Margaret wrote a letter, she concealed it beneath her vest, and in her solitary rides, contrived to drop the missive in a previously-agreed-on spot by the roadside. A man who waited hidden among the bushes came out directly, picked up the letter and conveyed it to another secret agent some distance down the river, from whence it was safely forwarded to its destination.

All this was brought to light by the confession of the man himself, fearing discovery of his agency and judging it most prudent—with a voluntary confession—to throw himself on the mercy of his patriotic neighbors. The baggage of Miss Moncrieff was examined and several other papers relating to military affairs were discovered. While she remained a prisoner, some British officers appealed to the Americans on her behalf. Her trial was postponed from time to time, until it was finally decided to give her over to her friends. The crime for which a man would have suffered the gibbet was eventually pardoned to one of her sex and age. Some months later, Miss Moncrieff was escorted to a place adjoining a British position, from whence she was conducted in safety to her father, with the stipulation that she never again enter within the American lines.

By her later autobiographical account, Miss Moncrieff was soon married—unhappily, and returned to England with her husband, an army officer. From this period on, her history offers only repulsive and painful details. Being treated with neglect and brutality, she fled her husband. Alone and utterly destitute, probably urged by the desperation of misery, she plunged into the abyss of vice, from which—despite making much noise in the fashionable circles of Great Britain and France as a theme of conversation among lords, dukes, and members of Parliament—there was no recovery to the world's good opinion.

MARY PHILIPSE MORRIS

Mary Philipse was the second eldest daughter of Frederick Philipse III, Speaker of the New York Assembly—a man with widespread mercantile interests. Philipse was lord of the old Manor of Philipseborough, an immense estate extending twenty miles along the banks of the Hudson River.[20]

Mary Philipse was born at the Manor Hall, 3 July 1730. Tradition tells us she was beautiful, fascinating, and accomplished. Her manners, uniting dignity with affability, charmed all who knew her. Her house was the resort of many visitors at all seasons.

In 1756, Colonel George Washington, then commanding the Virginia militia, found it necessary to confer with the commander in chief of the British forces in North America, General Sir William Shirley in Boston. Traveling on horseback, Washington stopped at the principal cities en route. The military fame he had already gained and the story of his remarkable escape the previous year at Braddock's defeat[21] excited curiosity about the brave twenty-four–year-old hero.

While passing through New York City, Washington was entertained at the home of an older friend from Virginia, Beverly Robinson, whose father had been governor of that colony. It was a long acquaintance that continued until it was severed by the Revolution.[22]

It happened that Mary Philipse, Mrs. Susannah Philipse Robinson's younger sister, was staying at that time with the family. Although she was slightly older than Washington, her charms made a deep impression on the Virginia colonel. He rode on to Boston, then returned, and was again made welcome by the hospitable Mrs. Robinson—and her sister. He romantically lingered until duty called him away; a friend thereupon kept Washington informed of important family events. In one missive a few months later, the intelligence came that a rival was in the field, and the consequences could not be answered for if the brave young militia colonel delayed a further trip to New York. These letters were somewhat playful in tone, but evidently written in the belief that an attachment existed on Washington's part and that his future happiness was concerned.

Washington could not at that time leave his post, however deep his feelings for the fair object of his admiration, but neither the bustle of camp nor the seeds of war effaced Mary Philipse's image from his heart. It is now impossible to ascertain how far his demonstration of affection had gone, or whether Miss Philipse had discouraged the colonel's attentions—so deciddly as to preclude all further hope. The probability, however, is that he despaired of success and did not again see Mary Philipse until after her marriage to Captain Roger Morris—the rival of whom Washington had been warned.

A large part of the Philipse estate came by right of his wife into Roger Morris's possession but was seized from him by confiscation in punishment for his loyalism. Mrs. Morris was included in this attainder, so that the whole interest might come under a 1779 act of the legislature.[23]

Many years later in Canada, someone remarked to a Philipse descendant that there would have been a great differenece in family fortunes had Mary Philipse chosen to become the wife of the first president of the United States, instead of the wife of an exile and outlaw, and she herself attainted of treason. The descendant replied that her ancestor had been remarkable for fascinating all who approached her, putting them to her will, and had she married Washington, she "might have kept him to his proper allegiance. He would not—could not—then have become a traitor with such a wife as Aunt Morris."

MRS. MUNRO

Before the Battle of Bennington,[24] General Stark with several of his officers stopped to obtain a draught of milk and water at the house of Mr. Munro, a Royalist who chanced to be absent. One of Stark's officers walked up to Mrs. Munro and asked where her husband was. She replied that she did not know, whereupon the officer drew his sword and endeavored to intimidate her into a more satisfactory answer. General Stark, hearing the commotion, severely reproved the officer for his uncivil behavior to a woman; the offender went away abashed.

Mrs. Munro recalled Stark's words, "Come on, my boys!" as he marched away to battle. The firing continued till late; after a sleepless night, Mrs. Munro and her sister repaired at the earliest dawn to the battlefield, each carrying pails of milk and water. Wagons had not yet been sent to convey the casualties to hospitals and bring away the dead for burial.[25] Wandering among the heaps of slain and wounded, the two women relieved the thirst of the sufferers on both sides. Some, like the Hessians, were unable to express their thankfulness, save by the mute eloquence of their grateful looks.

BARONESS FRIEDERIKE Von RIEDESEL

Friederike Charlotte Luise von Massow, daughter of a Prussian minister of state, was born in Brandenburg in 1746. At the age of seventeen, she married twenty-five–year-old Lieutenant Colonel Baron Friedrich Adolf Von

Riedesel, who in time became commander of the Brunswick mercenaries serving with the British army in America. The Baroness is described as full in figure and possessing no small share of beauty. In the spring of 1777, with their three young daughters, she followed the Baron to Canada. Her journal and letters to her mother, first published in Germany two decades after the Revolution, vividly describe her travels with Burgoyne's army through various parts of the country and the occurrences she witnessed.

Her graphic picture of scenes of the war and American society is also an exhibition of female energy, fortitude, and conjugal devotion. Some of her foreign habits rendered her rather conspicuous—such as riding in boots, in what was then called the European fashion. She was sometimes even charged with carelessness in her attire. Subjected to dangers and privations from which even a soldier might have shrunk, she presents a touching picture of fidelity and tenderness. With her children, the Baroness proceeded to Fort Edward to join her husband. When the troops broke camp, she did not remain behind. A calash[26] was ordered for her further progress with the army. The first Saratoga action at Freeman's Farm took place in her hearing, and some of the wounded were brought to the house in which she stayed. Among them was a young English officer, whose sufferings excited her deepest sympathy and whose last moans she witnessed. Her diary gives a touching account of the scenes passed through at the memorable conclusion of Burgoyne's campaign: "With the battle at Saratoga on the 7th of October, our misfortunes began." Generals Burgoyne, Phillips, and Fraser—with the Baron—were to dine with her that day. In the morning she observed an unusual movement in the camp and had seen a number of armed Indians in war dresses. To her inquiries as to whither they were going, they answered, "War! War!"

As the dinner hour approached, an increased tumult, the firing, and the yelling of the savages announced the approaching battle. The roar of artillery became louder and more incessant. At four o'clock, instead of the guests invited, General Fraser was brought in, mortally wounded.[27] The table, already prepared for dinner, was removed to make room for his bed. The Baroness, terrified by the noise of the conflict raging without, expected every moment to see her husband also led in, pale and helpless.

Towards night the Baron came to the house, dined in haste, and desired his wife to pack up her camp furniture and be ready for removal at an instant's warning. His dejected countenance told the disastrous result of the battle. Lady Acland (see LADY HARRIET ACLAND above), in a nearby tent, was presently informed that her husband was wounded[28] and was a prisoner.

Thus through the long hours till day, the kind ministries of the thirty-one—year-old baroness were demanded by many sufferers. "I divided the night," she writes, "between Lady Acland, whom I wished to comfort, and my children, whom I feared might disturb poor dying General Fraser. Several times he begged my pardon for the trouble he thought he gave me. About three o'clock I was informed he could not live much longer, and as I did not wish to be present at his last struggle, I wrapped my children in blankets and retired into the cellar. At eight in the morning he expired."

All day the cannonade continued; like ministering angels, the women attended the wounded soldiers who were brought in. In the afternoon, the Baroness saw the house that had been assigned to her go up in flames. Fraser's last request had been that he be buried at six in the evening in the Great Redoubt,[29] and the British Army's retreat was delayed for that purpose. The generals with their retinues followed the honored corpse to the spot in the midst of a heavy fire from the Americans, for General Gates knew not that it was a funeral procession.

The women stood in full view of this impressive and awful scene, so eloquently described by Burgoyne himself: "The incessant cannonade during the solemnity, the steady attitude and unaltered voice with which the chaplain officiated—though frequently covered with dust which the shots threw up on all sides of him—the mute but expressive mixture of sensibility and indignation upon every countenance; these objects will remain until the last of life upon the minds of every man who was present." The deepening shadows of evening closed around the group, thus rendering the last service to one of their number, while each might anticipate his own death in the next report of the American artillery. "Many cannon balls," says Madame von Riedesel, "flew close by me, but I had my eyes directed towards the embankment where my husband was standing amidst the fire of the enemy, and of course I did not think of my own danger."

The following night the army commenced its retreat, leaving the sick and wounded, a flag of truce waving over the hospital thus abandoned to the mercy of the foe. The rain fell in torrents all day on the ninth, and it was dark when they approached Saratoga. Again the alarm of battle and the reports of muskets and cannon drove the Baroness and her children to seek shelter in a house, which was fired upon under the impression that the generals were there. It was occupied by women and crippled soldiers. They were all obliged at last to descend into the cellar, where the Baroness laid herself in a corner, supporting her children's heads on her knees.

Night was passed in the utmost terror and anguish, and in the morning the terrible cannonade commenced anew. So it continued for several days, but in the midst of the dreadful scenes, when the Baron spoke of sending his family to the American camp, his heroic wife declared that nothing would be so painful to her as to owe safety to those whom he was fighting. "The want of water," says the Baroness, "continued to distress us, and we were extremely glad to see a soldier's wife so spirited as to fetch some from the river. It was an occupation from which the boldest might have shrunk, since the Americans shot at everyone who approached the river. They told us afterwards they had spared her on account of her sex.

"I attempted to dispel my melancholy by continually attending to the wounded. One day a Canadian officer came creeping into the cellar, and was hardly able to say that he was dying of hunger. I felt happy to offer him my dinner, by which he recovered, and I gained his friendship."

At length the danger was over. On the seventeenth the capitulation was carried into effect. The British generals waited upon Gates, and the troops surrendered themselves prisoners of war. "My husband's groom," writes the Baroness, "brought me a message to join him with the children. I once more seated myself in my dear calash, and while driving through the American camp, was gratified to observe that nobody looked at us with disrespect; but on the contrary, greeted us and seemed touched by the sight of the captive mother with her children.

"When I drew near the main tent, a fine-looking man advanced towards me, helped the children from the calash, and kissed and caressed them. He then offered me his arm, and tears trembled in his eyes, 'Madam,' said he, 'I beg of you, do not be alarmed.' 'Sir,' I cried, 'a countenance so expressive of benevolence, and the kindness you have evinced towards my children, are sufficient to dispel all apprehension.'

"He then ushered me into the tent, where I found General Gates engaged in friendly conversation with Generals Burgoyne and Phillips. General Burgoyne said to me, 'You can now be quiet and free from all apprehension of danger.' I replied that I should indeed be reprehensible, if I felt any anxiety when our General was on such friendly terms with General Gates. All the British generals remained to dine with the American commander.

"The gentleman who had received me with so much kindness, came to me and said, 'You may find it embarrassing to be the only lady in so large a company of gentlemen. Will you come with your children to my tent, and partake of a frugal dinner, offered with the best will?' I replied, 'You show me so much kindness, that I cannot but believe you are a husband and a father.' He informed me that he was General Schuyler.[30]

"The dinner was of excellent smoked tongue, potatoes, butter, and fresh bread. Never did a meal give me so much pleasure. After our dinner, General Schuyler begged me to pay him a visit at his house near Albany, where he expected that General Burgoyne would also be his guest. My husband advised me to accept the invitation. We were two days journey from Albany; General Schuyler carried his civilities so far as to solicit a well-bred French officer to accompany me on the journey.

"We reached Albany, where we had so often wished ourselves, but did not enter that city with a victorious army, as we had hoped. Our reception, from General Schuyler and his wife and daughters was not like the reception of enemies, but of the most intimate friends. They loaded us with kindness, and behaved in the same manner towards General Burgoyne, although he had earlier, without any necessity ordered this splendid establishment to be burnt. Burgoyne said to Schuyler, 'You are too kind to me—who have done you so much injury.' 'Such is the fate of war,' Schuyler replied, 'let us not dwell on this subject. 'We remained three days with that excellent family, and they seemed to regret our departure."

On the way to Boston, General Riedesel brooded continually on the disastrous events and in his captivity was not able to bear his troubles with the spirit and cheerfulness of his wife. He became moody and irritable, and his health was much impaired. "One day," says the Baroness, "when he was much indisposed, the American sentinels at our door were very noisy in their merriment and drinking and grew more so when my husband sent a message desiring them to be quiet; but as soon as I went myself, and told them the General was sick, they were immediately silent. It is astonishing how much the frail human creature can endure, and I am amazed that I survived such hard trials. My happy temperament permitted me even to be gay and cheerful, whenever my hopes were encouraged. I had it in my power to be useful to those who were dearest to me, and that without my exertions, I might have lost those who contribute so much to my felicity."

The prisoners at length reached Cambridge (see HANNAH WINTHROP above); Baroness Riedesel was lodged in one of the best houses of the place. Few of the officers were permitted to visit Boston, but Madame von Riedesel went to visit General Schuyler's daughter, Mrs. Carter, and dined with her several times. She describes Boston as a fine city but the inhabitants as "outrageously patriotic." The worst treatment came from persons of her own sex, who gazed at her with indignation and testified contempt when she passed near them. The Baroness had no admiration for Mr. Carter who, in consequence of General Howe's having burned several villages and small towns suggested cutting off our generals' heads, to pickle them, and to put them in small barrels. As often as the English should again burn a village, to send them one of these barrels.

Towards the approach of winter, the prisoners received orders to set out for Virginia.[31] In commencing their journey in November 1778, the Baroness had the accommodation of an English coach. They were often without food and were obliged to halt frequently. "We reached one day a pretty little town," relates the Baroness, "but our wagon remaining behind, we were very hungry. Seeing much fresh meat in the house where we stopped, I begged the landlady to sell me some. 'I have,' quoth she, 'several sorts of meat; beef, mutton and lamb.' I said, 'Let me have some; I will pay you liberally.' But snapping her fingers, she replied, 'You shall not have a morsel of it. Why have you left your country to slay us, and rob us of our property? Now that you are our prisoners, it is our turn to vex you.' 'But,' rejoined I, 'see those poor children; they are dying of hunger.' She remained unmoved, but when at length my youngest child Caroline, who was then about two years and a half old, went to her, seized her hands, and said in English, 'Good woman, I am indeed very hungry,' the woman could no longer resist, and carrying the child to her room, gave her an egg. 'But,' persisted the dear little one, ' I have two sisters.' Affected by this remark, the hostess gave her three eggs, saying, 'I am loathe to be so weak, but I cannot refuse the child.' By and by she softened, and offered me bread and butter. I made tea, and saw that our hostess looked at our teapot with a longing eye, for the Americans are very fond of that beverage, yet they have stoutly resolved not to drink any more. I offered her a cup, and presented her with a paper case full of tea. This drove away all clouds between us."

On the banks of the Hudson, at a sloop captain's house, they were not so fortunate—being given the remnants of breakfast, after the hostess, servants, and children had finished their meal. The woman, a staunch republican, could not bring herself to any courtesies toward the enemies of her country. They fared a little better after crossing the river. When they wished to warm themselves in the kitchen, their host followed, and taking them by their arms, said, "Is it not enough that I give you shelter, ye wretched royalists!" His wife, however, was more amiable, and his coarseness gradually softened, till they became good friends.

Passing through a wild, grand, and picturesque country, they at length arrived at Virginia. At a day's distance from their place of destination, their little stock of provisions gave out. They reached a house and begged for some dinner, but all assistance was denied them, with many imprecations upon the Royalists. "Seizing some maize, I begged our hostess to give me some of it to make a little bread. She replied that she needed it for her black people. 'They work for us,' she added, 'and you come to kill us.' An officer offered to pay her one or two guineas for a little wheat, but she answered, 'You shall not have it, even for hundreds of guineas, and it will be so much the better if you all die.'

"The roads were execrable and the horses could hardly move. My children, starving from hunger, grew pale, and for the first time lost their spirits. One of the wagoners who transported our baggage at length gave them a piece of stale bread of three ounces weight, on which many a tooth had already exercised its strength. Yet to my children, it was at this time a delicious morsel."

Their destination was Charlottesville, Virginia, where General Riedesel expected them with impatient anxiety.[32] This was about the middle of February 1779. They had passed in their journey through the states of Massachusetts, Connecticut, New York, New Jersey, Pennsylvania, and Maryland, and in about three months had traveled six hundred and twenty-eight miles.

NOTES

1. A Canadian fort on the Richelieu River, twenty-five miles northeast of Montreal.

2. Across the Vermont border, forty-five miles northeast of Fort Edward, site of a bloody engagement weeks in advance of the first battle at Saratoga.

3. Generally known as Saratoga's "Second Battle of Freeman's Farm." The British suffered more than six hundred casualties, the Americans only one hundred sixty.

4. The American commander.

5. Later to serve as Jefferson's secretary of war, 1801–1809.

6. In Italian, "mixture." An elaborate fête to celebrate Sir William Howe's impending retirement, before the British commander's army evacuated Philadelphia. Some doubt exists whether teenaged Peggy Shippen was allowed to participate in the adult extravaganza.

7. On 19 June 1778, the day after the British withdrew from Philadelphia, Washington appointed the undeniably heroic but difficult Arnold military governor of the city.

8. Contemporary opinion assessing Peggy Shippen's innocence or complicity in the Arnold/André plot to betray West Point to the British is best voiced by Carl Van Doren in his study, Secret History of the American Revolution: "Peggy could hardly have done more than confirm a powerful will like Arnold's in its own decision. Even if it were actually she who proposed the treachery—and there is no first-hand evidence that she did—the final responsibility must lie with the mature and experienced Arnold for undertaking to carry it out."

9. André designed the harem costumes and ladies' hair styling for the event.

10. That meeting was to coordinate the following year's joint campaign with French General Rochambeau.

11. The Haverstraw, New York, home of quixotic Joshua Hett Smith, brother of an important Royalist judge and undoubtedly a coconspirator.

12. A strategic village a dozen miles upriver from Arnold's Robinson farmhouse headquarters, just across the Hudson from West Point.

13. Important colonial military post, built in 1755 fifteen miles below Fort Anne, on the portage between Lake Champlain and the Hudson River.

14. Fraser, leader of Burgoyne's advance corps, was killed by the third shot from Tim Murphy, one of General Daniel Morgan's Kentucky sharpshooters, in the second Battle of Saratoga, 7 October 1777.

15. "Bonnie Prince Charlie," who eventually fled from the Scottish Isles to safety in France.

16. A few miles east of Inverness.

17. Sixty miles south of Raleigh.

18. See Note 9, Chapter 11 above.

19. A strategically located village near the entrance to the Hudson River Highlands, about forty miles north of New York City.

20. Before the Revolution, in which the Philipse Family saw all its property confiscated by the State of New York, Frederick Philipse III was considered the wealthiest man in America.

21. Washington's horse was killed under him, and several bullets passed through his uniform coat.

22. In 1777 Robinson, colonel of the Loyal American Regiment, led a successful British foray through the Hudson Highlands. Later, in 1780, Robinson became the British army's spymaster "running" Major André. His country home across from West Point served alternately as a hospital and headquarters for Benedict Arnold and other Continental army generals (see MARGARET SHIPPEN ARNOLD above).

23. The three Morris children could not be held guilty of "corruption of the blood" and after their mother's death in England at ninety-six, their reversionary rights, long since purchased by John Jacob Astor, were exercised and became the cornerstone of Astor's immense nineteenth-century fortune.

24. On 16 August 1777, General John Burgoyne dispatched two parties numbering 1,190 Hessians and British to seize American military stores and horses at Bennington, Vermont. They were met by a superior force of Vermont and Massachusetts militia and Continentals under General John Stark and Colonel Seth Warner and were decisively defeated.

25. Almost nine-hundred of the enemy—compared to eighty Americans—were killed, wounded, or captured.

26. A light carriage with a folding top.

27. See Note 14 above.

28. He had been shot in both legs.

29. Anchor of the defensive British entrenchments thrown up after the first battle of Freeman's Farm.

30. On 4 August 1777, after bitter Congressional wrangling over Burgoyne's easy capture of Fort Ticonderoga, forty-four–year-old Major General Philip John Schuyler—fourth-ranking officer in the Continental Army—had been replaced as commander of the Northern Department by Major General Horatio Gates.

31. After lengthy discussion, Congress decided that General Gates had exceeded his military authority in extending parole to Burgoyne's entire army. Nullifying the terms of surrender, the legislators allowed only Burgoyne to sail back to England.

32. Being moved from pillar to post, the Baron and Baroness would not make it back to Germany until late in 1783.

INDEX

About the Author

LINCOLN DIAMANT studied American History at Columbia University and was a writer for CBS News before he became a biographer and historian of the American Revolution. He is author of eight books, including *Chaining the Hudson* (1994) and *The Broadcast Communications Dictionary* (Greenwood, 1989). He has lectured extensively on American History and has served as a commentator for Fox Television.